CLOSE UP

John Fraser

CLOSE UP
An Actor Telling Tales

OBERON BOOKS
LONDON

First published in 2004 by Oberon Books Ltd
521 Caledonian Road, London N7 9RH
Tel: 020 7607 3637 / Fax: 020 7607 3629

www.oberonbooks.com

Published in paperback in 2005

A catalogue record for this book is available
from the British Library.

ISBN: 1 84002 504 2

Printed and bound in Great Britain by
Marston Book Services Ltd, Oxfordshire

Every effort has been made to trace the photographers of all pictures reprinted
in this book. Acknowledgement is made in all cases where photographer
and/or source is known.

CONTENTS

*Sixteen pages of photographs (I–XVI) can be found between
pages 152 and 153.*

ACKNOWLEDGEMENTS

First and foremost I want to thank:

my dear friend Adolf Wood for so generously affording me the benefit of his intellect and his vast experience in shaping my material;

his wife Dawn Keeler for networking selflessly on my behalf, and for her indestructibly sunny nature;

Frank Barrie, whose encouragement at an early stage inspired me to continue;

Val West for making the London Shakespeare Group possible;

the late Kenichi Watanabe-San for all those years of loyal support;

and Gary Raymond and Delena Kidd for making the dream come true.

And finally, I want to thank Gordon Dickerson, who for entirely philanthropic reasons has been my champion.

I should also like to thank all at Oberon Books for making the publishing of this book an unalloyed pleasure: Ian Higham, for his imagination and his dedicated expertise; Stephen Watson, for his attention to detail and the archaeological research needed to strengthen my feeble grasp of history – particularly my own; Charles Glanville, for his refusal to give up, when there is room for improvement; Emma Schad, for her sweetness and her industry; and above all, James Hogan, for his unfailing support and his overwhelming generosity.

It remains only to thank my agent, the lovely Helenka Fuglewicz, Julia Forrest for her meticulous editing at an early stage, and all at Edwards/ Fuglewicz for believing in me.

For Rod
for putting up with me for twenty-seven years

Prologue: Whit Ye Get

MY AUNT GATTY was a philosopher.

The world will remember her for: 'What's fur ye, 'll no go past ye.'

'*Che sera sera*,' she would doubtless have added, if she'd had an inkling of what it meant.

Who can dispute it?

As I sit on my terrace on a hilltop in Tuscany, I ponder the inevitability of it all. And I marvel that a life that started so inauspiciously should end up so blessed. From a semi in a council estate in Glasgow to a mediaeval farmhouse that stands alone upon a promontory, overlooking a forest where wild boar root for truffles. The vines have yielded their grapes some weeks ago, the wine has been pressed, the last of the figs have been bottled or made into jam, and the white peaches are ripening at last on the tree beyond the terrace. This has been a good year, with no late-spring frost to blight the blossom.

Rod still swims every day, though by September the registration on the pool thermometer is too low for my threshold of pain. It is a joy to watch him cut through the water, from the statue of Persephone modestly emerging from the oleanders at one end, to Apollo swaggering at the other, his bow slung across his shoulders, his faithful hound crouching at his feet.

One of my earliest memories, seen from the top of a tram, was of a mysterious bower framed with box and peopled with naked statues: the Villa d'Este in Pollokshields. I thought it the most beautiful garden on earth.

Statues are an integral part of every city in Italy, which is perhaps one of the thousand reasons I lost my heart to this country. When we finally came here to live, I was free to make the garden of my dreams.

A frolicking *putto*, his chubby legs astride the globe, bashes a tambourine in the middle of the lawn between the cypresses. His plinth covers the lid of the septic tank. The trees were planted ten years ago, and are now towering above the house. Every inch of its ancient stone walls is covered, right up to the shuttered windows and the overhanging eaves, with tightly clinging, small-leafed creeper, which, with the onset of autumn, is beginning to turn into a riot of saffron yellow, of deepest orange speckled with scarlet and gold.

The *campanile* of the little church on the opposite hill rings out morning and evening for mass, but no one any longer swings on the ropes. The bells are struck with mechanical hammers, operated electronically by Don Ottorino, who at the moment is having one of his mid-week bouts of sanctimony. He plays a tape of 'Ave Maria Gratia Plena Dominus Tecum' on loudspeakers in between passages of plainsong which there is not a soul to hear except me. I have told him a half-truth – that I am not a Catholic – but he still treats me as one of his flock.

'*Siamo tutti bambini di Cristo,*' he assured me.

If he only knew.

All the peasants are out of earshot of the loudspeakers, thronging the fields in brightly coloured aprons and battered hats, harvesting maize.

From my terrace there is not another house to be seen, only the church and the rolling, deeply forested hills; but immediately behind us is a working farm, with six pigs being fattened in the barn for Christmas, and white rabbits with pink eyes breeding in the dark in rows of hutches, while the geese and chickens, the ducks and the guinea fowl roam free.

In a large compound surrounded by a wire fence eight feet high, fifteen pedigree red and white hounds are confined during the long hot summer. On the first of October they are let loose at last to plunge through the undergrowth in pursuit of their quarry. During the hunt, it is far from rare for a hound to be ripped almost apart by the razor-sharp tusks of a savage wild boar as the beast is brought to bay.

In their frustration during the summer months, the dogs frequently ululate like a pack of wolves howling, and at night the sound frightens our guests half to death...

But I sleep soundly, wrapped in the silence of the Tuscan hills, a silence broken sometimes in my dreams by the distant shoogle and bump of Aunt Gatty's sewing machine.

'What's fur ye 'll no go past ye...' I hear her mutter between her teeth.

'We're aw Jock Tamsen's bairns...'

'Mony a mickle maks a muckle.'

And Aunt Gatty's top tip for a contented life:

'Get on with it! And if you don't get what you want – WANT WHIT YE GET!'

ONE
The Formative Years

1 THE BEGINNING
Five years old

IT WAS NOT my first day at school, for that would have been in September. So why was my father walking with me through the snow, past the coalman fixing a nosebag to his shaggy Clydesdale steaming between the shafts of his loaded cart? Was it because of this icy wind which had pounced from the sky during the night, and was now biting us to the bone like a rabid beast? That freezing winter's day was the only day in all my childhood that I can remember my father escorting me to school. The cold, like an earthquake or a tornado, confirmed the power and the indifference of the elements.

My chilblains were throbbing. Regularly as clockwork every winter we had chilblains. They were a fact of life, painful and inescapable. Everybody had them, didn't they? My mother would rub the inflamed lumps with a raw onion till we all smelt disgusting, but it hardly made a difference.

Seeing our windows turn to swirling wafers of ice, my Aunt Gatty had quickly run me up a balaclava made of Harris tweed which tickled my ears and chafed my chin; even inside my woolly gloves my fingers ached; I would have whimpered had I been on my own, but my father was trudging through the deepening snow by my side.

My nose was red and running so I wiped it with my handkerchief. My mother would enjoin us, last thing, as we left for school – 'Don't forget your milk money! Take a clean hankie!'

At the school gates Tubby Paterson's mother said to my father: 'Your wee lassie's dropped her hankie!' Daddy frowned, and we looked down the snowy track to where my handkerchief lay barely visible in the snow.

'His name's Johnnie,' he said. 'He's a laudie.'

'Uch, he's too bonny to be a laudie!' Mrs Paterson said with a laugh.

I ran to retrieve my hankie, angry with Tubby's mother for her mistake, and with my father for being there to hear it, but most of all with my Aunt Gatty, whom I loved, for fabricating the androgynous headgear which had brought upon me this humiliation. Let the frost nip my ears! And freeze my hair! I snatched the offending monstrosity from my head and ground it underfoot.

The Early Birds, as Miss Martin described these pupils who appeared regularly in the playground just as dawn was breaking, had made a slide. You clear the

5

snow to the ground frost, then you belt along the trench at the bottom and skid as far as you can. The frost is soon buffed up to black ice, and the slide becomes a fixture while the cold spell lasts. Most of us wore crescent moons of steel on the soles and heels of our shoes in those days, to protect the leather from wear; toe-caps and heel-caps are essential for making a good slide.

Tubby Paterson. Mucky Brown. Nobby Clark. Cheesey McBride. I longed to have a nickname, but in all my life I never succeeded in acquiring one. At playtime Tubby said, 'Your Daddy was dead fu' on Saturday all right!'

'He wasn't drunk!' I protested. 'He's ill!' Our mother had reiterated this fiction so often, we all believed it. At least, we were confused.

'He was giving away pennies down at the shops! He couldn't stand up!'

'Drunks don't give away pennies! They need all the pennies they can get to buy whisky. Drunks only give away kisses!' I dreamt this up because I was cornered.

Tubby wasn't a bad chap, but I was still glad when he did a purler on the slide and burst his lip.

To prove he was a hard man, after school on the way home he offered me a Woodbine from a packet of ten.

'Have you been tickling your mother's handbag?' I asked him.

'Pru money,' he said. In those far off days, to save for their funerals poor people used to take out a policy with the Prudential Insurance Company, the premiums for which were paid in small instalments collected weekly by a man in a bowler hat.

'She'll think it's my Dad,' Tubby said. 'He's aye at the Dogs.'

Tubby's mother was a creature of habit, and she always emptied the household's ashtrays into their fireplace. Summers are short in Glasgow, and Mrs Paterson saw no reason to change her ways just because there was no fire in the grate, so in warm weather Tubby had a glut of butts. My initiation had been one hot day when Tubby, Cheesey and I had been giving each other watering-can showers on our bald lawn in our underwear. A neighbour complained to my mother, so we pooled our pocket money to buy a quarter of Imperials (Very Strong Peppermints) and we set off for Tubby's to smoke butts in our soggy underpants till we made ourselves sick. Afterwards we sucked the peppermints to cover the smell of tobacco on our breath.

But once summer had fled, we were forced to experiment. Rolled-up brown paper – no good. Tea-leaves in a clay pipe for blowing bubbles – better. Cinnamon sticks, bought from the chemist when we could scrape together tuppence between us – smouldered nicely. When you got fed up re-lighting, you could eat them. I didn't like proper cigarettes.

My Aunt Gatty had been pretty. She was all but illiterate but this would not have been a bar to marriage in 1918; it was whispered that there had once been a fiancé, but then it always was with 'Spinsters of this Parish'. The carnage of the trenches had scuppered her chances. At the age of eighteen, she had contracted erysipelas which overnight had turned her hair the purest white I have ever seen.

Erysipelas is a skin disease usually found in undernourished people. It first appears as a red patch on the face, shaped like a butterfly: if untreated, the bacterium can invade the blood and often proves fatal. It is also known as Saint Anthony's Fire.

This early brush with death had left my Aunt Gatty as deaf as a currant bun. She could just hear if you hailed her like a taxi, which caused consternation in public places. There were frequent misunderstandings which resulted in a degree of umbrage and dudgeon on Aunt Gatty's part that disqualified her from acceptable company. She was forty-one years old and in this isolated state when I was born in 1931. She was my mother's older sister. Though I loved my mother much more, it is entirely due to Aunt Gatty and her Singer sewing machine that I have prospered.

She lodged with our family, and in lieu of payment for her keep, she clothed us all by treadling her Singer sewing machine, like Hopalong Cassidy riding the range, every evening after she had finished doing the same thing all day in a factory. There she was on 'piece work', earning a pittance as a seamstress, her weekly wage determined by the quantity of work she finished. On a treadle sewing machine. She had calves like a Sherpa's.

She was a fast worker. Wouldn't you be? She was also a thief, on a grand scale. She suffered no qualms. Politics were, if not below her or above her, then certainly beyond her, but she understood the principle of exploitation. She conceded that few fingers came stickier than hers, but she stole only from the workplace: these proceeds, she maintained with some defiance, were her due.

In our council house, my Aunt Gatty's room was the only one with a single occupant. My parents had the main bedroom, my two sisters and I shared the other – Chris and Jean in a double bed, myself in a single in the corner – but Gatty slept and treadled alone.

Her room was big enough to hold a small bed, a chair and the sewing machine, and once Gatty was inside it was hard to budge the door for two reasons. One: no amount of banging on its panels could be detected by the occupant whilst she was basting the pleats on a kilt for your eponymous or thundering across the plains of an overcoat for one of my sisters. Two: once the door was slammed against intruders, she would heave her loot accumulated over the years from underneath the bed and spread it fondly round her feet – bales of tweed and silk and cotton and barathea; linings and trimmings and linen stiffened with glue for lapels; velvet and calico and cashmere and tulle; buckles and buttons...

Buttons... Buttons covered in cotton and silk and velvet and satin. Buttons of staghorn and mother-of-pearl, of silver and of leather, of bleached bone and bright-painted wood. Zippers and hooks-and-eyes, and slim volumes of needles and bulging satchels of pins. And to prevent the cotton thread from knotting or snagging on my Aunt Gatty's flakey thimbled fingers, a lump of beeswax exquisitely scarred as if by the winds of time, an aromatic nugget of craft and industry, this rippling, warm, organic artefact that smelt like a warm puppy.

Every Friday night, stranded amidst the choppy seas of Aunt Gatty's booty, I lay beside her on her bed; while she read me *The Dandy* I sucked her ear-lobe. We had Cinnamon Balls and Lillian Cream Caramels as well, best eaten simultaneously, but Gatty's earlobe was my preferred comforter. I was five years old and not retarded in other respects.

Another obliging reader was my next door neighbour. She was six years older than I was. She had little to rejoice in except her name which was Lulu Bold, for she had a hare-lip and a cleft palate and she spoke in snorts and snores and explosive puffs of air which no one could understand – including me, though I pretended to as she vainly strived to introduce me to the arcane wonders of the *Girls' Crystal*.

When the weather was fine, this festival of unintelligibility took place on our garage roof. The garage was car-shaped. Lulu and I sat on 'The Bonnet' which sloped a little, while we leant against the higher part which had eaves. Throughout this late-weaning part of my childhood, Lulu Bold remained unsucked. At least by me. She was often in hospital having patches of skin removed from her thighs and her arms to graft onto her upper-lip, but it never made much difference except to add to her suffering.

There had once been a car in our family but for as long as I could remember the garage had been empty and rotting and infested with wood-lice. At this time I had a rabbit called 'Nero' who should have been re-christened 'Houdini', for he would have gnawed his way out of Alcatraz. After his fifth escape in so many weeks, I had taken the extreme measure of putting his hutch onto the garage roof. At first, the drop deterred him, but he soon learned to fly.

My father was an engineering merchant with his own business till the bottle got him. He was the kind of drunk seen only in Glasgow on a Saturday night. How he ever got home remains one of the great unsolved mysteries. I never saw him tipsy. By the time he arrived at the door he was on all fours, or swaying with his feet astride and clamped to the ground as if to stop the world in its trajectory. This degree of drunkenness was ugly, fearsome and disgusting; but it was as nothing to what invariably followed.

My father was not only a chronic alcoholic, he was also epileptic. Epilepsy is not a disease, it is a symptom, like a bellyache; stomach pains can be the result of many causes, from cancer to dyspepsia, and so it is with epilepsy.

In 1914 my father was wounded in the trenches on two occasions, once in the arm, then in the leg; they were both minor wounds from which he fully recovered, so he was sent back to Flanders to fight again. In 1915, third time lucky, a bullet went through his neck: he was left for dead in the mud surrounded by decomposing corpses for four days, before the Red Cross found him only just alive. During these four days, unable to move and delirious with pain, rats had gnawed at his wounds, leaving a patchwork of scar-tissue on the left side of his neck like a relief-map of torment. With macabre symmetry this was repeated almost identically on the right side. My father's favourite story when he was drunk was the story of the rats ripping at his throat.

'I've called Doctor Dunne,' my mother would reassure him if she could see the shadow of the fits coming on. Doctor Dunne prescribed Paraldehyde, a viscous transparent fluid that lolloped like mercury in a glass of water without dissolving. The smell of it, like a blocked drain, was enough to knock sober citizens off their feet, but it quietened my father when he could conquer his retching to swallow it, and averted his seizures if we caught it in time. He was also prescribed pills called Luminal, a powerful sedative and pain-killer; if we had acceded to his demands for it in ever-increasing quantities, it would have killed him, so my sisters and I were dispatched to the kitchen to chop up aspirins to the requisite size, rounding off the corners with a nail-file, till in his catatonic state, my father was fooled and ceased his importuning. He had spent three years in hospital while the Great War gorged on a generation of young men, before he was deemed fit to take up civilian life. During that time he was fed laudanum to ease his terrible pain and to still his terrors. Three years on opium. Is it any wonder his story ended as it did?

'I've seen more doctors than a butcher's seen black pudd'n's!'

My father, drunk as always, was sawing doggedly with his dentures at the rump steak my mother had bought for him from her meagre housekeeping allowance. Since he drank so much, she reasoned that he should eat well to counteract the effects of alcohol, and red meat then was the life force. Suddenly he dropped his knife and fork with a clatter and ripped the collar from his neck. Here we go.

Revealing his scars – 'One wee bullet! In one side and out the other! You think that was one wee bullet?'

He had yellow slug-scum in the corners of his mouth, and he slopped Lea and Perrins Worcester Sauce in great squirts over his steak.

'Marne and Wipers. Up to our oxters in mud. The bastards got me when I was having a shite behind the wireless carrier. Sorry Teeny! That just slipped out! Don't listen to me, son, your father's a foul-mouthed old blether. No offence. No offence where none is intended. Four days and nights… Sorry son.'

He was chewing slowly like a ruminant. This story was his 'Goldilocks and The Three Bears'. 'Sloshing in corpses. Putrid broth. Flies gumming up your eyes. Your nose, your ears. And at night the rats came.'

Now he was into his stride, his food was forgotten.

'They smelt my blood from the China Sea. They came from all the sewers and the shite and they squirrumed between my legs and they ripped my breeks and my semmet [trousers and vest] till they found my NECK!'

He hurled his plate to the floor where it shattered, but no one knelt to clear up the mess.

'They found my neck – with the blood going black and the pus all wet and crusty round the edges. Oh the bastards!' He gasped like a landed fish. 'The bastards. They found the hole in my neck. They found it. And by Jesus Christ they fed off my living flesh!' My father's anguish was like ammonia, you couldn't breathe it. 'I heard their yellow teeth grinding at my tubes and yanking at my gristle. The pain was the Heart of the Sun, but it was the filth…the filth of these –'

His whole body shuddered like an unsaddled horse.

'They were after my head! They wanted to eat my HEAD!'

He planted his flag on the peak of his pain and began the descent to reality.

'One wee bullet doesn't leave scars like this, son.' He made an ineffectual gesture of apology in my direction. 'It was rats' teeth that killed your father. Damn badgers!'

With 'damn badgers!' we knew a fit was on its way. The rats were now the size of badgers.

My mother maintained until her death that it was this unimagineable experience in the war, not simply the physical damage to his nerves and tissues, that caused my father's epilepsy. Alcohol abuse can cause fits. My mother believed, however, that my father got drunk as he felt 'the shadow of the fits coming on'. No one will ever know; but to my mother's shame and chagrin – against the odds, I believe she loved my father to the end – the cause of his death a few years later in a mental hospital was attributed on the death certificate to 'Chronic Alcoholism', with no mention at all of his ordeal in the trenches.

When my father was safely in hospital six hundred miles away we were happy, though he once arrived back on the doorstep in his pyjamas. He had hitch-hiked all the way from Chepstow next to Wales, in what we thought of as the deep south of England. The authorities believed that his epilepsy and his alcohol abuse were the result of his war-wounds, and he was always treated in Army Hospitals. By the time he arrived home that summer he was already drunk.

During my father's convulsions his neck and chin would spasm uncontrollably and he would snort like a motorbike starting up; he would try to smash his head against the wall or the floor with the strength of a caged wild beast, so one of us had to dive for a cushion while my mother prized open his jaws to prevent him from swallowing his tongue or biting it off. Her fingers were at risk but by then she was adept.

After the fit had passed my father would look up like a child reborn into a terrifying world and whisper 'Teeny?', which was his pet-name for my mother.

'Yes, John, I'm here,' she would assure him in a voice that would make the angels weep, and she would stroke his brow with her chapped hand.

In these piteous moments of calm after his torment I almost loved him.

2 THE ROT SETS IN
The Sweet Taste of Applause

Once upon a time
When the Pigs drank wine,
The monkeys chewed Tabacca;
The Wee Bull Dugs,
Pit Oan their Cluggs,
And waddled through the Watter.

I STILL REMEMBER the thrill of their applause... Five years old, with the sideboard for my stage...

On her windswept croft on the island of North Uist, every year Old Mairat my great aunt would choose two fat chickens from the small flock clucking round her back door and wring their necks under the outside tap; while the birds were still warm, she plucked all their feathers and singed the stubborn ones round the parson's nose with a candle; then, slipping her hand up the rectum, she pulled out their innards, and re-repacked the liver and the kidneys in greaseproof paper. She would stuff the parcel of offal into one bird with its head still on, then stuff six hardboiled eggs in their shells into the other.

Laying the carcasses head to toe, she bound them in muslin. Then she wrapped this precious gift in thick brown paper and trussed it in a safety net of knotted string studded with sealing-wax and sent it to us all the way from the Outer Hebrides – because the pickings there are better for chickens than any pickings she could imagine for chickens in the city. Two or three days in the post at that time of year could only improve their flavour.

The main meals in my youth were Dinner at midday, and Tea at six o'clock. As a word, as a meal, as a concept, Lunch did not exist. Chicken was our once-a-year Christmas luxury, and turkey was undreamed of. We sometimes spent Christmas with my Aunt Flora, my Uncle Bob and the Cousins, Tommy, Christine and Moira. After we were finished dinner, Auntie Flora organised ferociously competitive team games, like 'Flounder Racing', which involved flipping paper fish across the carpet with cardboard fans, and pitched battles, with tangerines and walnuts as missiles, and firework sparklers as the prize.

But nothing caused our childish hearts to beat faster than Auntie Flora's Surgery. Like Roald Dahl, my fearless aunt pandered shamelessly to children's fascination with the ghoulish.

A volunteer was grabbed from the family circle – my mother's convincing protests stifled by a hand clamped over her mouth. The victim, my poor mother, was then forced to lie upon a table behind a sheet suspended from a washing line, with a lamp rigged up behind the whole contraption. The silhouette show was performed by Auntie Flora and Uncle Bob with a saw, a trowel, and an outsize butcher's cleaver (made of cardboard); it was gruesome in the extreme, with my mother screaming and gouts of blood (tomato sauce) splashing onto the sheet during each 'operation'; but the aftermath was worse. All the lights were switched off, and in the total dark, the organs which had been so graphically excised in shadow-play were removed from a bucket and passed round the spectators from hand to hand, for our confirmation. This procedure was a bloodcurdling climax to the whole macabre affair.

'Oh my poor sister!' mumbled my Auntie Flora. 'Auntie Tina's HEART!' she cried, passing round a tennis ball cut in half, embedded in a disgusting lump of several soaps stuck together and jellied by immersion in warm water.

'Bob! Pass me her stomach!' Auntie Flora yelped. Round came a slippy, chamois leather pouch, filled with steaming mashed potatoes which squeezed out as you held it, sticking to your hands and spattering onto your lap.

'The guts! The guts! Let's have her guts!'

'Guts coming up!' cried Uncle Bob, warming to his task as he distributed handsfull of lukewarm spaghetti aslither with unidentified rubbery bits.

'What's this we've got here?' asked Uncle Bob.

'The tripes!' hissed Auntie Flora. 'The TRIPES!'

'Right!' confirmed Uncle Bob. 'The tripes! Auntie Tina's tripes coming up!' Steaming hot face flannels knotted with bits of elastic were pressed into our hands.

'Oegh!!' Auntie Flora growled. 'Oh this is too horrible for words!' There was an unbearable silence. Broken by shuddering exclamations of disgust.

'What have we got for them now, Flo?' whispered Uncle Bob, building up the tension.

'Her EYES!' Auntie Flora screeched. 'Oh, Great Gordon Highlanders! It's Auntie Tina's EYEBALLS!' My mother moaned piteously in the darkness, as reluctant hands fumbled for – two peeled grapes! Squashy, slippery peeled grapes!

We all shrieked like banshees and Moira wet her knickers.

Pandemonium!

Lights up!

Picking over the exhibits to see how ingeniously we had been fooled!

Filthy and sticky as we were, we all threw ourselves into my mother's arms in gratitude that she had survived her ordeal unscathed.

The massive clean-up was punctuated by pulling crackers and blaring in each other's ears with carnival hooters.

In the evening everyone was expected to do A Turn.

Though out of practice, my mother played 'Velia' on the piano. Uncle Bob sang 'Oh Sweet Mystery of Life At Last I've Found You': it was terrible, but we only had Richard Tauber on a crackly record to compare it with.

Tommy did a couple of card tricks. Tommy Cooper without the laughs.

And Chris did an imitation of Mrs McWhirter walking her dog.

I was persuaded, with little difficulty, to deliver my poem. I insisted on ten minutes of preparation, however, then I made my entrance and, sliding a chair over to the sideboard, I climbed up onto the top between the sherry decanter and the candlesticks.

I was a big success. Probably because the poem was short. But my appearance caused consternation.

'Why are you dressed like that, Johnny?' My Auntie Flora had a wart on her chin that trailed wisps like a spider plant, and she wanted to know, as well she might, why I had a cushion stuffed up my jersey, a tea-cloth wound round my head, and one of her aprons tied at my waist.

'I'm a grown-up,' I explained, skidding off the polished surface onto the floor. Since I had been required to recite in public, I had to adopt a persona that commanded respect, and who else fitted that description better than my poor harassed mother?

Chris, Jean, and I, and the cousins, Tommy, Christine and Moira, were all accommodated for the night on a couple of mattresses on the floor. We lay in a tangle of limbs singing campfire songs like 'She'll be comin' round the mountains', and popular ones like 'Amapola', 'South of the Border' and 'Little Sir Echo', till at last we toppled one by one into the bottomless pool of a profound sleep, from which we emerged at lunchtime on Boxing Day, ready for more.

I never see my father at these parties. He must have been in hospital. The only time I see him he is drunk and having fits...

But the pig poem had been made up by my father especially for me. He had taken me through it, some time when he had been normal, like any other Dad. But I can't remember him doing it.

All I can remember is the poem.

When I turned six, my big sister Jean used to take me every Saturday afternoon to Crossmyloof Ice-Rink. She would lace me into the smallest pair of skates on hire, while we were jostled by customers rushing to the ice, trampling the sodden coconut matting like ponies with metal hooves. Tucking me under her arm, Jean would launch into the juggernaut of churning limbs which whined and sliced all round us to the strains of 'It looks like rain, in Cherry Blossom Lane' blaring from the loudspeakers, or 'I had my thrill, on Blueberry Hill'.

In 1937 the world was obsessed with soft fruits.

Jean was thirteen and the object of much admiration from flying squads of pimply youths, who would sweep her off into corners, abandoning me to my fate below eye level, where my little legs scissored vainly against the tidal waves of skaters whose indifference to my welfare in pursuit of their own pleasure threatened to chop me into bite-sized pieces.

Jean would invariably find me at the end of the session wailing my heart out, convinced that I should never see my sister or any of my family ever again. Every week I promised not to be a baby, and every week Jean promised not to let me out of her sight, and every week turned out the same. We both must have weighed up the pros and the cons of our Saturday outings and come to the conclusion that the emotional turmoil which seemed to be unavoidable in the overcrowded rink was more than compensated for by the dubious joys of skating.

Many distant moons ago my mother's eldest sister had emigrated to America and had found a good position 'in service' as a lady's maid in New York. Aunt Effie was another spinster like my snow-haired deaf Aunt Gatty, and she would send us parcels from time to time, wonderful, mysterious parcels containing her mistress' discarded finery for Chris and Jean to dress-up in – a crushed-velvet negligée trimmed with maribou, a pearl-satin evening cloak, a reticule in midnight blue silk containing a powder-compact complete with dispirited puff, and a stump of lipstick in a spangly dispenser. These parcels used to make me wonder for a moment whether the indiscriminate accumulating of trinkets might be a family trait; perhaps Aunt Effie's fingers were as sticky as my Aunt Gatty's?

On my sixth birthday, the Parcel of Parcels arrived from the United States of America, and it was addressed to me and to my cousin Moira.

There were two Redskin outfits: the chief's fringed trousers for me, and the beaded squaw's skirt for Moira. We had feathered head-dresses, a bow and arrows, a tomahawk with a rubber blade, and sticks of warpaint for slashing our cheeks with coloured stripes. To crown it all, there was a wigwam with room inside for two, and in lieu of a peace pipe, a large tin of peanut brittle to share at our pow-wow.

Bribed by a small quantity of the crunchy toffee, Chris and Jean and Tommy helped us to erect the wigwam before disappearing in search of more adult pursuits.

Moira and I were hoarse with our battle-cries and panting from the exertions of our war dance.

'You can have the last piece of peanut brittle,' Moira said magnanimously. She was a year older than I was, and I looked up to her as a woman of the world. She was trying and failing to find a comfortable position, cross-legged, with her back against the centre-pole.

I bit off a peanutty piece for myself and handed her the rest.

'Redskins share and share alike,' I told her, glowing like a traffic light with bonhomie. 'I wish we had some Redskin Irn-Bru.'

Fired, no doubt, by vivid memories of Auntie Flora's shadow play, Moira suggested we try a game of 'Sudgery'. Marvelling at the winged imagination of my older cousin, I followed her eagerly indoors to find instruments suitable for our purpose.

We returned with a motley assortment of kitchen utensils and toilet accessories, and under Moira's firm instructions I flung aside my feathered headdress and removed my fringed tunic and my undervest. She then surveyed her prospective patient – me – and I could tell by the way she stuck out her lower lip that I failed to measure up to her requirements.

'Take everything off!' she whispered. Her whispering was a clear indication to both of us that we were embarking on dangerous waters, and that naughtiness couldn't begin to describe the wickedness we were up to.

'I will if you will!' I whispered, feeling as if I was drowning in a vat of undiluted evil, and the sheer excitement of it left me short of breath. Even as a pre-adolescent, I was discovering that guilt is a powerful aphrodisiac.

We sat there in our birthday suits, all thoughts of pretend operations abandoned in the light of this unforeseen development.

We examined each other's number one equipment as if our lives depended on it, and the rapture I experienced that day in sniffing Moira's bum has never been exceeded in all my adult fantasies.

I knew nothing about sex. I didn't know what it was. I had no idea what it was for. Moira and I enjoyed playing 'Sudgery' so much we knew it must be wicked; so wicked we knew that it had to be kept a secret. I played 'Sudgery' with my favourite cousin whenever the opportunity arose, which wasn't often, but we were never found out.

But that first time in the wigwam, how do you explain that among the instruments we had collected for our 'Sudgery' I picked out my mother's perfume spray? Attached to the bottle there was a rubber ball covered in cream lace, which you had to squeeze to make it 'Skoosh!' Without instruction or encouragement, I discovered somehow that it was bliss to slip the nozzle into Moira's front bottom and go 'Skoosh!' 'Skoosh! Skoosh!' 'Skoosh! Skoosh!'

Moira must have had the most fragrant front bottom in the Northern hemisphere.

I started off right. What went wrong?

3 FAMILY MATTERS
Even Dysfunctional Ones

MY MOTHER had black hair shot with grey that fell to her waist, but she wore it in my lifetime wound round a laddered stocking at the base of her neck in a curl as thick as a blood sausage. She had a lean upright figure, square shoulders, a slender waist, narrow hips and strong legs. Her eyes were the colour of molasses, with an almost oriental slant.

Both my parents wore dentures. This was a legacy of the soft water in Glasgow which a hundred years ago had so little lime in it that caries and rickets were endemic among its citizens. The council rectifies the situation now by adding tons of lime to the waters of Loch Katrine, the city's reservoir. The prevailing philosophy among the poor at that time was that a total extraction got the costly business of visits to the dentist over with once and for all.

My mother's hands were red and calloused from scrubbing floors and pounding the weekly wash in our gas-boiler with a scrubbing-board and a bar of venerable soap, hard and veined like ancient ivory. She smoked thirty 'Capstan' cigarettes a day, which was her only indulgence. Often there was only mashed potato for dinner with a dollop of butter. She never complained.

Sometimes she wept when my father was late for the fifth night running, and she couldn't bear to think of the evening ahead let alone think of the future for her children. She was shy, and reserved with neighbours; she was tolerant beyond her understanding, wise beyond her experience, and fundamentally good. She never wore a scrap of makeup, and she was heavily wrinkled by the time she was forty. In an early photograph, wearing a wide hat and leaning over a wall, I thought she looked like a young Ava Gardner. It is rare for children not to describe their mothers as beautiful, for offspring see in their mothers an idealised version of themselves.

My eldest sister Chris was ten years older than I was. She was dark, with fine bones and the same narrow eyes as my mother. As a child she was an extrovert, and the leading light of the Dramatic Club; at the age of eleven she was voted The Most Popular Girl In The School. Then adolescence struck, and overnight her personality changed. Gone forever was the popular hoyden, and in her place was a painfully shy girl who was self-effacing to a fault.

My sisters' bath night, particularly before some special occasion, became a prolonged and noisy secret ceremony. Amid yelps and giggles, Jean was shaving the fluff from Chris' armpits, and removing the downy hairs from her legs with evil-smelling wax heated up in a miniature frying-pan over a methylated spirit flame. These arcane rituals were conducted behind locked doors, and added fuel to my insatiable but thwarted curiosity about the truly extraordinary mystery of being female. I later found a chamber pot under the bath, full to the brim with little towels soaking in bloodstained water. There were whole wildernesses of ignorance upon which I dared not trespass; my only salvation was that I knew by instinct when questions would cause consternation, so I didn't ask them.

A story was repeated to me by Betty MacAteer, our local sibyl, who was incalculably old; she had already started at Queen's Park Secondary School. She spoke of an occasion so long ago that the details were lost forever in the mists of time: one day a glass coach had drawn up outside our front door and two men in black had carried out a white shoe-box which was borne away inside the coach resting on a satin cushion. I learned much later that the glass coach was a hearse and that the shoe-box was a coffin containing the remains of my still-born older brother.

My middle sister Jean was only seven years older than I was but she spoilt me in a way that my mother never did. All of us three siblings were preternaturally close – no doubt due to the Wagnerian dramas caused by my father's illness – and we remained close. There must have been some disagreements between the three of us, but I can remember none.

We lived in the outskirts of Glasgow in a semi-detached house on a council estate called Mosspark. Perhaps because the estate was new, and the houses had not yet had time to fall into disrepair, delusions of grandeur were endemic. Many tenants had persuaded themselves that their sojourn at the council's expense was temporary, and that soon they would be on their way to proper suburbs like Giffnock or Bearsden.

Like Mrs McWhirter across the road, whose Pekinese was bald around the middle because she carried it everywhere under her arm, with one hand on her hip. A cigarette was stuck in her mouth like a fixture; she never inhaled but let it smoulder, so that her upper lip and the tip of her nose were stained indelibly brown; the smoke drifting into her eyes compelled her to wink at passersby, and since she was a plain woman and as old, it seemed to me, as anyone can get before being sat in a rocking chair in front of the fire, her apparent invitations found no takers.

Her husband brought the booze home twice a week in his briefcase. Most days the case swung with his stride, light as a feather, but he was not endowed with the talent for mime required to disguise the greatly increased weight when it was filled with bottles. People muttered through their net curtains, 'There goes Pa McWhirter wi' his bag fu' o' Bells!'

Then they'd rummage in the sideboard for a 'Nip' to cool their indignation. This love-hate relationship with alcohol is to blame for the habitual drunkenness which is the unacknowledged shame of the Scottish nation.

The tram-ride from Sauchiehall Street takes you along the boulevards of Pollokshields and Dumbreck, where the toffs live in their detached stone mansions, so if you were a stranger you might think you were on your way to visit a person of quality. But then the great shoogly vehicle, squelching sparks from its overhead conductor, lurches round the bend into Mosspark, and you are confronted with row after row of pebble-dashed semis, their front doors painted an identical green by the council, and opposite, behind a high spiked fence, the dreary desolation of Bellahouston Park.

In 1937 this Park became the site of the Empire Exhibition, the biggest trade fair ever to be mounted in these islands. Within six months the vast space – about half the size of Hyde Park in London – was landscaped and transformed into a Space-Age City. The Empire Tower was built on a man-made hill in the middle, a slab that scraped the sky like a cosmic exclamation mark – a pointer to the Greatest Show on Earth!

All the colonies were represented, each with its own pavilion, vying with its neighbours for attention. Australia housed a globe of the world the size of a minor planet suspended without visible means of support in a vast blue space that twinkled with stars, revolving slowly in defiance of gravity. New Zealand had gilded naked figures of a male and a female on plinths adorning the entrance, untramelled with a fig-leaf, brandishing their pudenda tantalisingly out of reach above your head.

Battery-driven buses hummed on pink tarmac along avenues flanked with crystal palisades between fountains bathed in coloured lights that danced to music from loudspeakers clamped to poles fluttering with the flags of all the Commonwealth. Customers were thus insinuated past the cultural and business side of things, which was the point of the whole exercise, to the outer limits where the glass and steel fantasies crumbled into a sleazy sideshow which racketed on day and night for six months, and for which I had a season ticket.

This little passport in blue rexine with my child's laborious signature snapped behind cellophane gave me access daily with no charge to a tawdry wonderland that held me spellbound.

One of my favourite stalls was the freak show, with its Siamese twins who were not Siamese at all, but two game girls from Wigan, I am sure now, stuck together with latex rubber, though there was a two-headed foetus pickled in a jar in case you made a complaint. There were three giraffe-necked women from Burma, sitting in a booth in their tribal dress. The printed notice on the side of their 'cage' assured us that if the brass rings that held up their heads were to be removed, their necks would break. There was a bearded woman with a curling appendage that reached to her chest which looked genuine even right up close (the beard, I mean, looked genuine, and for that matter so did the chest), and a troupe of perfectly-formed midgets from all round the world, two to three feet high, with old wrinkled faces and treble voices. There were fire-eaters and sword-swallowers, Indian and African dancers, and a lethal-looking guillotine where a bulgy woman in glittering scanties had her head cut off. The severed head was wrapped in newspaper and flung into the audience (shades of Auntie Flora's Sudgery!) where, unparcelled, it turned out to be a cabbage.

There was ice-cream and candy-floss and toffee apples. There were dodgems, the waltzer, the Big Wheel and The Wall of Death, with motorbikes hurtling in a thunder of blue fumes, horizontally skimming past your elbows as they rested on the parapet.

And the whole squalid magnificence reeked of joss sticks and cheap scent and stale makeup and patchouli and a damp and acrid musk which I found intoxicating and compulsively groiny.

I visited the Empire Exhibition almost every day of its existence for six months: such an early saturation in this sordid funfair existence has had an effect on my life which has been incalculable.

Thank God.

My father had been born one of seventeen children. They all survived infancy to overpopulate the globe. My Daddy was somewhere in the middle. The family was not Catholic, just prolific. This army had been brought up in a terrace house with three bedrooms, a tin bath, and an outside lavatory in Barrhead, a small town midway between Glasgow and Paisley. My grandfather, no doubt exhausted by siring this prodigious progeny, died before I was born. My grandmother, however, the brood mare for her husband's perpetual motion, lived to a ripe old age; when we visited her I didn't like to eat there because the old house smelt of overpopulation and fishy soap. My father's brothers and sisters all married and had children though none broke their parent's record of seventeen. I have legions of cousins throughout the world: Frasers to right of me, Frasers to left of me...some of them in America, in South Africa, in Canada or Australia. In my travels they have sometimes turned up at the Stage Door announcing their blood-ties. I liked to muse that people are like breeds of dogs. I am a Fox-Terrier, so my relations will be recognisably Fox-Terriers. On the contrary, they turn out to be Great Danes or Chihuahuas, or more often than not one of the Heinz 57 Varieties.

My mother also came from a large family, though only half the size of my father's mighty one: there were five girls and three boys. The MacDonalds were brought up in a tenement in Govan, a ship-building area, since my maternal grandfather, Black Roderick, was the Captain of a dredger on the Clyde. In photographs he has a square beard that reaches half-way down his chest and a braided skipper's hat straight out of Gilbert and Sullivan. Both my mother's parents died before I was born. Perhaps my extended family is so numerous because it is so short-lived. Like those millions of newly hatched turtles that are eaten before they reach the sea.

4 THE OUTER HEBRIDES: NORTH UIST
War Declared

MY MOTHER'S FAMILY the MacDonalds were immigrants from the Western Isles – from the Island of North Uist in the Outer Hebrides to be precise – and although they spoke English – Scottish English – their original tongue was Gaelic.

I was taken once by my Aunt Gatty for a holiday near Claddach Kyles, on the eastern shore of the island where the remains of my mother's family still lived.

Apart from the expense, the journey from Glasgow in those days to the Outer Hebrides was long and uncomfortable. Eight hours on the train through Glencoe and Fort William, the tops of the mountains only visible if you crouched on the floor of the compartment, to Mallaig or the Kyles of Lochalsh, where you boarded the little McBrayne's steamer and grabbed a seat inside, if you were lucky, for the sleepless night ahead. The Cuillin Hills of Skye in silhouette filled the dawn, and after calling at Portree and Dunvegan, the brave little boat would set out into the Atlantic, heading for its first stop in the Western Isles, Stornoway on the island of Lewis. Throughout the interminable journey we grazed on the sandwiches and a flask of tea my mother had prepared for us. At dusk, two days after our departure from Glasgow, the steamer coasted into Lochmaddy Bay.

The island of North Uist is like a rumpled purple blanket spangled with mirrors – countless lochs abounding in fish – but the land between is treeless because of the shallowness of its top soil and the unremitting winds. You hardly miss the trees because the heather grows as high as your eye; and the bogs, aglitter with dragonflies in the summer, provide the peat which is the island's staple fuel. There are ancient circles of great standing stones. The locals call them 'Faerie Rings', but I expect they are Druid relics. The Vikings landed here millennia ago and left a legacy of flame-haired amazons and names like Ludovic and Magnus.

You can spear flounders on the silver beaches if you have the knack, and dig up winkles when you see their tell-tale 'eye' catching the sun in the wet sand.

The cattle look like bison crossed with snub-nosed yaks and they have a horn-span like the wingspread of a skua, and orange pelts that sweep the turf. My cousin Malcolm coaxed the pale yellow milk from the lovely beasts by hand, but I spurned the tumbler he filled straight from the cow, which my Aunt Gatty promised me was the best thing in the world for a growing boy. Just because I was city bred, did they really think I would fall for it? Just because the spout issued from the ginger depths of undergrowth between the legs of an animal I had never seen before, did they really think I couldn't tell by the size and shape of the pink and wobbly teat that jetted blood-warm and frothing into the glass, what it was? And what the big hairy beast was doing?

Malcolm's house smelt of peat and cream, and the earthen floor was scattered with clean white sand from the beach once a week.

The Uist people's necks are locked in a religious yoke. The Wee Free Kirk is a joyless, Calvinist sect whose ministers preach nothing but Hellfire. Grace is said in Gaelic before every meal. The only activity permitted on a Sunday is the long walk to the Kirk, and many cover ten miles on the Sabbath going to all three services, morning, afternoon and evening. All food to be consumed on Sunday has to be prepared the day before and the wash-up must be left till the following morning. The only reading permitted is the Bible or Bunyan's *Pilgrim's Progress*. Sunday papers can be bought and read on Monday. On Saturday night Old Mairat, an incalculably ancient relation who lived alone, used to separate the cockerel from the hens. I had my own bedroom under the eaves, so I could get on with *Coral Island*, ready at the slightest creak from the stairs to stuff such wickedness under the pillow.

There was a pump over the kitchen sink and no other plumbing in the house. The lavatory was on the shore, a hole in a plank in a tiny cabin erected on the edge of a small cliff. When the wind was high you had to chase your used piece of newspaper round the cubicle as it kept gusting back up the hole. There was a bucket of sand with a trowel in it, and the sand, if you were quick, could be used to weight the paper down. But it did nothing to stifle the stench.

Malcolm was the big brother I had always longed for, a gentle youth with a loping stride and a soft, confident way with the animals. Even at eight years old, watching him herd the cows out onto the moors, and whistling without his fingers to Kirsty the collie to round up the sheep, stirred emotions which I didn't understand.

Aunt Gatty had kept up her Gaelic, and she had to act as my interpreter with my younger cousins since children are taught English only once they go to school. Communicating in this way was a noisy affair, what with the state of my Aunt Gatty's 'lazy drums', as she was wont to call her all-but-useless otic appendages, but where there's a will there's a way. Malcolm was in his teens, but through lack of practice, he was halting in English. This in no way diminished my adoration of him, and my feelings were the start of a pattern pre- and post-adolescence. Girls were my chosen companions and my trusted friends. But boys held a mystery for me long before I recognised its origins as sexual.

There were other holidays in the Isle of Arran and in the fishing village of Stonehaven. I can see the clouds of midges that tormented us, and the horrible clegs [horseflies] that stick to you, sucking your blood till you swell up like a bladder, and I can remember downpours of torrential rain.

But mostly the sun is blazing in my memories because my father is not there...

There are jam sandwiches and tea that tastes funny but delicious from a flask, and there are sand-dunes like cool velvet caressing your toes and the sea so cold you have to have 'chittery bites' after 'a dook' – biscuits to stop your teeth from chattering after a swim...

We used motor-car inner tubes for life-belts, since only my big sister Chris was a strong swimmer, and all the women's nipples almost pierced their woollen swimsuits with the cold.

There was a seaside concert party that performed under a concrete awning on the promenade. Six chorus-girls wearing tartan tutus swung their purple knobbly knees erratically into the air, while a crooner in a kilt with a vibrato like a musical saw warbled 'Blue Moon'.

They had a 'Tableau' with the crooner again, a Pastoral Scene with a trickling hose for a waterfall and a flock of three insanitary old sheep.

And they had Frank and Doris Droy, who had seen better days.

They had played 'The Metropole' in the Trongate, for God's sake. And they had no rivals in their field.

They were true sophisticates.

The show I remember was presented after tea and designed for adults, who were more able to appreciate the subtlety and the sophistication of their humour.

Frank and Doris – The Droys – performed short, black-out sketches, and to set the tone Frank would first remove his dentures.

It was a classroom sketch. Frank, minus his teeth, was the teacher. Doris was his pupil. She had a very short skirt, revealing ripped navy-blue bloomers. As the lights went up she was revealed picking her nose and chewing it.

Frank chalked a big 'F' on the blackboard. 'Whissat?' he frothed.

Doris stopped chewing and studied the symbol through narrowed eyes. At last she shouted: 'K!'

Frank threw down his pointer in disgust, and pulled a few gurning faces with his toothless gums. 'Every time I write "F" you see "K"!'

Blackout.

On the walk home the sky was full of the cries of gulls as they wheeled keening round the harbour. The wind tasted like Bovril on the lips; as the evening catch was unloaded, the smell of fresh mackerel and whiting and cod assaulted our senses as if the very essence of the sea had erupted in a fountain under our noses, seasoned by the tang of damp mortar and lime from the fishermen's stone cottages.

The peat smoke, the tea-pot mashing on the hob, the honeyed steam from fresh scones just out of the oven, homemade raspberry jam and slabs of butter beaten with spatulas and rolled into little corrugated balls so that it spread like cream...

Then home to Mosspark and school again, to the worry and the bald lawn and the grey skies and the drizzle and the chilblains and the drunkenness and the constant dread...

Then war was declared with Germany.

The wireless looked like a bakelite model of an art-deco cathedral, and we all stood round it in the congregational silence reserved for sermons. The lugubrious tones of Neville Chamberlain, the Prime Minister, dubbed in history books The Great Appeaser, broke the news to the nation. '...The United Kingdom and Germany are now at war...'

Daddy was upstairs in bed sleeping it off. My Aunt Gatty looked expectantly from my sisters to my mother and back again, waiting anxiously for an upgrade in the decibels in order more fully to appreciate the enormity of the calamity which she could read in all our faces. Not wishing to butt into their grown-up grief, I asked in a tactful whisper, 'Shall I go and put on my gas-mask?'

We had been issued with these masks some months before, and gas-mask drill at school was a welcome break from lessons. We loved to sing and shout inside them till the perspex window steamed up, and by blowing and manipulating the rubber you could make the most satisfying, the most unforgettably epic farts.

I was gently dissuaded from donning my mask straight away. In spite of the prevailing mood of despair I was elated, in anticipation of a new dimension in our humdrum lives, something quite different and impossible to predict.

My big sister Chris joined the WAAFs. She was so pretty that they wanted to use her photograph on the recruitment poster. They must have thought better of it, for in the end they used a plain girl instead. Later on in the war Jean did voluntary work in the evenings behind the counter at the YMCA canteen. She was jailbait at barely sixteen, but she broke a few hearts.

'Quickly! Into the cupboard!' Mummy commanded.

To a child who lacked the experience and the imagination to envisage the consequences of being bombed with high explosives, the air-raids were hugely exciting, and I never felt the slightest tremor of fear. I loved being dragged rudely from my bed in the middle of the night by my big sisters, because I knew that if the air-raid siren shrieked its baleful warning after midnight, the following day pupils were allowed to stay off school till after midday.

The bass rumble of the Luftwaffe's bombers laboured like a gramophone running down; the deep, undulating rhythm of the engines was punctuated by the boom-boom, boom-boom of the anti-aircraft guns, a double beat on the timpani. It was a challenge to interpret this war-music, so new and exciting to our ears. There followed the fire-cracker rattle from the fighter-planes as the flak burst in purple stars round the great hulks with their cargo of death and destruction. Gazoom! The Spitfires slashed through the clouds firing in sleek arcs from their gun turrets as girders of light from the powerful searchlights in Bellahouston Park criss-crossed the clouds.

'Come away from the window, Johnny!' Mummy was pulling her shabby flannelette dressing gown over her nightie. Chris and Jean somnambulated down the stairs sharing an eiderdown, a two-headed conglomerate of sisters.

'And straighten the blackout!'

We had thick black sugar-paper blinds at all our windows, and the panes were mullioned with sticky-tape to prevent shards of glass flying everywhere if a landmine blew them in.

A voluntary home guard of tin-helmeted air-raid wardens patrolled the streets outside; too old or unfit for the call-up, they took their responsibilities seriously, just waiting to seize their opportunity to nab you for chinks round the edge of your windows; even a tiny sliver of light might help the Jerries to pinpoint their aim and blow us all to smithereens.

We're always hearing that wartime brings out the best in people. It also brings out the worst. Power corrupts, and absolute power corrupts absolutely… Having admired Mister Hodge slapping his butter into shape with his wooden paddles on the marble counter of his grocer's shop, and garrotting his barrel-sized cheddar into wedges with his curling steel wire, perhaps we should not have been so surprised that giving him a whistle turned him into a Gauleiter.

'Lights out!' he would shriek at the least provocation, blowing his whistle like the referee at the annual Celtic versus Rangers carnage. 'Book that traitor!'

Most of our neighbours had an Andersen's corrugated-iron capsule buried in the garden, but if you didn't have a shelter but were lucky enough to have a staircase, during the air-raids the government had advised people to take refuge in the space underneath. Nothing, of course, would survive a direct hit, but the area below the stairs was believed to offer the best protection against falling masonry.

All of us, except my father who was in hospital, huddled together inside the cupboard by the light of a guttering candle in a saucer. We didn't talk much, as we were straining to hear whether the deadly drone was approaching or receding, or whether another wave of bombers was on its way to blitz the shipyards in Clydebank only ten miles away.

'I hear a brass band.'

We all looked at Aunt Gatty.

She held up her hands as if to say 'It's not my fault!' and repeated emphatically: 'I hear a brass band!'

She had at last acquired a hearing aid. It was a primitive machine by today's standards, and it weighed about as much as your average car battery. It had to be strapped to her body with a stout belt round her middle in the vain hope of concealing it under her cardigan. She was used to people shouting into her ear, but it was hard for her to adjust to the idea of potential communicators having to shout even louder into her cardigan. The wire from her ear made her look like a large bag of dynamite about to be detonated. The instrument seemed to be of the whistling variety, like some kettles, and she spent a lot of time interfering with her navel to force the tricky whistler to its knees. With typical nonchalance, she called her new technology her 'Radar', and its antics infuriated her.

'It's playing "Colonel Bogey"!' she protested.

The ground shook as a Big Bertha flattened John Brown's shipyard along with ten streets around it, which was confirmed the following morning in the *Daily Record*. Flakes of whitewash floated about our ears in a miniature blizzard.

Aunt Gatty was now picking up police messages. She repeated them to us for our confirmation – 'Double two five eight? Come in double two five eight? Meet me at the corner of Ashdale and the Avenue. Over?' For a moment Aunt Gatty looked expectant, her lips popping open to reply to this curious invitation. Then the penny dropped that her Radar was promiscuous and indiscriminate.

'Now I'm gettin' the poalis,' she said, wresting the troublesome tonnage from around her waist and turning down the whistle to a peep. 'Keep tuned in. It'll be the nine o'clock news next. This contraption's got a life all its own.'

Then the All Clear sounded, the high steady note which proclaimed that the warplanes had wreaked all the horror there was to be wreaked for one night, that they had emptied their lethal bowels over the sleeping shipyards and were heading back home to Adolf, so that it was safe once again for us to return to the comfort of our beds.

5 THE MAD CEMENT MIXER
Evac You Wee

I CAN'T REMEMBER why my mother didn't come to Central Station. All the other mothers were there to see off the 'Evacuees', which was a new word to everyone, but to Scots ears alone it suggests little children. Forget the Evac. What we hear is 'You-Wees'. All those motherless bairns with labels round their necks – there wasn't a dry eye in the house.

Miss Malcolm insisted on kissing me goodbye in place of my mother, and it was not an experience I should like to repeat. My father must have been ill, I suppose, and my sisters generously giving me the chance to stand on my own two feet, but I had a struggle with a feeling, for the first time but certainly not the last, of being abandoned. At eight years old, along with several other boys and girls from my class in primary school, I was setting off for a little border town called Newton Stewart in Kircudbright, pronounced Kirkoobray, far from shipyards or military installations or other prime targets for Jerry's bombs.

When we reached our destination we were herded into the black stone Presbyterian Kirk to be given the once-over by the mugs whose arms had been twisted by the council to give house room to these poor brats from Glasgow for the duration of the war. During this processs of allocation we felt as stray dogs must feel in a dog-pound, where the healthy, the beautiful, and the winsome are the first to be saved from the needle. We all looked eager and metaphorically wagged our tails.

I was billeted with a family called the Broughs, Ma, Pa, and son Kenneth. That I didn't stay the course was due to Vera Lynn.

'We'll meet again' was bad enough, but then it was 'Goodnight children everywhere, Your Mummy thinks of you tonight…' It was 'Daddy' in the song, and it was meant for children whose fathers were away in the forces, but every time I heard it, in my head I changed 'Daddy' to 'Mummy' for obvious reasons… 'Lay your head upon your pillow, Don't be a kid or a weeping willow…' Show me the You-Wee who could remain unmoved in the teeth of such an onslaught!

The cracks appeared at tea-time, when Ma Brough had served up meat-loaf, mash and baked beans. My favourite. Then Vera Lynn started and I couldn't eat a bite.

It was not till much later, however, when the whole household was asleep that the dam broke.

'Ma!' Kenneth shouted. 'It's the ludger!'

We shared a bedroom and an antipathy for each other that flourished like a hot-house plant. He was an only child, and I was a cuckoo in the nest, so his resentment of me was understandable. He was a month or two younger than I was, and I tried hard to ingratiate myself with him by lending him my copy of *The Last of the Mohicans* and teaching him the Fangle Slanted Wrapover Anchor Dog that I had learnt at the Cubs, to no avail. He had a grey, mottled complexion and hair like a lavatory brush, and there were a hundred occasions when I could cheerfully have broken his nose. Like when he kept referring to me as 'The Lodger'. But my hands were tied in that direction, since Ma Brough made me acutely aware in not so subtle ways how grateful I should be to her and Pa Brough for taking me in, and to Kenneth for allowing me to share his bedroom, and – the implication was clear – for putting up with my tricky, city ways.

I know families were paid by the government for the keep of evacuee children, but when I once overheard Ma Brough complain to her husband that 'the price is too high' she may, on reflection, have been referring to the emotional price, for she didn't seem to me to have a lot of love to spare. She was not an instinctual, earth-mother sort of woman, and she disliked me only a little more, I suspect, than she disliked her own son.

Since I mentioned hands earlier, I ought to mention at this point that Pa Brough had only one. The other, he informed me the first time I met him, had been chewed off by a mad cement mixer. He didn't wear a false one, just a woollen 'sock' to cover the stump. Disabled as he was, he was adept at most manual tasks – I watched him spellbound as he tied his tie – and he always treated me with a slightly embarrassing formal respect, as if I was a young prince in a fairy tale being reared in the forest by the woodcutter and his goodly wife. He rarely called me anything but Master Fraser, and he sought my opinion on everything. I believe Pa Brough detected something fine in my nature, which, if he was not mistaken, I attribute unequivocally to being brought up entirely by females. Not just any old females, naturally.

'Ma!' Kenneth shouted, now at our bedroom door. 'He's blubbing!'

Ma Brough took a moment to throw on her dressing gown and came reluctantly to investigate.

'What's all this about?' she said, sitting on my bed and sizing up the situation. With a sigh of exasperation she said, 'He's homesick.'

'Shall I get a bucket?' Kenneth asked her.

She shook her head. 'Back to bed and go to sleep. And no Ifs or Buts.'

She stroked my brow perfunctorily, and patted me firmly on the shoulder.

'He'll be all right in a minute,' she assured Kenneth.

What she meant was: 'Or else!'

She added, 'He won't be keeping us awake much longer!'

But she was wrong, and I wasn't all right.

I was pining.

At the little country school, I was taught to knit, one plain one purl, making squares which the teacher sewed into lumpy, multi-coloured, stretchy things which she called blankets; I couldn't imagine in my nightmares anyone being desperate enough to consider using any of these hideous artefacts to keep warm; they were just an excuse to keep the You-Wees busy and out of mischief, since the teachers couldn't cope with the explosion of pupils in their rural classrooms.

At dancing class I learnt the Eightsome Reel, the Gay Gordons and the Highland Fling. I wrote home three times a week, brave little notes relating how I had spent my days, because I knew no words that could express the anguish in my heart, and I didn't want to be a worry to my mother.

Billy McFarlane took me to a slaughterhouse, where I saw a bullock hoisted with chain and tackle, its great astrakhan head hanging helpless beneath the weight of its tonnage, a bolt into the skull, the slash of the butcher's knife across its throat, the neon fountain of blood gushing into basins the size of cartwheels to be made into black puddings. The slaughterman threw the 'wizzle' at us, the bullock's penis which is sometimes dried and made into a whip. It slapped across my bare legs, and I ran as if Auld Nick himself was after me, and I didn't stop till I had shut myself into the bathroom in Ma Brough's billets and scrubbed at the black smear on my legs until my skin glowed pink.

Pa Brough took Kenneth and me sailing. He swung the boom and mastered the rudder and lowered the sails at the end of the day and tied us up to the jetty with a deftness that defied belief. He could be forgiven for his pride in refusing to accept his disability.

Then, on the way home – Kenneth had run on ahead while Master Fraser and Pa Brough were walking back through the woods and talking man to man – he stopped and asked me to undo his flies…

I had seen him tie his tie every morning, single-handed. I had seen him eat his breakfast and drink his tea. I had just seen him manage a boat like a professional helmsman, but now he wanted me to unbutton his trousers…

When I hesitated he rebuked me.

'You're not refusing to help your old friend to relieve his bladder, are you Master Fraser? Just undo my flies, laudie, that's all I ask.'

Perhaps that's all it was. Perhaps he was tired with being clever and overcoming his handicap. I didn't know why else he would ask me to do such a thing.

But no one had ever asked me to do such a thing before. In all my experience, no boy had ever asked another boy to do such a thing. I didn't know what I was afraid of, but I was. And leaving him to wet his trousers, if need be, I ran ahead to catch up with my arch enemy, which no doubt gave Kenneth a big surprise.

Newton Stewart, the village life, the Broughs, the even tenor of a sober household without a sniff of alcohol, it was a different world, a healthier world most people might say, but I was pining.

My mother came to visit me just before Christmas, saw the desolation in my eyes and took me home. I didn't care if I was melted by the Jerries as long as I was with my mother.

Finally, neither did she.

6 SHENANIGANS
And a Proper Education

I HAD BEEN TAUGHT the breast-stroke on a kitchen chair before being propelled for the first time into the arctic sorbet of 'The Baths' in Pollokshields. Municipal pools in my youth were Spartan places for bathers who could avoid turning blue only by serious swimming. There were scalding showers belching steam beyond the shallow end like a vision of paradise to sustain your floundering under the instructor's remorseless disapproval. Only on odd days in July and August when the sun stopped flirting from behind the clouds and came out for a steadfast gaze at our city – on the same latitude as Moscow – did the prospect of 'The Baths' appear to me as a pleasure and not as a penance. It was on such a day that at the age of eleven I had my first sexual experience with an adult. In today's language, I was sexually abused. I told no one because I loved every moment of it.

The day was a scorcher. The queue for 'The Baths' snaked round the block, and each individual on entry was given a numbered ticket. On the hour, a whistle was blown, a shrill policeman's whistle with a dried pea inside to make it trill, and the pool had to be cleared for the next customers. There were cubicles all round the pool with half-doors which left your shoulders and ankles exposed; because of the crowd, everyone had to double up in the changing rooms. I had to share my cubicle with an English soldier.

He was probably all of eighteen years old. The landscape that he revealed to me between his legs was Shangri-La; magical, mysterious and bosky, and it cradled a gigantic length of superhumanity that grew larger by the second and finally stood right up to wink at me. I was flabbergasted. When this miraculous club erupted, spurting milky fluid over my hairless belly, I caught a flicker from the far end of the dark tunnel of my ignorance. Pete – for such was the soldier's name – fondled me, but not excessively. He seemed content to exhibit his virility rather than to foist it, and I watched enthralled. I saw him on two other occasions. My mother was mildly concerned at my new friendship with a mature adult, as well she might be, and she invited him to tea. He came in his uniform, and any suspicions she might have entertained were dispelled because she wanted them to be; she had no words in her vocabulary to address me on such a subject. She saw that Pete was no drivelling monster, and she swallowed her fears. A year later, when he had long since disappeared down south he wrote to me and to my mother inviting our entire family to his wedding. We didn't go. Chris said she expected he was hoping for a present.

Child abuse is the most horrifying crime on the statute books, along with rape and murder. But in my case I was not abused; I invited Pete's intimacy by my blatant curiosity. There was no penetration and no force and above all there was no fear. I believe there are many cases similar to mine, where the fuss made by adults when they find out causes more harm than the 'abuse'. This is not a defence of paedophilia, but there are degrees of 'abuse', and there must be many instances like mine when there is no harm done and the experience can be taken in a child's stride. Having said this, over many years I have wondered whether I enjoyed my first homosexual experience because I am homosexual, or whether I am homosexual because I enjoyed my first homosexual experience. I will never know, but as long as doubt remains, childhood must be protected at all costs, in case unsolicited initiation at a tender age damages forever a person's chances of a stress-free, loving relationship. Or even influences sexual preference, although I seriously doubt this latter possibility. At every turn, within the family, at school, in films, in advertising, on television, in print, and all around us for twenty-four hours of every day, heterosexuality is promoted because it is normal. This barrage of promotion makes no difference to the minority who discover, usually to their dismay, that they are attracted to their own sex.

In the wake of this incident with Pete there was a family conference. (Minus my father, of course, who was in hospital. He was always in hospital.) It was not about the fragility of my moral fibre, however, but about my academic future. It was time for me to go to secondary school.

'You will be going to the High School For Boys,' my mother told me. The High School was one of the two top grammar schools in Glasgow, and its fees were way beyond our means. I had passed the entrance exam, but my average results had failed to qualify me for a scholarship.

'But how – ?'

'Your Aunt Gatty is going to pay,' my mother said, kissing her sister on the cheek.

It will be abundantly clear to all who have read this far in these memoirs that I loved my mother ferociously. But it was my deaf Aunt Gatty with her Singer sewing machine and her calves like melons that treadled me out of the hopeless rut of my father's drunkenness and set me on the first rung of the Ladder of Life. The climb was up to me.

7 TATTY-HOWKING
And Thunderbolts

1943 WAS MY Year of the Thunderbolts.

It began in the Highlands, on a great hunting estate in Ross-shire, a far cry from the council estate in Mosspark where my family huddled behind windows latticed with tape to keep them from splintering when next the Hun was bombing the shipyards in Clydebank.

I was billeted with thirty of my schoolmates, Poppy Garland the science master and Marge the housekeeper in a shooting lodge belonging to the illustrious family which had made its fortune selling Worcester Sauce (though I never found out whether they were called 'Lea' or 'Perrins' or neither), situated on a bluff above the Cromarty Firth, near the town of Alness, in a country of beetling crags and black torrents north of everywhere.

I was twelve years old, and I can time the first Thunderbolt to within a month. It was September when I first noticed my balls.

To mix metaphors and confuse sportsmen round the world, that intimate discovery was the starter's pistol for the Thunderbolt Marathon which was to follow.

The Thunderbolts came in the shape of Beauty, Love and Death in that order.

For the first time I caught a glimpse of the alarming and wonderful possibilities that being a fully-fledged grown-up might afford me.

In 1943 most able-bodied young men were in uniform fighting the Jerries or the Japs, and school holidays were adjusted so that children could take over the jobs of the farm-labourers who were serving at the front and help to dig potatoes and bring in the harvest grain. 'Tatty-Howking' is back-breaking work, but the sense of adventure compensated for our aches and pains. 'Stooking' wheat then forking it up onto the trailer was more noble employment, though with our puny arms we had to work in pairs to avoid being knocked over by the weight of the sheaves. We were placed eight to a room in tiered bunks, and we were asleep before our heads touched the pillow.

I had never properly heard music till I heard it on Spotty Calder's portable gramophone – 'Prélude à l'après-midi d'un faune', 'The Swan of Tuonela'… Till then I had been happy with 'South of the Border' and 'Blue Moon'.

Awareness of beauty arrives hand in hand with adolescence. Along with the havoc hormones wreak with our hearts and our reproductive organs, it seems that they also galvanise our senses and wake us to the wonders of the world. Before puberty I can't say that I found solace in Debussy or Sibelius, or gazed awestruck at sunsets or picked wild gentian with a pang in my heart, or cherished solitude, appreciated company, felt tenderness for strangers. But then the Thunderbolts struck, time after time, and I would rise, dazed, only to be felled again like a bouncing puppet: Rodin, Delacroix, Gauguin, Michelangelo.

'Is there no pity sitting in the clouds that sees into the bottom of my grief?' Shakespeare's Thunderbolt left me for dead.

Ella Fitzgerald, J D Salinger, Thomas Hardy, Rider Haggard. They expressed my glorious torment with such unbearable beauty.

In the fields we worked alongside Italian prisoners of war. They were a mixed bunch, as soldiers tend to be. But there was one who was exceptional.

> A feeling of sadness and longing,
> That is not akin to Pain,
> And resembles sorrow only
> As the mist resembles the rain. (Longfellow.)

This exactly decribed my feelings for Remo.

A year before, these inchoate yearnings for Remo might have seemed, in my innocence, to be spiritual, the longing for an older brother to look up to and admire; but after my experience with Pete at the swimming baths in Shawlands, I could no longer deny that at the most profound level they were sexual. When working, his shirt would ride up from his coarse army trousers and the sight of his tight belly with the dark hair curling up from below his belt sent my blood spouting through my veins. Perhaps he construed my lingering glances as hero-worship, for he was always kind, and I clung to the hope that this dark longing made me special for him, as he was special for me.

Kelvin McNeish, known as 'Keavie', was the captain of our rugby team; he had frizzy orange hair, no eyes to speak of, and from the evidence of the bath at the end of the game, every inch of his body was densely covered in freckles like a speckled hen. He always had white stains down the front of his trousers, but there was no evidence of imminent blindness or of monkeyhair growing on his palms.

'Isn't Remo nice?' I ventured towards Keavie one night, as I passed him bravely grappling with his manhood under the blanket as I climbed the ladder to the top bunk.

'I've got another bone on!' he confided through gritted teeth.

Keavie was engaged yet again in single combat with his problem, which wouldn't lie down till he had punished it. I would have been only too happy to assist, had he had less freckles and different coloured hair, although he never asked anyone for help, and refused to acknowledge that he got anything but pain from his exertions.

'Phawooh!' he would groan after one of his short, sharp, but innumerable bouts. 'That's better.'

There was silence from below, so I thought I might try again.

'There's something just wonderful about Remo. Don't you think so, Keavie?'

'Which one's Remo?' he asked sleepily.

'The dark, good-looking one. Rides on the step of the tractor. Sings songs. Plays the fool. Don't you think he's specially nice?'

'Italians are all nice. They're not really our enemies. It's that Mussolini's fault. They invented ice cream.'

'And spaghetti.'

'You wouldn't believe it!' he groaned. 'I've got another bone on!'

At the end of a hard day's work, Remo would buffet me and cuddle me without restraint as all Italians do with children. His need for love was as great as mine, but this open tactile affection was not sexual on his part but sensual, like nuzzling a puppy. At no time did he caress me or embrace me in an inappropriate way, but my response was unlike a puppy's response. I held onto him too long. I buried my face in his neck. I beamed my love at him from a furnace-sized pain deep inside the walls of my chest, and he accepted it as his due.

Remo was an ordinary boy: a farmer, a bricklayer, who knows? But he seemed to me imbued with the beauty of a prince in a fairy tale. His obsidian eyes had purple shadows under them and lashes like breakers on a dark shore. His lips had commas at the corners, and since he was always laughing, his teeth, though uneven, were so white against his dusky complexion that I rushed to the mirror to compare them with my own. He was short and stocky and clean, though he smelt strongly of natural sweat, and this smell was a profound delight in my nostrils.

He sang our 'Pop' songs in an execrable accent – 'Padebeebaa – Izza Dee Chadanoogah Choo-choo!' – and gave me his chocolate (we had different lunch-boxes) and stood on his hands against the hay-barn pulling funny faces and shouting newly learned obscenities in English till he ran out of ideas, when he would continue in Italian.

'Fahkeen Buster! Bahgger me! Knee-Kerss! Dio Lupo! Porca Madonna!'

He was the most intoxicating human being I had met in my life, and I have no doubt that Remo was the spark that ignited my lifelong passion for the Italian people.

When it was time to go back to Glasgow I didn't know what to do with my breaking heart.

Remo hugged me for the last time and he knew.

His lovely eyes glistened for a moment before he burst out laughing again.

8 THE PIPE BAND
The Wonders of the Kilt

AT THE HIGH SCHOOL I linked emotion with sensation for the first time and fell head over heels in love with Gerry. It was a physical relationship, consummated in our fumbling schoolboy fashion as often as possible, which wasn't nearly often enough. The early stages of this fabulous new adventure were facilitated by the happy chance of our national costume. We both wore kilts.

Because we were in the pipe band. The Officers' Training Corps was compulsory, so I joined the band and opted for the big drum because you get to wear a leopard skin. The pelt has a hole cut just below the neck so you can slip it on like a poncho. The head, with glass eyes squinting and fangs agape, hangs between your shoulder blades, and the spotted part of the hide protects your uniform from the layers of blanco you have to lavish on the tighteners. I wore a Glengarry bonnet, a kilt with a long hairy sporran and spats.

In some ways the big drummer is the conductor of the band. He marches in the middle, his bass 'Thud-Thud!' keeps the marchers and the other bandsmen on the beat, and the same bass notes delivered at double speed signal when to start 'Scotland the Brave' or 'Heeland Laudie' and when to stop. That's the easy part. The difficult skill to acquire is how to whirl the sticks above your head, individually and together and across the top of the drum from one side to the other with as much panache as you can muster without losing the beat or your sticks over the heads of the rest of the parade.

The drum was as big as I was. I could barely see over the top. To avoid tumbling head over spats I had to stuff the leopard's tail into my sporran.

Gerry was a piper, which takes a lot of puff and application; unlike a drum which any moron can hit so long as he has a sense of rhythm, the bagpipes are a musical instrument which requires a lot of practice and an ability to read sheet music. Gerry was not a born musician but he had a go, and with the noise that bagpipes make it is difficult for all but the initiated to know whether the instrument is in tune and what series of notes the piper is supposed to be playing.

At the end of one rehearsal we were changing into our civilian togs to go home. The others had already gone, and the bandmaster, our physics teacher, had left us to lock up because his wife was in hospital having a baby. His waistcoat was stained with food droppings, and he always wore a watch-chain, so he was known as 'Chains and Slavery'.

There is a myth, fostered by the Scots themselves, that real men wear nothing underneath their kilts. Without any premeditation, Gerry and I started to make a joke about this, and one thing led to another. It is quite extraordinary how quickly all tentativeness was abandoned, and how passionately we were exploring each others' bodies like starving men at a banquet. He had musky skin almost free from adult hair, and a brown body smelling of hay that I could never have enough of. He had only one ball then but perhaps the other one has dropped by now, because he turned out to be quite fertile. He became a successful business-man and fathered three girls.

At school we did not mix in the same circles. Although we were in the same year, we were not in the same class. My interests and hence my friends were artistic or literary, and I played rugby, which was the school's official game, though I was only in the second fifteen. Gerry was an academically-handicapped tearaway, who excelled only at football in the quad – and football was looked down on.

Our only common ground was our lust for one another; otherwise we were separated by the great social divide. And of course our guilt. And our terror of being found out. So all our meetings thereafter, which were all too few, were conducted in great secrecy, and in going about school business, we made no pretence of being friends.

Nonetheless my passion for Gerry lasted three years: at that age, a lifetime. Then he discovered girls, and I was devastated. As we grew older he was bewil-dered by my constancy and repelled by the heat of my emotions. In self-defence, perhaps, I regressed from being the lover to being the beloved; though any consummation was out of the question.

Spotty Calder's acne was improving and he would only don his glasses when he absolutely had to, but no amount of attention to his appearance could make him attractive. He would close his eyes when speaking to you and his lids would flutter as if you were trying to poke them. He was a terrific swell since he lived in Newlands and his house had two front gates. They drove their Bentley in one gate and out the other. They had a lavatory on the ground floor; just the pedestal and a washbasin with a mirror above it and clean towels on a rail. The proper bathroom was upstairs. Spotty asked me over one evening; thereafter I felt that an invitation to Buckingham Palace would hold no terrors for me.

The Calders had two pugs called 'Grrs' and 'Bee' who couldn't breathe and had to be given oxygen when they weren't being kissed. The parquet floors of the house were very highly polished and difficult for dogs with breathing problems to manoeuvre, so they mostly snored on Chippendale carvers and were fed by hand.

The family was very musical and Spotty played duets on the piano with his mother. He had a roomful of gramophone records filed neatly on shelves from floor to ceiling, old 78s, the kind that Elyot breaks over Amanda's head in *Private Lives*, though they were without exception 'Classical'. He played these records exclusively with wooden needles which he had to sharpen on a little strop before each playing.

Spotty's father never removed a lighted pipe from his mouth even when he spoke, so that the air around him was always blue. I can't imagine what he made of his son, for Calder Senior was exceedingly hearty while Calder Junior was not.

It was a trial for me to sit and listen to Mozart renderings which even I could tell were clumsy with Spotty and his mother swaying to each cadence as if they were in concert at the Wigmore Hall. I didn't understand or appreciate the music. I didn't know whether to put on a blissful expression and concentrate hard on their fingers fumbling over the keys, or to gaze into space in a knowing yet enigmatic dream, or to look thunderstruck, or to seem bereft; all I could think of was what I could say at the end of the ordeal that would not reveal my ignorance or expose my hypocrisy. What I really wanted to say was 'Have you done?'

Poor Spotty used to shower me with presents. For instance, the first Biro pen I ever saw, which was miraculous to us, a pen that wrote wet, without an ink well. It weighed a ton. Or a record of 'The Polovtsian Dances' from *Prince Igor* which he knew I liked. These presents were accompanied by notes with strings of XXXXXXXX's at the end. I'd catch him gazing at me in class and he would blush. I felt sorry for him.

To know that I was loved by Spotty the way I loved Gerry eased my sense of isolation and was a comfort of sorts. Although, as I already knew from Gerry's rejection, there was no comfort in any of this for Spotty.

9 MISSING THE MATCH
Appearances Are Deceptive

MY PARENTS' DEATHS were so close together that I remember them as opposites rather than as separate events; during this short period I proved to myself in a subconscious way that I had a talent for acting.

On a Friday evening in October my Aunt Gatty had gone to see a relation who was recovering from a stroke. There is always an ample supply of catastrophes in large families to satisfy the cravings of the most ardent doom-watcher, and by this time, with marriages and children, our family was the size of the Golden Horde.

My mother and sisters were paying their nightly visit to the lunatic asylum where my father lay dying. I was not allowed on these visits I am grateful to record, since I was judged to be too young at thirteen to be exposed to the harsh reality of wardsfull of mental patients. My mother knew my father was dying because 'His nose was sharp...' I set little store by her prediction, thinking, 'It could be blunt again by tomorrow.' But she was right.

I was listening to *ITMA* on the wireless and putting dubbin on my rugby boots in preparation for the match the next morning when there was a knock on the front door. I had never seen a policeman without his hat. Over his shoulder the bald patches on our front lawn glinted after the drizzle in the feeble chink of blue light from the dowsed, black-out street lamp.

Verifying that I was alone in the house, the Bobby took a notebook from his pocket and read in a monotone, 'I regret to inform you that John Alexander Fraser of 20 Mosspark Street, Glasgow, passed away at six thirty-five p.m. on Friday the 16th of October 1944.'

'Sorry, son.' He put on his hat and left.

I sat in the easy chair poking the horsehair back through a hole in the arm and listening to Lulu next door with her multiple scars playing *Für Elise* on the piano. Could we dare to hope for a life free from paralysing anxiety and shame? Free from the stink of booze and the snarling violence and the pitiful suffering and the panic and the degradation? Would I see my mother smile again as she was smiling in the photo looking over the wall? Could we all link arms and go singing down the street?

My mother and sisters had been too late for my father's final moments. As they returned home I beheld their grief in wonder. 'They loved him!' – I thought. It was incomprehensible to me.

They remembered him as he had been before the bottle got him, when according to the whispered testimony of my sisters and my Aunt Gatty, he had been a wit, a gentleman and a dandy. When the family was rich. When they had all lived in a fairy tale before I came along to spoil it.

My mother never spoke of these early days of her marriage. Perhaps it was too painful remembering how they had gone forever…the Gala occasions when the whole family would dress up to grace the Royal Box at The Alhambra for a performance by the Wilson Barrett Company. (The manager of the theatre, who ended up in prison for embezzlement, lived just along the road.)

My mother would be sheathed in floor-length satin with a silver-fox stole slung carelessly around her naked shoulders; her elbow-length white kid gloves had little pearl buttons at the wrist which had to be done up with a hook. These relics lay yellowing in tissue paper in my parents' bedroom-drawer to bear witness to the truth of the picture painted by my sisters of this Golden Age before I was born. My father in his dinner jacket with a camellia in his buttonhole, Chris and Jean in their party-frocks with matching scarlet velvet capes and patent-leather pumps. Confused about all the talk of a Maid and a Chauffeur, I always saw the Maid wielding the wheel of our motor car in her pinny and her pokey-hat starched cap…

For me, the prospect of life without my father was too sublime to contemplate…

When I returned to school after the weekend, Keavie confronted me in the cloakroom. Ginger Keavie. I could see by the set of his mouth and by his heightened colour that he was angry. I was about to explain when he interrupted me.

'No excuses!' he said in his posh Bearsden accent. 'You completely screwed up the game against Allan Glen's! You know we don't carry reserves! No matter what!' he interrupted me again. 'No matter what – if you're ill or you can't make it – our number's in the book!' We had no telephone. 'You have to ring me! Do you understand? So I can find a replacement. If this ever happens again, you're off the team for good. Is that clear?'

He thrust his face so close I thought I caught a glimpse of eyeball behind the dense fringe of his ginger lashes, but I may have been mistaken.

'I'm sorry Keavie,' I said. 'My father died on Friday night.'

I experienced a new sensation as I said it. I felt noble and tragic and set apart. As Keavie's face grew less ripe in colour and he put his arm round my shoulder,

I revelled in his pity. The teachers took me aside one by one to offer me their condolences, which I accepted with fortitude though my heart was singing. I was acutely aware of everyone's sympathetic glances as I sat in a corner acting bereaved.

My mother was the same age as my father – forty-eight – though she looked much older. My sisters have told me she had faults but I thought she was perfect and since my father was the opposite, I compensated for this imbalance by loving my mother too much.

She had been so busy nursing my father that she had told no one of the pain she had been suffering for months. A swollen valve of the heart was diagnosed, and she was ordered instantly to bed. She died a few days later on a Friday night, six weeks to the day from the night my father died.

I wept because my Aunt Gatty and my sisters were weeping, but it was not grief I felt but shock. I knew what dead was. Dead was gone. Like my father. Gone, with a chance to start again.

But start again? Start what? And for what reason? There could be no life without my mother...

I was taken to kiss her for the last time, since it is the time-honoured custom – 'To verify that the earthly remains are of the deceased and no other.' Her head lay on a satin pillow in the frilly casket; she looked like a piece of wedding-cake in a box. Her long hair was brushed out on the pillow and the broad streaks in it were only a little whiter than her lovely face.

Feeling as if I was falling into emptiness, I bent over to kiss her brow. It was as cold as steel.

I knew then that if I continued to believe in God I should execrate him.

The next day there was a knock on the door and I went to answer it. Keavie McNeish stood there, dangerously immobile. Since we were not on visiting terms, the freckled sight of him with his feet planted firmly on my doormat suddenly brought home to me that it was Saturday evening and long past the final whistle.

Without preamble he said, 'I suppose your bloody *mother's* dead!'

'Yes.'

'What?'

'Yes, she is.'

'Oh very funny! Very fucking funny!'

'Do you want to see her? She's not being cremated till Monday.'

'Listen, Fraser. You have a warped sense of humour!'

'I'm sorry about the match, Keavie. My mother died. That's the truth. I'll be in on Monday after the funeral.' I knew the routine by now.

Keavie's freckles seemed to swirl like artificial snow-flakes in a glass globe.

'You're — You're not serious?'

By then I was probably crying. I can't remember. Whether I cried or not felt all the same.

'I'm sorry, Johnny. I'm... I'm so sorry. How was I to know?... Fucking Hell! Will you ever forgive me?'

At any other time I would have been mortified to invite such a swell into our shabby house but I was past caring about niceties; he had ventured into the lower depths, beyond the outer limits of Bearsden and Pollokshields to find me, so I asked him to stay for a cup of tea.

At school, despising myself for my hypocrisy over my father's death I refused to demean my mother's memory by baring my overwhelming grief, and I behaved almost cheerfully.

To an outsider it must have seemed as if my father meant the world to me and my mother had meant nothing.

This was my first, and perhaps my best, performance as an Actor.

10 VE Day
And Children's Hour

AT THE AGE of twenty, my sister Jean was considered by all my friends to be 'A Top Turn', which is a Variety term for the Star at the top of the bill. Having spent her childhood in Chris' shadow, Jean's lack of confidence gave her a vulnerable, eager-to-please quality which men found irresistible. She had the figure of a sylph without being in the least thin, and during her evenings behind the counter at the YMCA in Eglinton Toll, serving young lads in uniform a long way from home, she attracted a host of admirers. One of these was a young Welsh rating in bell-bottoms called Glyn who had an Adam's apple that went up and down like a monkey on a stick, and he was so deeply in love with my sister that she had no alternative but to invite him back to our house for him to meet her family, now so sadly depleted.

After the introductions, we had tea: tinned salmon and salad, and some prunes and swiss roll to follow. Aunt Gatty had even made some custard, and she was civil to the nervous young lad, though she kept looking at him with suspiciously narrowed eyes. She later confided to me in the kitchen that she was afraid he might be 'a Pape'. Running the tap so he wouldn't hear us talking about him, I asked, 'What makes you think he's a Catholic?'

'I can tell a Pape a mile off!' was one of Aunt Gatty's more frequent assertions. 'He's wearing perfume.'

Glyn had splashed on some aftershave to create a good impression.

'He seems a nice chap.'

'It's no good if he's a Pape.'

Aunt Gatty went up to her room and shut her door with a bang. Within minutes the house was shoogling. Her sewing-machine was her pet bucking bronco in her own private rodeo.

Chris and I retired tactfully to give Jean and Glyn the chance to get to know each other. I had to do some homework, and Chris pretended to listen to the wireless. We knew that heavy petting can lead to rape, but we were confident that we were just a scream away. Love's Young Dream had to have an outlet or it would be forced to resort to the area behind the dustbins on the way to abominable disgrace, like Wendy Carson.

47

When Germany capitulated in May 1945, the government declared a National Holiday to celebrate Victory in Europe. The 8th of May was nominated as V E Day, and in Glasgow the rejoicing converged upon George Square.

Jean dressed up for victory in a red jumper, a blue skirt and white shoes, with a Union Jack draped around her neck. I stuck a paper flag in my breast pocket, and together we took the tram into town and elbowed our way into the jubilant crowd that had assembled in Glasgow's main arena under a blizzard of bunting, red, white, and blue, not forgetting the yellow Standard of Scotland and the White on Blue Cross of St Andrew's.

A band played 'Ah belang tae Glasgow, Dear Auld Glasgow Toon…' and 'There'll be Bluebirds Over, The White Cliffs of Dover, Tomorrow, Just You Wait and See…' and 'There'll always be an England – As LONG AS SCOTLAND'S THERR!' and 'Land Of Hope And Glory…' and everyone sang along linking arms and swaying to the music. Strangers kissed, and drunks danced with incongruous partners; cannons roared from somewhere behind Queen Street station, and lights that had been dark for six years were switched on and the city was suddenly ablaze.

> **BISTO! THE FLAVOUR TO SAVOUR!**
> **LEWIS'S ARGYLL STREET**
> **COME TO THE CA'D'ORO!**
> **BETTY GRABLE IN 'CALL ME MISTER'**

We were conga-ing in a snake through the monumental sculpture, past Rabbie and Sir Walter, under the raised hooves of Albert and Victoria, when I saw that Jean was weeping, and I knew it was not with joy.

I hauled her aside. In my own estimation at fourteen years old I was not only an adult, but since both our parents were dead, I considered myself the head of the family.

'What's the matter? We've won the war! What's to be sad about?'

'I'm engaged!' she sobbed, as if 'engaged' meant she had only weeks to live.

'What?' I asked, nonplussed.

'Glyn asked me to marry him and I said "Yes".'

'You don't seem very happy about it.'

'He's the sweetest boy in the world,' she said, 'but I don't want to marry him.'

'Then why did you say you would?'

'I couldn't bear to disappoint him!' Her face screwed right up and she bawled like a baby.

At fourteen I was not Socrates.

'You have to tell him, pet. We're talking about lifetimes here. Yours and his. Not dropping a stitch or losing at Peever. You have to tell him you're really sorry but you've made a mistake.'

She did. And next time someone proposed to her, she asked time to think it over.

If I were to cite one reason for choosing Scotland as your birthplace, and only one, it would be the educational system. I am grateful to record that in my day it was shamelessly elitist, for it set my modest abilities on such a bedrock that they appear to more advantage than they would have done if they had been left to flounder without the discipline of a Scottish curriculum. Clever students in Scotland are pushed to the limit. There are no half measures and there is absolutely no let-up.

Historically, education was the only means of escape from poverty, the only highway to a better life. Parents from the poorest families dreamed of sending their offspring on to university to redeem the shame of their straitened circumstances and to make them proud. To this day education in Scotland is sacred.

This is why I can never forget or underestimate my Aunt Gatty's sacrifice in spending all her hard-earned wages to give me a secondary education that was the equal of any to be had in these islands.

It was widespread practice when I was young to allot pupils to streams A, B or C according to merit. But at the Glasgow High School for Boys, as well as those categories, there was another one. If you were considered to be especially clever you were put into the S stream (S for Special is often for backward children, but not in The High School), and you were quite blatantly crammed. Normal classes were composed of about thirty pupils, but in my S class there were only five of us for languages and for science.

I wanted to study Art as one of my subjects, but such an idea was dismissed by the 'Rector', our Headmaster, as frivolous.

'You can take up Art, as a hobby, later. But while you are in our clutches, Fraser, we are going to make sure that you develop your brain. You will not take Art while you are at The High School. Art is for later. Art at school is for boys with difficulties. You will study Higher Maths, Physics, Chemistry, English, History and Latin. You will also take Lower French and Ancient Greek. Is that clear?'

I believe the Scottish Higher Leaving Certificate is considered slightly less advanced than the English A Level because it is often taken at a younger age, although passes in the requisite number of these exams qualify students for university entrance.

At the age of sixteen I passed all my exams, gaining Highers in Maths, Physics, Chemistry, English, History and Latin. I also passed Lower French and Ancient Greek.

And I was not the cleverest boy in the school. There were about four much cleverer than I was.

I was elected Captain of my House, and settled down for a year in the sixth form, as I was too young to go on to university, which my teachers and particularly my sisters were quite determined that I should do.

After that Christmas dinner so long ago, perched precariously between the curly brass candlesticks and the sherry decanter on the sideboard, I had basked for the first time in the glow of the limelight with my pig poem. Thereafter the craving for applause never left me.

Everybody needs approval; self-worth is a prerequisite for a happy life. Why is it that artists in general and actors in particular need praise in such distilled form and in such quantity? At least we don't set out to run the country or exploit the workforce or conquer the world. Our megalomania feeds on vanity and not on power, which may be pathetic but it seems to me harmless. And to devote your life to a harmless pursuit is an achievement, albeit of a negative kind.

I believe passionately that the life of an artist is positive and affirming. This is with hindsight, of course. I had no such highfalutin' principles when I wrote to the BBC while still at school, begging for an audition.

There was plenty of Drama being broadcast in those days before television, and I was one of the millions of avid listeners who tuned in daily to 'Auntie Kathleen' on *Children's Hour*. My audition was successful, and since there were few child actors in Glasgow at that time, during my last year at school I was employed on a regular basis. Working with professional actors and being accepted among their number confirmed me in my determination to try my luck in the theatrical profession. My sisters were appalled, as well they might be, but not appalled enough to stop me.

11 THE PAGE TO HERODIAS
The Park Theatre

I SHALL BE INDEBTED to Spotty Calder forever, since in 1947 his hearty, pipe-smoking, tweed-jacketed Dad got me, at sixteen years old, my first job in the theatre.

Unlikely though it seemed, Calder Senior was friendly with an odd man called Clarrie McMurdo. There might have been a masonic connection. Mr McMurdo ran a tiny professional theatre club called 'The Park Theatre', which was confusing since the theatre was nowhere near a park; the premises were situated on the first and second floors of a large terrace house near Charing Cross in Glasgow where Clarrie McMurdo also resided. Alone. His moderate wealth had been inherited – something to do with Pitman's Shorthand. With The Park Theatre Company, later to emerge in 1950 in a new imago as The Pitlochry Festival Theatre Company, he was realising his life's dream.

Clarrie McMurdo was running to fat. He had soft white skin with a hectic blob of colour on each cheek, and he always had what looked like cottage cheese between his teeth. Spotty's father had arranged for me to meet Mr McMurdo since he knew that I hoped to make the stage my career, and The Park Theatre was short of an ASM.

Assistant Stage Manager is an imposing title which belies the humble reality of the post, which is the absolute beginner in the theatre, the tea-boy, the prompter, the dog's body, the prop man. In this capacity he is called upon to exercise some ingenuity in finding furniture and 'Props' for each production, usually with no budget at all. At my interview I lied about my age (sixteen), assuring pink, cheesey Mr McMurdo in my baritone voice that I was seventeen and a half. I got the job.

It's almost impossible to understand how in the dark people in my youth were about sex in general, let alone about deviance. I thought there was me, David and Jonathan a bit, but not really, and Oscar Wilde. And a few men with haunted eyes in the Gents at Central Station. My first year out of school was a revelation to me in this respect, though much of what I observed was mysterious. But the theatre isn't the real world after all. As Mr Calder would have put it: 'Hardly typical!'

How's this for mysterious?

A mounted policeman would arrive at the front door of The Park Theatre Club every other day. From the top floor of his house, where he lived in a world of Ming and Delft and Meissen serried on shelves behind glass, Clarrie McMurdo would run down, taking the stairs three at a time as if the house were on fire. As he approached ground level he would reduce his speed, then, panting on the pavement, he would stand with his thumbs down the seams of his trousers like a private on parade and gaze up in rapture at the effulgence of the policeman's boots.

The policeman never dismounted. They would talk sometimes for half an hour. I never heard what they discussed, but at the end of it, the policeman would swing his horse around, tip his fingers to his checkered hat and trot off while Clarrie McMurdo stood rooted to the pavement unable to resume his life while the faintest clip-clop of his hero's mount could be heard in the distance or the merest breath of horse-flesh and boot-polish could be savoured in the evening air.

The only explanation for Mr McMurdo's behaviour was, succinctly, unrequited love. But what about the policeman? Was he flattered? Was he cruel? Was he kind? Was he thick? Answers on a postcard.

The first part I played on the professional stage was that of the page to Herodias in Oscar Wilde's *Salome*.

In the opera by Richard Strauss, using a translation of Wilde's play as the libretto, the role of the page is sung by a woman, and the character is in love with the captain of the Guard. Salome and Herod, peacocks with gilded claws, cascades of precious stones, geysers of purple prose ejaculating through the steam of lust, the Dance of the Seven Veils, the Baptist's head on a platter, the naked seductress being crushed to death with the soldiers' shields, the inspiration to Aubrey Beardsley as well as to Wilde and subsequently to Richard Strauss – we're talking decadence here, not 'Puss In Boots'. So in our production of the play, the part of the page was taken, as Wilde intended, by a boy. Me.

In 'Hodge The Grocer's Shop' in 1947 there were on sale bottles of a savoury sauce called 'Dad's!', and the injunction on the label was 'Take Plenty Of It With Everything!' Make up on the stage at that time was used in this manner. Everyone used a ton of it at all times indiscriminately. If you were playing a butler with one line to speak – 'Dinner is Served' – you spent an hour in front of your mirror before the curtain went up with an arsenal of grease-sticks on a filthy towel in front of you, painting on your mug the image of this butler as a man; his life, his worries, his appetites, his disappointments. With Leichner Nos 5 and 9 and 20 and 19 and Dark Lake and Carmine we painted portraits on our faces, spending painstaking hours every night in constructing an image of a character from fiction.

This excessive use of paint was a relic of the eighteenth century, when theatres grew to the size of Drury Lane. On the vast stages the actors were reduced to the size of puppets lit by forests of candles twinkling in suspended chandeliers and in free-standing candelabra and in funnels floating in a trench filled with water as a fire precaution all along the front of the stage. Footlights, wherever they still exist, are referred to by old hands as 'The Floats'. Candle light is golden but hazy, and those grand theatres built after the Restoration were directly responsible for 'Ham' acting, for the use of graphic make up and the gestures of melodrama. Playhouses were intimate in Shakespeare's day and plays were performed in daylight. Only wigs and beards were used.

Even after the advent of gas, followed shortly afterwards by the limitless versatility of electric lighting, for many years actors were reluctant to relinquish make up, which they considered an integral part of their characterisation and the badge of their trade.

A word about the filthy towel. This was before washing-machines or Kleenex or Nivea were invented. The fastidious members of the company washed their towels once a week. In the provinces actors were poorer than church mice. We wore rags for dressing-gowns. We would have been ostracised had we worn anything finer. We used liquid paraffin as a skin cleanser, cheaper than any brand cream, and we bummed slivers of wash-house soap from the next fella. We burned corks for covering bald-patches or playing Othello.

However ingenious our economies, the principal tool of our trade was make up. We could no more consider appearing in public without make up than we would dream of attending church without our trousers. Plasticine for false noses, or false chins, little gobs of screwed-up paper stuck to our cheeks with spirit gum for warts if you were playing Bardolph or a Witch in *Macbeth*. Or diverse peasants in Chekhov or Brecht. Then there was crêpe hair sold in plaits; when unravelled, its kinks were removed over a steaming kettle and applied to the pre-gummed face with a pair of scissors and a damp flannel for bearded or moustachioed roles. Unsubsidised repertory companies could not afford wig-makers. We had no professional help, so actors had to be artists then. Olivier was a genius at make up. Gielgud was a dud. There you go.

Grotesque though everyone looked in the mirror, in costume and under the lights we didn't look so much like a bunch of freaks. But even if we had, freaks were more fun than ordinary.

When preparing for the first time to play my role as the Page to Herodias, I was flattered when several of the maturer members of the company almost came to blows over who should help me apply my make up, an art of which I knew nothing, since I had arrived in this exotic milieu straight from a Boys' Grammar and had never attended a drama school, let alone seen the inside of a theatre dressing room in the whole of my life.

The director had stipulated that I should play the part of the Page to Herodias naked, except for a loin cloth (see above, ref 'Decadence'), but it was my mentors who insisted that my eyeshadow should rival Elizabeth Taylor's in *Cleopatra* and that my toenails should be painted silver and that my lips should be outlined and shadowed to make them look like an advertisement for Michelin Tyres. One particularly pushy Thespian dug out a ruby from his work-box and could not be dissuaded from straddling my lap to affix it between my eyes.

I was also advised to camouflage my Glasgow pallor with a body-wash – or 'Bole' as it was affectionately called then, after the clay our ancestors used as warpaint. The eagerness to smooth this liquid over my adolescent frame and to smear the lipstick on my almost innocent lips among these senior members of the company aroused even my suspicions.

By the time my admirers had tarted me up everyone said I looked wonderful. My appearance might pass muster, but I was seriously concerned about my lines. There were not many, but they opened the play and they set the mood for what was to follow.

I was well aware that I would have to do my best to cover up my Glasgow accent, since I could find nothing in the script to explain how an Egyptian slave might have a provenance in Albion which in Herod's day was off the map.

The vowel sound 'O' as in 'No' is closer to 'Aw' in Scottish than to 'Ay' which is how the English pronounce it. The 'A' as in 'Bath' is closer to the 'A' in 'At' than to the 'A' in 'Art', etcetera, and there is no differentiation between the long English A and the short one. In spite of these confusions, any Scotsman worth his salt can master these English sounds if he has to, unless he is Sean Connery.

The difficulty is with the 'oo' sound. There are two pronunciations in English for this vowel, but only one in Scots. In Scotland all 'oo's are short, and the 'oo' in 'foot' is pronounced exactly the same as the 'oo' in 'moon' and it takes a very long exposure to English English for a Scotsman to work out the difference.

Try saying this aloud, transposing all the 'oo' sounds into the short round Scottish 'oo', for these are the opening lines of Oscar Wilde's *Salome*, which were entrusted to me on that memorable night : –

Look at the moon. Oh, Look! Look at the moon!
How strange the moon seems
She is like a woman rising from a tomb!
She is like a woman rising from a tomb!
She is like a dead woman
I fancy she is dreaming of dead things!
The moon, look, look, the moon is the woman's tomb...

Everything was a success at the Park Theatre. It seated only a hundred and fifty customers, there was a mailing list, and every production played to capacity.

On the opening night, the mounted policeman, looking insignificant out of uniform, was ensconced in the middle of the front row. My sisters and my Aunt Gatty sat behind Spotty, who was accompanied by his Mum and Dad, who coughed noisily during the decadent bits.

At the curtain, tumultuous applause. Chris and Jean had no standards by which to measure the play, the production, or the performances, so they joined in the mutual admiration and the general rejoicing.

Only Aunt Gatty was forthright. Patting her trusty Radar, she said 'My! You fairly knew your words!'

In his review in the *Sunday Post*, Gordon Briggs complained that –

'John Fraser's Egyptian transvestite would look at home in Gomorrah if his tones did not reflect the Gallowgate.'

(The Gallowgate was one of the worst slums in old Glasgow.)

Thereafter I took elocution lessons.

TWO

Wavering

1 SELF-IMPROVEMENT
And National Service

Dodds: 'Poor tired Dick had hot toast for his tea.'
Me: 'Poo-err tie-urrd Deck had hoat tow-ust furries tea.'
Dodds: 'Pooah tie-ard Deek hed heart taste faw his tee.'

MR PERCIVAL DODDS, failed actor, pretentious humbug, dirty old man and self-styled 'Phonetic Therapist', had given up on me.

He always started the elocution lesson with some tongue-twisters of the 'Poor Tired Dick' variety, so he could fast forward into automatic pilot and get his hands on Doris Wylie's tits.

He stood behind poor Doris, his favourite fantasy inducer, and clamped her to his moth-balled belly with one hand squeezing her ribs and the other poised on her diaphragm with a lecherous thumb brazenly paddling between her breasts, his eyes tight shut, his chin on high as if he were howling at the moon. A picture of dedicated pedagogy.

Intercostal Diaphragmatic, he called it.

'Breathe...In...Out. In...Out...Up...Down...' It was as obvious as that.

'Her-humm-ah! Her-humm-ah!' He gave Doris a final squeeze as if he was wringing her dry and put her down.

'IN THE THEATRE,' he pronounced in stentorian tones, 'WE PROJECT THE VOICE, NOT BY VULGARLY SHOUTING LIKE HOOLIGANS AT A FOOTBALL MATCH, BUT BY VOICE PRODUCTION! WHICH COMES FROM THE DIAPHRAGM YOU SEE!'

He adjusted himself inside his trousers and continued, 'Miss Wylie will show you...'

'ONCE MORE INTO THE BREACH, DEAR FRIENDS, ONCE MORE...' she began.

'Bravo!' yelped Percival Dodds.

There were three other girls to choose from, but they weren't as pretty as Doris Wylie; then there was me and Eric Mansefield, all aspiring to be thespians or hoping at least for one reason or another to acquire an accent which would not label us the moment we opened our mouths.

Nothing wrong with national or regional accents, but if you're in the business of communicating, of travelling the world, of teaching English to foreigners, or of acting on the professional stage, then acquiring the basics of received pronunciation is essential.

A Liverpudlian Henry the Fifth would be unconvincing. Or a Glaswegian Lord Peter Wimsey.

After my *Salome* debacle, I wanted the choice, that's all, and almost in spite of Dirty Dodds – for he had no interest in any of his pupils if they were not of the female sex and complaisant with his shenanigans in the name of Intercostal Diaphragmatic – I began to get the hang of it.

'Jeck Spret could eat nay fett –' I started.

'Bbllle, bbllle, bbbllbbblllebbllley,' went Dirty Dodds, shaking his jowls at my efforts, but I knew I was getting better when Aunt Gatty said I sounded like a Pape.

After my parents died my family was moved by the council to a two-bed-roomed ground-floor flat in a tenement alongside the tram depot in Battlefield. Within a short time both my sisters were married and the two young couples had a bedroom each, while I slept on a folding bed in the living-room. Aunt Gatty went to live with her sister, my Auntie Margaret. Jean's husband was studying to be an accountant, and the lack of space and privacy drove him to saw through the floorboards in his bedroom and create a 'Study' in the foundations of the building where he could crouch among the spiders at a table with his books under an anglepoise lamp, but could not stand upright unless the trapdoor was open. When we were all at home and queuing for the bathroom it felt like the Siege of Leningrad.

The Park Theatre was closed for re-wiring after a minor infringement of fire regulations. The dimmers in the lighting box had got red-hot and set fire to the stage manager's trousers. I was now out of a job.

National Service was then compulsory, and I had received notice that I was due for call-up in a year's time. I was now seventeen and a confirmed pacifist. The war was won and over but the principle of joining a killing force was repugnant to me. When I explained this to my sisters the sky fell in.

The word 'Conshy' still had a hateful resonance so soon after the war, and my sisters were mortally ashamed of what they construed to be their little brother's cowardice. They wept for a week and tried to reason with me. I appeared adamant but my resolve was wavering. I was frightened of going into the witness box to defend my position, since God was the only copper-bottomed ally that I knew of, and I had stopped believing in God altogether when my mother died.

Crumbling, and secretly relieved, I justified my pusillanimousness to myself: 'It's selfish of me to put my principles above my family's happiness.' And since I was unemployed I volunteered to join the army straight away and get my National Service over with.

I had never been in the company of so many toffs. They had names like Christopher and William, unabbreviated, and Jonathan and Jolyon and Richard, unabbreviated, and Harcourt and Edward, unabbreviated. They had all been to Eton or Harrow or Marlborough or Wellington. Some had titles, and others had two surnames handcuffed together with a hyphen. They must all, I mused, have two front gates.

The percentage of upper-class recruits in my intake was phenomenally high because it was the end of the school term, and students had volunteered, like me, to do their National Service before going on to university. There were others of course, like Phil the Geordie who might as well have been speaking Latvian, and Al the Jewish Cockney – 'Got a friend in the business!', and Fat Donald with knock-knees and no conversation, only jokes – 'Heard the one about…?' And Reg, the engineer, terminally depressed at seventeen, for there was nothing to recommend him, ugly, stupid, charmless, not a redeeming feature. He went on to become a millionaire building bridges in Zaire.

Along with Jolyon and Richard and Harcourt and Christopher I was selected for training to be an officer. My large number of Highers passed at the age of sixteen impressed the examiners; besides, I had been working like a man possessed on my elocution lessons, for Gordon Jackson had cornered the market in fresh-faced young Scotsmen, and I realised that if I wanted to work, I would have to cast a wider net.

Jolyon asked me, after a short acquaintance, 'It's very difficult to place your accent. Where do you come from? Let me guess. Tasmania? The Isle of Man?'

At least he didn't suggest that I came from the Gallowgate.

I completed my basic at Aldershot, where all cadets served under the preposterous mountain of self-importance called RSM Britten. His name confused him. He thought our country had been named after him. He weighed about twenty stones, and sported a nailbrush moustache. When he wasn't commanding parades, where his cultivated falsetto shriek could fell jets in mid-flight, he rode a bicycle, which under his monstrous girth looked like an awkwardly shaped suppository in the process of being inserted.

At the Officer Training Wing in Catterick Camp, Yorkshire, after the punishment of assault courses and cross country marathons and ditch digging and pontoon bridge building, and between learning how to operate and service radio-receiver-transmitters, how to live with and not be defeated by the internal combustion engine, how to erect field telephone-poles and how to interpret teleprinter-print-outs – in short how to be a really useful person in the event of another war – I wrote, directed, designed and made the costumes, composed the music and the lyrics for and played the lead in a revue with the recherché title of *Up Your Jumper*. No megalomania here worth digressing about.

It included my skit on Alexander Korda's film of *Caesar and Cleopatra* with Vivien Leigh and Claude Rains. I of course played Cleopatra, in football boots with wired-up cardboard tits that lit up when I put my hands on my hips. My Royal Signals training had not gone for nothing after all. The show was scheduled for two nights. We played to full houses for a week. This did not dampen my enthusiasm for pursuing my career in the theatre.

With a pip on my shoulder, I was posted to Bad Oeynhausen, a beautiful spa town in Westphalia surrounded by barbed wire because it was the Headquarters of the British Army Of The Rhine. BAOR. It was my first time abroad and I felt I was on course for the life I had imagined for myself, a life that had to include travels far and wide to satisfy my burning curiosity.

I was eighteen years old and I was a Duty Signals Officer in charge of a space the size of an aircraft hangar, buzzing with serious and important activity. This was the nerve centre of the forces in Germany, where messages were transmitted and received from other headquarters around the world, messages often classified SECRET or TOP SECRET or TOP TOP SECRET. I had forty fräuleins under my jurisdiction, all pounding their teleprinters and quaking at my approach: forty young women, our defeated enemies and now my slaves. I was their *Obermeister*. And they all made eyes at me. Ferociously. I had never been exposed to predatory female lust on such a scale. It frightened the life out of me.

I was billeted in a Palladian villa on a tree-lined avenue, in an attic room which I made into my first home. I had a bedside lamp, courtesy of the quartermaster, and a bakelite wireless set that I bought myself. It played 'Wild Again, Beguiled Again, A Simpering, Whimpering Child Again, Bewitched Bothered and Bewildered...' and Doris Day singing 'Che Sera Sera'.

I had a German civilian batman called Udo who had a room on the same floor of the villa. He had a pale, pale complexion, heavy hair which fell round his face like a wet mop, grey eyes and a sumptuous mouth. He was as thin as a whippet, about my age, and I fancied him hugely, but victor–vanquished situations don't always get you what you want even had I tried, which I was much too timid to do, though I looked at him a lot which he evidently noticed, which was of course my intention, for he would occasionally bang me gently on the head with his fist, which is not proper behaviour for a servant.

2 PLUMBING DEPRAVITY
And Failing to Lose my Virginity

TILL MY ARRIVAL in Bad Oeynhausen the Rhine Army Theatre Club had been run by a major in the engineers, a regular soldier called Roarie McAllister. He was an anglicised Scot who never drew a sober breath; pink gin was his tipple. He had a moue like a suckling infant seeking his mother's breast. He got some shows on somehow: *The Man Who Came To Dinner*, *The Last of Mrs Cheyney*, *The Magistrate*, culminating in *Private Lives* – as it always does sooner or later – with myself at eighteen playing Elyot when he should be forty and Liz Anderson, the wife of a colonel in the RASC, playing Amanda.

Liz was a foot taller than I was and old enough to be my mother. I could grey up my hair with talcum powder but the disparity in our altitude was more of a problem. I got a pair of scissors and sliced up some newspapers – for the first time but by no means the last – and stuffed them into the heels of my shoes till, when standing, I was pretty well on points. Teetering round the stage was hard so I kept still, mostly, and held onto the furniture. Liz and I had a few compatible moments when she was sitting down.

In spite of the incongruity of our pairing, the production was a success. I was given leave from my duties as Signals Officer, and under the auspices of BAOR, *Private Lives* toured Germany for the services. This was a precedent; hitherto only professional theatre companies brought out from England had been entrusted with entertaining the troops of the Rhine Army.

In the cast was a voluptuous young woman called Anna Fields. Her father was a captain in the Pay Corps and her mother was a Berliner. This was a tricky situation so soon after the war, but Anna's father had married Greta in 1931 and during the hostilities he had passed her off as Hungarian. Anna was utterly blonde, big-breasted, slitty-eyed and quite determined to get me. Here was a woman – what am I talking about, Anna was a SIREN – who blatantly desired me. She was the apogee of all red-blooded males' expectations, and it was hard to regard her as anything other than a challenge.

Because I was a commissioned officer, when I was off duty it was legal for me to wear civilian clothes. Anna spoke perfect German, and to my alarm it became clear as the tour progressed that behind her foxy façade lurked the soul of an adventuress. In Hamburg and in Berlin and in Munich, as she sought out ever more outré and sleazy joints for us to sample, all of which were out of bounds to other ranks, I trailed after her in thrall, but with my heart in my mouth when it came to saying goodnight.

On the notorious Reeperbahn in Hamburg we visited a club with a glass dance-floor lit from underneath and a cabaret where the dancers wore G-strings, feathered head-dresses and nothing else; as they whirled past, the customers near the front were buffeted with mammaries. In England at this time, even in the lowest strip joint, nudes were permitted only if they remained stock still like statues with sequins or tassels stuck on to hide their nipples. At the bar, in the shadows at the back of the club, customers furtively masturbated into their trousers.

In Berlin she took me to a club where the cabaret was provided by transvestites. The clientele seemed straight enough, but the creatures who were performing twice nightly burst from the 'Herren' [Gents] with black-stockinged muscular calves above huge feet stuffed into bulging stilettos and elbowed their way through the crowd, their wrestlers' shoulders mocking their padded brassieres, blue stubble erupting under layers of pancake, their false eyelashes like bird-eating spiders, booming '*Liebchen!*' in bass voices and flinging great hairy arms round unprotesting customers. In Bradford men were arrested for wearing pink shirts.

'WHY?' I asked Anna.

'Why not? They're not doing any harm.'

'They don't look remotely like women. And even if they did, they're not. Who finds freaks attractive?'

'Other freaks I suppose! Come on.'

Instead of a dance floor 'The Golden Horseshoe' had a circus ring filled with sawdust. The waiters and waitresses constituted a freak-show: several dwarfs, three grotesquely fat monstrosities, a congenitally deformed cripple with two holes where once his nose had been, a chinless crone with bulging, goiterous eyes. They were dressed like clowns but they wore no makeup, for no amount of paint could exaggerate their grotesqueness. While they waited on the tables serving steins of beer a litre tall, the ring of sawdust in the middle was the setting for the show.

A Valkyrie, naked but for thongs cutting like razor-wire into her rolls of fat, strode shuddering into the arena leading a large white horse. The woman's vast wobbling buttocks were pitted like the backdrop for a firing-squad. Her high patent-leather boots chafed the pendulous 'W' of her crotch, where clumps of curly hair escaped from her pouch in a jungly fringe. She wore a top hat and brandished a mighty whip.

'*Meine Damen und Herren! Wilkommen. Ich bin von Kopf bis Fuss!*' she husked in true barker's fashion. '*Ein Zwei Drei! Oop-La!*'

Under her blandishments a customer rose sheepishly from a table at the back and made his way down the aisle to the accompaniment of cheers or jeers (they were indistinguishable). Once there, she yanked his jacket from his back and flung it to the ground, where his wallet spilled its contents onto the sawdust. With a swing of her high-heeled boot, she kicked it aside. Then there ensued a discussion, muted on the man's part as if pleading for clemency, ever more strident on hers, till with a slump of his shoulders, slowly and fearfully the man unbuttoned his shirt; when it hung loose, the Valkyrie snatched it from him, cruelly exposing his flaccid torso to the baying crowd. Startled, he suddenly covered his wilting nipples like Aphrodite emerging from the waves.

'*Achtung!*' she commanded, at the same time offering him linked fingers as an aid to mounting the waiting steed. Her hands were coarse and beefy and ingrained with dirt. Clumsily he scaled the horse's flanks and clung to its mane as the ring-mistress prepared for action. She retired to lunging distance and cracked her whip once on each side above her head, a silky swoop followed by a report like the crack of a rifle. At this signal, the horse began to trot round the ring with the man bouncing helplessly on its back with his eyes on the ground.

She cracked her whip three, four, five times in the air as the crowd whooped louder and louder. Then as if at their insistence she finally slashed it down to within an inch of the man's naked back. CRACK! He jerked upright at the nearness of it. The horse trotted placidly on, secure in the knowledge that the scourge was not for him; the lethal sting of leather was reserved for the Rider not the Mount.

She hit him in the end. She lashed him. Many times. The crowd grew quiet as the first weal appeared, releasing along with a trickle of blood a disgusting guttural grunt of satisfaction each time the thong made contact with flesh, while the victim's cries registered both protest and a kind of tortured ecstasy.

I leapt to my feet and, grabbing Anna's arm, I plunged towards the exit. There was a short delay while we sorted out the Deutschmarks with a bearded woman from Hieronymus Bosch, but once I had gulped a lungful of the drizzly night, my trembling stopped.

'Jesus,' was all I said.

What I was thinking was, 'I think *I'm* perverted? I think *I* have a problem? What is all this out there? Those people are sick! Sick and ugly and depraved! What's wrong with wanting a nice boy to love? What could be more tender? What could be more normal?'

'Everything's relative,' I muttered to Anna who skipped by my side as I put distance between us and 'The Golden Horseshoe'.

'That was a mistake,' she said, putting her arm through mine. 'I could never have imagined anything so horrible. I'm sorry.'

'It's not your fault! I wanted to see everything. And now I feel I have.'

'My Granma recommended it.'

After all the tension and the revulsion, I shouted with laughter and kissed her hard on the cheek.

'Your Granma must be quite a goer.'

'She read about it in the paper. She thought, since we're young, we might find a bit of decadence amusing.' Anna was staying with her Grandmother in the suburb of Schlossbergen.

In spite of her vamp's appearance and her taste for thrilling and disturbing excursions, Anna was a product of her time and of her class, and she was moderately committed to holding tight onto her cherry. She at least made a play of preventing my assumed ardour from going too far, *ie*, from pursuing foreplay below the waist, for which I was profoundly grateful. In Hamburg we had entwined our tongues, and I had kneaded her breasts and sucked her ears and made zoo noises of ungovernable lust, then howled with frustration when she ever so gently rebuffed my reluctantly wandering hands.

She was young as I was, and inexperienced, so perhaps she thought it usual for young men to blow hot and cold without an explanation. But she had apparently had enough of it.

It was our last night on tour. As we approached my hotel – I had asked her in for a night cap – she squeezed my arm.

'My Granma's broad-minded,' she whispered. 'I told her I wouldn't be home tonight.'

My heart thumped into my ribs. This was truly an emergency...

'They won't let us past Reception!' I stammered. 'I have a single room. They'll call the police...'

'I'm German!' She laughed her merry tinkling laugh, which made me want to break her nose. 'I sound like a Berliner! They won't turn me away!'

'I can't, Anna. Truly. There's too much going on in here...' Clutching my brow. 'I don't have any – you know – any –' I waved one hand in a futile gesture.

'We don't have to go the whole hog, do we? Just to lie together, naked, to sleep in each other's arms... To...'

'No!' I shouted, quite quietly since we were now in the foyer and already attracting suspicious looks. 'I'm sorry, Anna. I'm not in the right frame of mind...'

'It's our last chance! Mummy and Daddy watch me like a hawk. We'll never be able to get together in Bad O.'

'Nonsense. Where there's a will there's a way...'

She laid her head tenderly on my shoulder and twiddled the lapel of my first ever made-to-measure double-breasted finest worsted lounge suit. She kept twiddling it, in lieu of something else of mine that she had clearly set her heart on twiddling.

'That night club upset you, didn't it. You're so sensitive, darling. That's what attracts me to you. I can't bear big, rough men who're only interested in one thing.'

'There's more to life than sex...' (Coming from me?!?!)

'I believe you're a Puritan at heart. Is it because you're Scots, do you think?'

'Oh, I don't think of myself as a Puritan...'

'You're too much of a gentleman. You think all that...should wait till we're married? Silly boy. Come on...'

She started dragging me towards the lift. I couldn't have a row with her right there in front of the hotel staff and several of the guests who had been watching us in mild amusement. I shook her off and stared at her for a moment. This sweet girl whose only sin was to desire my body – but whose attentions, if they had continued, would have laid bare my deepest shame. If I had had any lingering doubts about how to behave or what action I ought to pursue, they were instantly dispelled by her use of the word 'married'. I turned and ran. I heard the revolving door spin behind me and my footsteps splashing on the pavement, otherwise I might have been tempted to record that I disappeared in a puff of dust.

That was Anna's lucky day.

3 TRUE LOVE
With all its Heartaches

HELEN OF TROY was played by a black American who is most often described as looking like a frog; but Eartha Kitt was so scabrously sexy, so witty, so naughty and so talented that she challenged the concept of beauty. She sang songs composed by Duke Ellington, and in the last act, slithering like a golden snake then grinding and bumping like a burlesque stripper, she lured her twenty-stone Faustus into Hell – 'See where Christ's blood streams in the firmament...'

Orson Welles had brought *Faust* to Germany, his own modern version, acknowledging Goethe and Marlowe and incorporating numerous acts of prestidigitation, an art of which he was particularly fond and at which he excelled. I remember him producing a rolled-up dollar bill from an orange. It was hard to see any relevance in this feat to the fable of the Doctor who sold his soul to the Devil for power, worldly riches and the love of women, but it went down well and Orson did a card-trick as an encore.

Micheal MacLiammoir, Orson's friend and mentor from the Dublin Gate Theatre, played Mephistopheles, and, disguised in a raincoat and a large Fedora, I played Gangster Number Two. The non-speaking gangsters were recruited from the ranks of amateurs throughout the tour. Orson was over six feet two and although he was not quite as fat as he became later in life, he was still huge, and in his presence mere mortals felt like midgets. He had a rumbling bass voice of great power and beauty but off-stage you had to strain to hear what he was saying. This tactic created a cathedral-like hush around him, transparently designed to inspire awe. I made a mental note: *Noise is bluster. When playing a powerful man keep the decibels down.*

Der Kunz Teater, then re-named The Rhine Army Theatre, was built on classical Greek lines and it stood in the middle of a gracious park shaded with magnificent mature trees, linden, oak and maple, Roman pine and monkey puzzle. It was June and the sky had a sea-green light in it as I left the stage door, meaning to strike across the park towards my quarters in Friedrich Strasse. I had gone only a few paces when a man approached me from the front of the theatre, where the audience was streaming out after the Saturday night performance. I could see by his peaked cap that he was a British Army Officer, and as he approached, my eyes dipped automatically to his epaulettes, a reflex in the uniformed services to ascertain rank, not least because if the insignia includes a red flash you have to salute it. I was safe. Only three pips. A Captain.

'Johnny? Do you remember me?'

A young man stood before me whose face I would never forget. I had seen him on two occasions, once at the Park Theatre where I had been introduced to him by a famous conductor at the Royal Opera House who was a friend of Clarrie McMurdo's, and once in the Lounge Bar of the George Hotel, which was known at that time as a haunt for homosexuals. I had been taken there by an actor in the company who wanted to show me the sights, but I had fled after five minutes, uncomfortable with the edgy, subterranean feel of the place. But not before I had taken with me the indelible image of a face, one of the handsomest faces I had ever seen, the face I saw now within touching distance of my own.

'You're from Glasgow! We met once.'

'Now stationed in Ehrwald. In the Austrian Tyrol.'

'Cushy posting! How'd you manage that?'

'I'm Medical Officer there.'

'A Doctor!'

I was breathless with excitement. Because of the company I had seen him in, I was fairly confident the young doctor shared my sexual orientation.

'Ian.' He held out his hand. 'Ian Hornton.'

'John Fraser.'

'I know. Actors. You're on the Marquee. In the programme. It's hard for you to be anonymous.'

We held the handshake a little too long.

'Have you time for a drink?'

'The Mess is just down there.' I pointed.

'Couldn't we find somewhere less public? More…civilian?' he said, pulling a wry face.

'Since we're both in uniform… I'm based here, and it's frowned on to go native.'

'Oh, what the hell. I speak German. Let's go to Heinrich's.'

He took my arm as if he'd known me all his life, and we strode off into the main part of town. Our common background made getting to know each other easy.

'You know Effie Morrison! What a character. She plays all the little boys on *Children's Hour*.'

'"Auntie Kathleen" gave me my first job... How long are you here for?'

'I leave at the crack of dawn for Innsbruck.'

'Oh. That's a pity.'

'It's a short business trip,' he explained. 'Had to sort through some records. We've just opened a new Clinic... I heard you were in the show. Orson Welles and Eartha Kitt...'

'How?'

We sipped our tankards of pale beer.

'Through the grapevine...'

'How do you mean, the grapevine?'

'Well, I've been asking about you. I tried to catch up with you a year ago in Glasgow. But The Park has closed now. I heard you were in Germany. In the Signals. It's not too difficult. We Medics...'

He had traced me... And come specially.

There was no time for beating about the bush, and in any case it was hopeless trying to hide that I was instantly and violently attracted to him.

'I work shifts, and I'm due a couple of days leave,' I said. 'Will it put you in an awkward position if I come up to Ehrwald in the middle of July?'

'Funny you should mention that. Yes it will, and you must.'

'What do you mean?'

'I'm being relentlessly pursued by the CO's wife. I drop hints like confetti at a wedding, but she's blind to them all. If you come up it might dawn on her that I'm not playing hard to get.' He smiled a heart-breaking smile. Then he looked hard at the table and almost whispered, 'I'm got, Johnny. If you want me. I'm got.'

With these two syllables I was catapulted into the bedlam of first love. The three intervening weeks before we could consummate our passion were among the most painful and yet the most exquisite of my life. In those days people wrote letters. The telephone was too public and too ephemeral a medium for outpourings of love. Those letters were written with your soul lying naked in your hand, they were written to be read and read again, to be pocketed as a poultice next the ache in your heart and committed to memory and kept under the pillow to colour your dreams. If these letters had been censored as they were during the war, we would have faced a firing squad.

Ehrwald is a village high in the Tyrol which had been requisitioned by the British forces as a leave centre. It was principally a ski resort but it was just as ravishing in summer with the snow-capped mountains surrounding sun-soaked valleys starred with wildflowers and clanking with cowbells, as it was thrilling in winter, thigh-deep in powdery snow cradled in the maw of icy peaks glittering against the sky.

For the remaining eighteen months of my national service I spent every leave in Ehrwald discovering love with all its heartaches, misunderstandings, tenderness and rapture, played out against a miasma of puffed sleeves and embroidered aprons and the flounce of dirndl skirts, of cocky little Robin Hood hats putting out their tongues of pink feathers and high-sheeny lederhosen burnished with thigh-slapping dances to the music of lilting accordions; of technicolour peasants quaffing litres of frothing beer from scenic mugs with silver lids, while Ian and I drank apfelsaft with our Wiener schnitzel in wooden chalets with brightly painted shutters and eaves half-way to the ground.

I learned the snow plough on the beginners' slopes, then swooping skywards in the ski-lift, we would come tumbling all the way down again between wildly erratic attempts at the slalom. Then there was the day we went to the Winter Olympics at Garmisch Partenkirchen and were dive-bombed by light aircraft. We ducked, but it was only the angry purr of the contestants' ski-suits in primary colours as they flew over our heads, spreadeagled against the sun.

There was the Passion Play in Oberammergau where the whole village, a crowd of ten thousand people dressed in peasant rags, parts to reveal the Lord Jesus arriving on a donkey.

After finishing his tenure as Medical Officer for the British Army of the Rhine in the Austrian Tyrol, Ian returned to Glasgow where he continued his studies to become a specialist.

He had the world at his feet. He was a fine doctor, a scholar, a good athlete, and a brilliant pianist, whose true loves were of course Mozart and Chopin, but he could play requests by ear and he would sing along with a hopeless hoarse voice – worse than Gene Kelly's – that was spellbinding and which made him a star at any venue with a piano. When I wasn't in Ehrwald, he was in Bad Oeynhausen. During the remainder of our national service we were like Castor and Pollux. As we were both commissioned officers from the same home town I don't believe anyone suspected anything untoward.

On demobilisation we both returned to Scotland, Ian to his studies and I to my life in the theatre. Although he was in Glasgow and I was in the highlands, we continued our affair over the next year at the same intensity, through letters and phone calls and at weekends whenever we could both get away. I was nineteen now, and I was beginning to worry that the price I might have to pay for our illicit love might be too high. I had seen enough of the world in the army and in Germany to know that I was not alone, that there were thousands, probably millions of men out there who were attracted exclusively to their own sex. But I did not want to be one of them.

I wanted a life full of love and friends and even children, a life that was not blighted by this curse of being queer, of being branded a criminal and risking a prison sentence if I persisted in loving Ian as I did, in having to find acceptance only among other homosexuals with whom I often felt nothing in common except our sexual orientation. I loved Ian more than I had believed it possible to love and want another human being, but I could see no future for us. Our meetings, of necessity, were clandestine and furtive, any prospect of a long term relationship doomed. For even if we managed to escape prosecution, in the Britain of 1950, two men living openly together would attract at best nothing but derision, and at worst a brick through the window. I could not fully express my doubts to Ian, who was braver than I was, and more willing to take a chance out in the open. Being an actor, I felt instinctively that any success that might lie ahead for me would depend as much on my appeal to the opposite sex as it would on my talent, and I was unwilling to jeopardise everything at this stage in my life.

We remained close right up until his premature death at the age of forty-three. By that time he was an eminent eye-surgeon, living in some splendour in a mansion on the Great Western Road surrounded by music and friends, and though I believe there were several lovers, none took up permanent residence with him. He never married and died from an overdose of pills and alcohol which may have been accidental, since he left no note.

During my two years in the Royal Corps of Signals, I not only mastered the intricacies of antiquated Signal Equipment, I also learned the workings of the internal combustion engine. I passed my driving test, and I learned to ski. I learned to fence with foil and sabre and I represented the Regiment in The Royal Signals Team. Fencing stood me in good stead later. There was a period in my career when I was always swashbuckling – *El Cid*, *Fury At Smugglers' Bay*, *Cyrano de Bergerac* and other stage productions.

And most importantly, I acquired a skill which gave me a lifetime's satisfaction and more joy than I can measure. I became an expert rider. I was taught by German grooms in the Headquarters of The British Army of The Rhine, on German Army thoroughbred horses, because I was a Commissioned Officer! The Other Ranks weren't allowed near these magnificent animals. I learnt dressage, cavaletti and jumping, which later got me the leading role in a film for Walt Disney called *The Horsemasters*.

All this at the taxpayer's expense.

To say nothing of the Wagnerian ravishment of my first true love affair.

I had been so reluctant to Serve my Nation, and how my Nation had Served me!

I should like to see compulsory National Service continued as a Peace Keeping Force on leaving school. Testosterone-fuelled young men need an outlet for their energies beyond beer and football. They should have the opportunity to live, to learn and to let fly, perhaps even to do some good and pick up some self-respect along the way, before knuckling down to a mortgage and the heavy weight of adult responsibilities. Even the privileged, destined for university, would gain from a year or two in a structured situation, helping others, instead of filling in their Gap Years pleasing themselves.

When I hollered this idea to my Aunt Gatty, she was not impressed.

'Mony a mickle maks a muckle!' she expostulated.

Most of my Aunt Gatty's aphorisms cannot be rendered comprehensible to those not acquainted with her byzantine thought processes. Her sub-text usually belied a direct translation. What I think she intended to convey on this occasion was:

'Hot air!'

4 THE GATEWAY TO THE HIGHLANDS
The Pitlochry Festival Theatre

THE LITTLE PARK THEATRE in Glasgow was wrapped up in 1948 and woke up two years later in a tent. By an amazing stroke of luck, in the time it took me to complete my National Service one theatre had closed and the other was about to open, and Clarrie McMurdo offered me a job starting the moment I was demobilised.

In May 1950, under a big top marquee erected on a raft of polished pine, The Pitlochry Festival Theatre was born. The town of Pitlochry is known as 'The Gateway to the Highlands'; it nestles in a valley in the Grampian Hills on the banks of the the river Tummel, and thousands of visitors arrive every summer to fish in the loch and walk the hills and admire the scenery. So the opening season of the theatre was planned with these tourists in mind. There were five popular plays, starting with *Macbeth* and *Mary Rose*. Still only nineteen, I was engaged yet again as an 'Acting ASM', playing tiny parts like Donalbain in 'The Scottish Play' and assorted messengers and servants.

I missed my entrance in *Macbeth* one night, and a colleague hurdled a guy-rope and grabbed me by my tabard, hissing 'YOU'RE OFF!' This is the stuff of actor's nightmares. It informs you that you have already missed your cue, that the play has come to a stop, that the audience is waiting and getting restless and that at the end of the week you will be out of a job. It is a much more alarming vocative than 'You're on!' which suggests that if you hurry you might still make it.

As a messenger I had to deliver some bad news, as messengers in Shakespeare are invariably required to do. Flustered and sixty seconds late – any unintentional hiatus in the middle of a play seems like an eternity to the actors, who often can find no way forward without crucial information or at the very least someone else to talk to – I sprang onto the battlements and threw myself at the feet of the King. 'MY QUEEN, YOUR LORD, IS DEAD!'

The leading actor playing the blood-soaked Tyrant slowly turned to me with a vulnerable expression on his face. He looked towards the audience, from whence there came no salvation… He sighed, scratched his spirit-gummed jowls and warily asked – 'And *my* Queen?'

Catching this life-line, quick as a flash I assured him, 'Dead too!'

He took a moment to consider this, then under his breath – though I heard him, and so did the front row of the audience – he muttered, 'There's a lot of it about.'

Before recording-tape was invented in the theatre we used a 'Panatrope' for music and sound effects. This lofty-sounding machine was quite simply a gramophone with front-of-house speakers, and the discs were recorded in bands for convenience: fanfares, mood music, dogs barking, pounding surf, thunder – ad infinitum. To pinpoint the desired music or effect, we ASMs would mark the disc with a yellow wax crayon. As junior ASM I was responsible for dropping the needle into the requisite groove when the Stage Manager gave me the cue-light.

The late Rosemary Kirkcaldy, who would become Mrs Joss Ackland, was spectacularly pretty: her pert little face was composed mostly of a pouting mouth and eyes emerging startled from a lather of blonde ringlets, and she was ideally cast as Mary Rose in J M Barrie's masterpiece, now in a more cynical age dismissed as being unbearably sentimental. In the second act, on 'The Island That Likes To Be Visited', somewhere in the Hebrides, Mary Rose is summoned by the Fairies and disappears for thirty years. The play gives no quarter to neo-realism. Haunting music has been composed and recorded for this lengthy disappearing act: behind a glissade on the harp and a swoop of violins, fairy voices intone, 'Ma-ary Ro-ose...' Up a notch and change key: 'Ma-ary Ro-ose...'

Suffering from first-night nerves, I must have put the record on the turntable upside down. The yellow crayon marks were clearly visible, but they were the wrong ones. When the cue came for Mary Rose's fairy voices I lowered the needle onto the pre-marked track. Where there should have been a bank of violins there was a roll of drums. The National Anthem exploded over the audience, producing pandemonium. The King-Pole swayed and the canvas trembled as I heard thundering footsteps racing round the perimeter of the tent on the polished pine floor. Joss, who was to marry Rosemary that very season, and who was in the thrall of a passionate and enduring love, arrived panting in the corner where I was operating the machine and laid me out. He didn't break my jaw, though some years later another actor did...

In 1951 Television had just started in earnest – as yet there were no commercial channels – and I was chosen to play 'Davie Balfour' in Robert Louis Stevenson's *Kidnapped*, which had been adapted into a six-part serial for the BBC. The Director had come up from London to scour Scotland for the perfect actor for the role. I was auditioned and got the part. Since the medium was in its infancy there were as yet no television critics: film critics reviewed whatever quality programmes were shown. After the first episode of our serial was broadcast, the doyenne of film critics, Miss C A Lejeune of *The Sunday Times*, devoted half her column to *Kidnapped*, heaping praise on me and ending with:

'This is potential Star material if I ever saw it.'

This review changed my life forever.

I was offered a long term film contract. I could choose one of the best agents in London, who shared my name, though we were no relation: Jimmy Fraser of 'Fraser and Dunlop'.

And at the age of twenty I made my first film.

5 THE RED PERIL
And the Wild Welsh Witch

VALLEY OF SONG was a gentle comedy, a Romeo and Juliet love story set in Wales, with two competing choirs instead of the feuding Montagues and Capulets. When it came out it was a *succès d'estime*, which means that it was neither a hit nor a turkey, but it brought me to the notice of casting directors and launched my career in films. I was offered another film straight away, but I didn't like the script or the part. I had been invited to join the Citizens' Theatre in Glasgow for a season, which I found a more attractive proposition, as I was keen to learn my craft and show off properly to my Aunt Gatty and to my sisters in my own home town.

My season there was memorable – to me at least – not so much for my performances and for playing the principal boy in a pantomime called *The Happy Ha'p'ny* with Stanley Baxter as the dame, but because of my brief but passionate affair with the Communist Party.

I had read Oscar Wilde's *The Soul of Man under Socialism*, I had dipped into Tom Paine, and I had even struggled with passages in *Das Kapital*, feeling clever and noble and dangerously radical. It must be remembered that I had never been to university and I had an intellectual inferiority complex. All my early adult life was spent trying to catch up.

I was intoxicated with the idea of joining the struggle to free the working class from the cruel exploitation which kept the workers poor and the bosses richer than any man in this troubled world deserved to be.

It seemed to me that the disparity between the rich and the poor was unacceptable in a civilised society, and was the cause of all our ills both physical and spiritual. What appealed to me about communism was its ideals, but I had not the faintest notion of what would have to be done, in its name, here in Scotland, to promote these ideals and to make the world a better place.

I attended weekly meetings which were held in West Nile Street. There was heady talk of protests, of strikes and marches, of workers' control and of commandeering pretty well everything without compensation, but nothing much actually happened.

To my dismay I soon found that I didn't like most of my fellow communists. They were on the whole aggressive and charmless and always ready to pick a fight, even among themselves. They believed that they had a monopoly on compassion; but instead of love, their hearts were full of hatred. My quest was for a humane society; their overriding enthusiasm was for destroying the one we had. They seemed to me to be motivated not by idealism, but by rage and resentment.

I am not exactly a pacifist, but I am no fighter and I take no pride in anger or in giving vent to it. Many people confuse anger with strength. We worship a wrathful God, after all. In argument I can be a firebrand, but in action I am an appeaser. A firebrand should be diametrically opposed to compromise and blinkered against opposing ideas.

So I was forced to face the fact that I lacked the conviction that only my views were the right ones, and that there was no room for debate. I lacked, too, the anger to be a revolutionary, and I had no appetite for the sustained aggression that is the first requirement for the arena of politics.

In youth I marched in protest for only one cause, CND. It's easy to be wise with hindsight, but during the Cold War, Mutually Assured Destruction seemed imminent if the peoples of the world stood by and did nothing.

In 1950, Stalin's iniquities had yet to emerge, as had the outrages of the Cultural Revolution in Mao's China, and the Khmer Rouge's atrocities in Pol Pot's Cambodia.

In Britain we were still seeing newsreels of Hitler's goose-stepping Nazis, and the allies' entry into Belsen and Dachau. I felt I could not love anyone who had never, even in the naïveté of their adolescence, leant a little in the direction of communism.

For youth always deals in the currency of extremes.

Had I lived in the United States, I would have been outed by McCarthy, and the Unamerican Activities Board would have put an end to my career. The irony has not escaped me that it is because we live in a liberal democracy that my youthful espousal of communism has not blighted my life.

After my painful entanglement with the Comintern, I was offered a film called *The Good Beginning*. This sounded prophetic, so I returned to London and started work straight away. I moved in with Rachel Roberts till I could find accommodation of my own. She was renting an apartment in Montague Mews with M, the future Countess of Ashdale. After making our first film together the three of us had become fast friends.

Rachel was a wild Welsh witch to whom moderation was a stranger. She was prey to every mania – klepto, dypso, nympho and perhaps others besides. She was the daughter of a Welsh Baptist preacher, which explained nothing, since I met her parents, and they were gentle, tolerant, civilised folk.

She always left the bathroom door open whether she was abluting or at stool, often singing raucously at the pitch of her voice, which was not a warning to keep out, but a celebration of being alive. With one leg up on the side of the bath, facing the hall and languorously soaping her groin, it was difficult to believe that this posture was not an invitation to further intimacy on my part, and perhaps it was, but I never took her up on it. Apart from everything else, we were always laughing too much.

Rachel confessed to me that she would sometimes pick up strangers in the street and submit to cruelty and degradation for their gratification. In the light of her tragic death, it is hard to escape the conclusion that she was a self-destructive masochist.

She could also be so obliging it could give self-sacrifice a bad name. When she spent a year at the Memorial Theatre in Stratford-upon-Avon, she methodically picked out all the young actors in the company who she guessed were wavering sexually (always a fair percentage in the theatre), and she would wheedle or beguile or force them in a strict rota system to go to bed with her. The drudgery of this self-imposed task was alleviated by the fact that most of these undecided young men were noticeably easy on the eye, *ie*, Laurence Harvey, Edmund Purdom, Robert Shaw and many others. Richard Burton was never a waverer, but Rachel pretended that he was and unselfishly took him to bed just the same. In the morning, if her wiles and her industry had proved to be efficacious, she would kiss her 'Good Deed' goodbye on the doorstep, assuring him: 'You see, Lovely? Stop worrying! You're not queer!' Goodness knows how many potential poofters she sorted out, or sent off as bent as a hairpin. In London I watched some come and go, but I was never one of them.

Her later marriage to Rex Harrison, I gathered from Carey, Rex's son by Lilli Palmer, was a prolonged battle for dominance. Rex was a cruel, manipulative man, and Rachel became his vicious adversary. Perhaps this mortal combat, inflicting pain and suffering punishment, followed by reconciliation, became as addictive to Rachel as her other manias, for not long after the Harrisons' divorce she killed herself. She drank weed-killer, which ensures a lingering and an agonising death. Hours after drinking the stuff, in her torment Rachel broke through the windows leading onto a terrace. The glass butchered her and it was loss of blood that finally killed her. Perhaps it was the end she sought

– screaming, savage, drenched in blood. For a woman of such wit and warmth and intelligence... It is hard not to believe in The Furies, or at least in the possibility of a Rogue Gene...

6 THE DREAM BOOK
Being Shrink-ed

IN *THE GOOD BEGINNING* I played opposite a young actress called Eileen Moore. I suppose she was quite boyish, though I never thought of that at the time. She was slender and extremely athletic, a fine tennis-player who was tanned from May to September. She was John Betjeman's 'Miss Joan Hunter Dunn', a golden girl with a radiant smile. I was wildly, high-tragically in love, in love with love, weeping myself to sleep with my stomach in knots. But where was the joy in it? It was Eileen's mind and her sweetness and a melancholy streak in her that attracted me, but there would be no end to my suffering if I could not make love to her. Inexorably there came the moment that could no longer be put off. I still hoped that at the starter's whistle my bursting heart would pump some blood in the right direction.

'It's a Far Cry to Aberfeldy!' my Aunt Gatty would no doubt have assured me.

As our naked limbs entangled, my indifferent organ made a mockery of my protestations of undying devotion. I not only loved Eileen, I respected her, which was fatal. This was a crisis that could no longer be ignored if I was to resist following through on the promptings to kill myself.

After the fiasco I walked through the night from Stanmore, where Eileen lived with her family, to my lodgings off Baker Street, ten miles or more in the driving rain, and my emotions were in a tumult. My feelings for Gerry and for Ian had been tumultuous too, but the ache for them had been composed almost entirely of desire.

Desire can be assuaged. But what is the cure for anguish?

We tried again. Eileen was tender and understanding, but it made no mechanical difference. We talked for most of the night which had been earmarked for love, and in the morning I telephoned the number she had given me. It was for her godfather, an eminent psychiatrist.

I had been eighteen years old when I had met Ian in Bad Oeyhhausen, and we had embarked on my first fully requited, consummated and passionate love affair. But I still hoped and prayed to the God I no longer believed in that in spite of my failure with Eileen a miracle would still save me from a lifetime of exclusive homosexuality and the social opprobrium concomitant with it; and Eileen's godfather was to be my miracle-worker.

I was determined to seek an escape from what I saw as the bondage of my homosexuality. Whenever I felt a glimmer of desire for a woman I would fan it feverishly with my hopes, but they were never strong enough to produce the furnace I needed to forge a proper relationship. There was no shortage of furnaces in my life but they were all blazing in the wrong direction.

Homosexuals then had three choices.

One. To conform to society's expectations. To marry and have children. Homosexuals in every society have done this since time immemorial and are still doing so in most countries. Only in the last fifty years and only in sophisticated cities like London and New York and Amsterdam and San Francisco is it acceptable for two people of the same sex to set up home together.

Two. To be celibate.

Three. To live a double life, fraught with danger – of violence or blackmail – and to live it alone.

It is possible to lead a decent and a happy life even if you are exclusively gay. But it isn't easy. In seeking a partner you do not, as heterosexuals do, at least in theory, have half the human race to choose from. Only a tiny percentage of your own sex will be as attracted to you as you are to them, let alone be compatible with you sexually and socially – before you even begin to investigate whether there is a possibility of mutual love. Your relationships will never have the respect and the endorsement of the whole of society.

And above all, you will never experience the universal and profound joy of raising a family.

I was determined that my disability, for I saw it as such, would not ruin the only life I had, for I had no enthusiasm for celibacy.

Eileen's godfather, Eddie, was a little round man of Polish extraction and Jewish (de rigueur for psychiatrists). He had a wide gap between his protruding front teeth that gave rise to his wife's nickname for him: 'Bunny'.

On my first visit I was so nervous I almost turned back at the door. Years of experience, however, had taught Eddie how to deal with frightened or reluctant patients. Instead of playing the stern father-figure he would later become to me, he beguiled me with his gentle charm. He suggested that we should not consider this our first meeting as a consultation, but rather that we should spend an hour getting to know each other a little, to see whether we liked each other enough to continue on a professional basis.

Of course, it worked. Here lay my only hope. Eddie would lead me gently through the thickets of my confusion and, with his gentle gap-toothed smile to reassure me, he would lead me out into the light.

I don't know whether it is good, or right, or necessary for a patient to like his doctor as much as I instantly liked Eddie, but our friendship made my sessions with him such a pleasure that trust was very quickly established, and trust is the bedrock upon which psychoanalysis is based.

He overstepped the doctor–patient mark most of the time. He played the violin to professional standards, and he would frequently invite members of the London Philharmonic Orchestra to join him playing string quartets. Even after a hard day's rehearsal, these musicians would join Eddie in his sitting-room, with only me and sometimes a couple of others for an audience, to play for their own pleasure. This is the definition of a true vocation.

Mirca, Eddie's wife, was Hungarian, and she used to provide a delicious buffet for these musical evenings, at one of which I tasted blinis and caviar for the first time.

I am impervious to chamber music, and continue to be so. But to my surprise, being right among the musicians – almost having to dodge their bowing elbows – I found the music rather thrilling. I dreaded the discussions afterwards, and usually left promptly the minute the performance was over.

'Could the Greek book have been an erection symbol?'

I was twenty-one years old and I was two weeks into analysis. Since Eddie was a Jungian, I was sitting opposite him, and not lying on a couch. A Freudian's relationship with his patient is strictly doctor–patient, but a Jungian conducts the proceedings on a man-to-man basis.

Eddie made me keep a dream book. First thing in the morning, or even when I woke up in the middle of the night, before those fleeting fantasies disappeared forever in the light of day, I had to write down my dreams so that Eddie and I could use them as a basis for discussion.

People's dreams are of no interest to anyone but the dreamer. Some bores have still to discover this. I make an exception of this dream, however, and I present a précis of it here, because Eddie proved something to me about which I was deeply sceptical, and proved it to me beyond any shadow of a doubt.

The dream I had just recounted to him was this: I was travelling on a tram in my native Glasgow to meet Eileen. As I descended, I passed an Indian in a turban, and I felt a Greek grammar book in my pocket.

'Could the Greek book have been an erection symbol?' was Eddie's response.

As a novice at this game, I was about to dismiss his suggestion as psycho-babble, when it hit me like a thunderbolt.

I hadn't written it down, which is perhaps another indication that I had tried to suppress it, but the whole point about my dream, and why it had disturbed me was that –

I COULD NOT GET THE GREEK BOOK TO LIE DOWN! I had studied Ancient Greek at school, and everybody knows the Greeks invented boy-love. The Greek book jutted out from my body at an angle of ninety degrees, and no matter how I juggled with it in my pocket, I could not disguise the shameful swelling nor make it lie down!

Now to the Indian.

Beards were uncommon in my youth, *ie*, as a rule only Indians wore them. I didn't write down that the Indian had a beard, but of course he had.

So: I have failed in my attempt to make love to Eileen and on my way to meet her I pass someone in a turban who is unequivocally male because he has a beard, and suddenly I have a protruberance in my pocket which won't lie down.

If that is meant to be a joke it isn't funny.

It proved to me with childlike clarity how devious and convoluted, how punning and Gothic in its deceptions, is our subconscious. It seems we will think up anything to avoid facing up to the truth.

I dropped my defences with Eddie. If he had said now, 'Could the tram ticket have been your mother?' – before, I would have dismissed the idea as rubbish – after, I might have been able to say, 'Hang on! Funny you should mention that! The tram-ticket sang me to sleep!'

'We must begin with your childhood.'

Eddie sat back in his chair. We still had over an hour till his next patient.

'Tell me your early memories… Whatever comes into your mind…'

At the beginning of my analysis, I went to Eddie three times a week, and my dream book, which he suggested I should keep, was full of flying dreams. I would soar above the world to great orchestral film-scores like 'Pop! Bubble, Bubble, Bubble, Bubble, Pink Champagne…'

I hardly needed Eddie to suggest to me that they were 'Freedom' dreams.

For I had found my saviour, and I was on my way to a Brave New World, where men were men and women were women and everybody was at it like knives – no problem – and I was one of them.

And what is life, after all, without hope…

Growing up surrounded by exemplary females, all of whom I had loved extravagantly, having a disastrous father and attending an all-male school where dirty talk was common, it became fixed in my developing consciousness that males had urges that repelled decent females, and that if we had to gratify these urges, we ought to leave the female sex out of the whole nasty business.

'Fear of Incest,' Eddie explained, 'to oversimplify.'

It was clear that I loved women. But I dared not think of them below the collar.

'You will never be one hundred percent heterosexual.' You might say Eddie was stating the obvious. 'If such a condition exists…'

'You think the entire population of the world is bisexual?'

'The entire population of the world is sexual, and given the appropriate circumstances, I believe everyone is capable of sexual attraction to his or her own sex.'

'Everyone?'

'It would be hard to prove. But I believe that, yes. And I believe you are also bisexual. I believe that being bisexual will be your natural state, if that is what you truly want, and if we continue with your analysis. But being Bent… or Straight… or being anything at all in the whole spectrum of sexuality doesn't mean that you have to act on it.'

'What makes you so sure I can be bisexual?'

'You love women. That's a start.'

'Love doesn't always lead to sex. Nor sex to love.'

'That's true. But they go best together.'

'Now you're being moral.'

'I'm also thinking of your quest for happiness.'

'Have I told you about the time I sexually abused my father?' I asked him.

Even in doctor–patient relationships, there is sometimes an irresistible urge to take control. I was gratified by Eddie's reaction, a puzzled mixture of disbelief and reproof.

'It was my turn to sit by my father's bedside till he went into a coma. He was drunk on booze or Paraldehyde and Luminal or a mixture of all of them. The fits were over, but he wouldn't go under. He'd just had some semolina, which was all he could keep down. And my mother had made it with water because we'd run out of milk. His teeth were sitting in a mug on the dressing table and there was a blob of pudding stuck to the end of his nose.

'"Tell yer mother it's no good fobbing me off with blue pudd'n. I may be no weel but I'm no' daft. Blue pudd'n doesnae do anybody any good. That pudd'n was blue!"

'The cord had come out of his pyjama trousers when my mother had been wrestling with him to get him ready for bed earlier, and since re-threading it is a bit of a performance, she had finally put him to bed wearing only the top of his pyjamas. When I caught a glimpse of all that paraphernalia swelling out of a thick nest of hair, I experienced a lurch in my stomach of excited curiosity. I had never seen a mature male organ – or a female one, for that matter – in my life before, and as my father lay there sliding into drugged sleep, all I could think about was his nakedness under the rumpled sheets within a few inches of my fingers and my popping eyes.

'I got as far as lifting the sheet to have a better look, but I didn't have the courage to touch his cock in case he woke up, though I wanted to. If I had, would I have been arrested, do you think, for adult abuse?

'You could say it was just curiosity, but I have absolutely no curiosity – now – about the intimate bits of the opposite sex, and the thought of doing something like that to my mother is so appalling it makes my blood run cold.

'So I can't share your certainty about bisexuality being my natural state…'

'You were pretty keen on your cousin Moira?'

'That's true. But I was a child, I can't get back to that place in the adult world…'

'We can try,' he said. 'Together.'

As I was leaving, he smiled. 'I love the English language. How clearly it differentiates between childish, and childlike. So many adult problems would disappear, if we could stop being one, and start being the other.'

7 MY FIRST PIMP
Stephen Ward

IT WAS ONLY because of my contract with The Associated British Picture Corporation that at the age of twenty-one I could afford the fees for psychoanalysis.

I was six months along the road, as I fervently hoped, to my recovery, when I reached the first milestone. Impatient to test the efficacy of my analysis I defied Eddie's advice and paid my first visit to a brothel.

I would never have had the courage or the resource to plan such an initiative without the co-operation of my friend Stephen Ward, the osteopath who killed himself after being accused of living off immoral earnings in the Profumo Affair.

In my first film, *Valley of Song*, which I made at the age of nineteen, I had played opposite a hairdresser's daughter from Dundee called M. She is now the Countess of Ashdale. She was a graduate from The Royal Ballet School, the kind of exquisitely beautiful creature one expects to see forever spinning on top of a music box. She had dark hair parted in the middle, deep dark eyes and a seductively crooked smile. She was tiny, with a waist a wasp would envy, and her little feet pointed always at quarter to three. She was living with Stephen at the time, and the three of us became good friends.

We lunched together every Sunday in the apartment above Stephen's surgery in Devonshire Place. Stephen always did the cooking, and he made a memorably delicious roast leg of lamb with onion sauce. He was a cultured man with great charm and a rich baritone speaking voice that was the envy of many an actor.

We had finished the wash-up. I collapsed in a pile of cushions on the white shag carpet in the studio with *The Sunday Times* and *The News of the World* on my lap, while M decided to take Wong Pie, her Japanese Tschin dog, for a walk. I fear the libidinous atmosphere in the flat must have affected the dog, for although he was little more than a puppy, M told me he was already on bromides. Without them he rogered everything he could keep between his paws from dawn till dusk – discarded clothes, the cushions, Stephen's patients' legs when they were least expecting it, the weekly shopping if left on the kitchen floor, and, by splaying his legs, even M's Gucci handbag when he was desperate – with the result that without medication there was an awful lot of mess to clear up and the young dog's overactive little organ was a running sore.

Jean Metcalfe was introducing *Family Favourites* on the Light Programme. Frank Sinatra… 'No love, no nothin', until my baby comes home…' Nelly Lutcher husking to her piano, 'Fine Brown Frame…'

Stephen rubbed his thumb on the paper to smudge the chalk. He was a gifted artist, and he augmented the considerable income he made as an osteopath manipulating the bones of various luminaries of the aristocracy – and providing seamier services, it transpired at his trial – by drawing saccharine portraits of debutantes and dowagers, of their household pets and their bloodstock, in red and white chalk and charcoal on soft brown paper.

The walls of his bedroom at the top of the house flaunted his true proclivities; you couldn't slip a playing-card between the frames. He never claimed that these posturing creatures were all his conquests, but to draw the female figure at that time, naked, in such detail and with such manifest lasciviousness, was like brandishing a heavily-stamped passport at a customs official. He had clearly 'been there'.

Stephen was a compulsive drawer, just as my Aunt Gatty was a compulsive knitter. If there was a moment's pause, Stephen would get out his block of brown sheets, his box of coloured chalks, and start to draw.

Since my presence in Devonshire Place precluded any forays into Shepherd's Market or Park Lane, where the sad little tarts that obsessed him walked the streets openly in those days, he was settled with his pad on his knee in front of me and sublimating his demon lust in conversation.

'Smell is what gives them away. I can tell in the darkest night the latitude if not the longitude of where they come from by their smell. Southern girls smell of musk, with perhaps a hint of garlic. The Northern ones smell of lemon, with perhaps a hint of fish and chips. In the east, even in their deepest clefts, they smell of chop-suey…'

I kept silent and very still, dreading that he would insist on my confirmation of these sexual aperçus, but he was happy to continue reminiscing.

'Oh happy days! She's really the Honourable Mrs Fotheringay, but she calls herself "Mrs Feather" for professional purposes. She runs the best brothel in London. Never been in trouble with the law. She's a godsend to the gentry. They know their sons are safe. The girls are all checked regularly. Much safer to send "Young Jeremy" to Mrs Feather than to throw him to the lions in Soho!'

I was wearing a polo-neck sweater but I noticed that he was drawing my head and shoulders as if I were naked. I suspect Stephen was pansexual.

'Where does Mrs Feather operate?' I asked casually, my heart pounding. In a flash of inspiration I had conceived the notion of sorting out all my problems with one audacious transaction. I would follow hot in 'Young Jeremy's' footsteps and pay a prostitute to make a man of me.

My adult life had been a battle to fend off respectable young women determined by fair means or foul to relieve me of my virginity. The prospect of being in control in a situation, of being the pursuer and not the pursued, if only because I was the customer and She, The Mysterious She, was the goods, was irresistibly tantalising.

Stephen inclined his pebble-glasses towards me, behind them his eyes moist with emotion. 'Elvaston Place,' he crooned. 'I have her phone number if you want it.'

'Why not?' I cleared my throat to cover my confusion.

Since M had not returned from walking Wong Pie round the block, Stephen had time to make good his word and he wrote Mrs Feather's telephone number on the back of an envelope. He emphasised that I must say 'Raymond' had recommended her to me. I never discovered whether Raymond existed or whether the name was simply a password.

'I shall want to hear about it in living colour and graphic detail if you go,' he whispered, as we heard M's fairy footsteps mounting the stairs, though I can't confirm he actually dribbled.

8 MRS FEATHER'S BORDELLO
No Luck

IT WAS ONE of those endless sunny evenings in June when the party in the street never stops. There were girls in pretty frocks or T-shirts discreetly punctuated with their nipples, boys in cut-away vests and jeans – everywhere you looked there were flickers of nakedness to titillate my inflamed yet cruelly thwarted lust.

On the telephone Mrs Feather had been doggedly amenable. To my request, 'When would be convenient?' she had replied, 'That's up to you, John. I like to stick to first names, it's more discreet. Don't you agree? When would suit you?' The morning seemed too desperate, the afternoon too clinical, and the night too depraved, so I settled for mid-evening, a compromise which I hoped would be construed as being civilised without appearing greedy.

As I emerged from the Gloucester Road tube station at a quarter to eight, the still-blazing sunshine seemed to capture me centre stage and pin me in a gigantic spotlight. All eyes were on me, and my tawdry mission lay revealed. I should have made my furtive tryst more post meridian and under the cloak of night.

Would there be a roomful of houris in frilly corsets and black suspenders – snaking their legs about the furniture, passing their pointy tongues suggestively over rosebud lips – as I made my entrance at the top of a grand staircase to the strains of a honkey-tonk piano? Or would there be a corridor with rooms to left and right, some with the door locked on the moaning occupants, others enticingly ajar, wide enough to see by the dim red light the half-clad figures inside sprawling on rumpled sheets thrusting their groins at me and beckoning lewdly, murmuring, 'You want a good time, Dearie?' Or would I be invited to peep through a hole, or a one-way mirror at a gigantic bubble-bath filled with sporting nymphs, while a grotesquely painted Mrs Feather, like a pantomime dame, asked me with a leer, 'What's your fancy?' Perhaps there would be an identity parade, with the whores in slit-satin cheong-sams and platform shoes chewing gum and smouldering through their ringlets as I walked along the line…

24 Elvaston Place was one of those Kensington mansions nowadays favoured by Arab countries for their embassies, but in the fifties often converted by avaricious landlords into tall, thin, hardboard cubicles, each with a gas-ring and 'Use

of Toilet on the Landing', advertised in the *Evening Standard* at exorbitant prices as 'Flatlets'. There was only one bell outside 24, and it was without a name. The bell was an original Victorian antique of the kind that must be burnished daily to maintain its lustre and be sharply pulled to make it work. The brass was mostly black and gleamed only in patches. My first attempt to make my presence felt produced no answering jingle in the hall. My second might have summoned the Fire Brigade.

Through the frosted glass panels in the front door a figure bore down on me. Was it too late to leap the steps and sprint through the blameless summer folk thronging the streets and plunge undefiled out of the pitiless glare into the bowels of the Gloucester Road tube like Orpheus without a backward glance... 'And stay a fruit for the rest of your life?'... I hesitated and was lost. The door, held by a chain, opened a crack, and a woman's voice said, 'Yes?'

'I'm a friend of Raymond's,' I said faintly. 'John.'

'Just a minute, John.' The chain was unhooked. 'Nice to meet you, John. I'm Mrs Feather.' She held out her hand, and as I took it she pressed her other hand on top and gave mine a conspiratorial squeeze.

Mrs Feather would have looked at home on the platform of the Women's Conservative Association. She was about sixty, neither well- nor ill-groomed, just tidy, with fine grey hair held at the back of her neck in a sensible coil. She was thin and small, and though her calf-length floral frock was of chiffon, it was a day dress with nothing glamorous about it. She wore not a hint of makeup on her unremarkable face.

'Isn't it a lovely evening, John?' I wished she'd stop calling me 'John'. She led me past a palm in a porcelain jardiniere framed by a window draped with heavy lace, her Cuban heels squeaking on the mosaic tiles, till resting her hand against the jamb of a door with 'Lounge' dimly visible on it beneath tired cream paint – the building must have been a small hotel at one time – she turned back to me and flashed a chipped and nicotine-stained smile. (The Honourable Mrs Fotheringay was like her doorbell, a bit neglected under the veneer.)

'You don't know Raymond!' she teased.

'Well,' I blushed. 'He's a friend of a friend sort of thing.'

'I know just the sort of thing,' she said, pursing her wrinkled lips in a suggestive moue, and with a kind of saucy flounce, she opened the door.

Where was the music and the raucous laughter? Where were the pink lampshades, the acres of yielding flesh, the fish-nets, the tidal waves of cheap scent impotent to disguise the overpowering reek of females rutting?

We were in a perfectly ordinary Kensington drawing room, with candlesticks on the mantlepiece, a cut-mocquette suite, a Japanese lacquered screen, a nest of tables, and a few 'Good Pieces' against the *Eau-de-Nil* walls.

In the corner of the Chesterfield sofa, however, sat a solitary figure; she looked about eighteen, slight and blonde, with a retroussé nose and wide grey eyes that I caught for only a moment before she returned her gaze to the large piece of apple pie she was eating enthusiastically with a fork.

'You don't know Sheila, do you?' How would I know Sheila?!? Sheila! Not Zsa-Zsa, or Dolores, or even a suitable English soubriquet like Samantha, or Maxine, or even Shirley, for God's sake, but Sheila!

'Sheila, this is John.' Sheila smiled not too sweetly and readdressed herself to the apple pie.

'Let me get you a drink, John,' Mrs Feather said. 'What would you like?'

'I don't mind.' I wanted to get through the ordeal without being noticed. Had I made a ludicrous mistake? Mrs Feather and one hungry girl did not seem, even by the Pope's standards, to constitute a brothel. Behind Stephen's wet-lipped innuendo, had there been a ghastly misunderstanding? Was this simply a Dating Agency, where randy young toffs were introduced to an 'Escort' for the evening?

'John, dear.' I was now 'John, dear'! 'Gin? Whisky? Sherry?' Mrs Feather persisted. 'A glass of wine perhaps?' Then lowering her voice she added, 'Or would you prefer something soft!'

I had no way of knowing whether the double entendre was intended but I was in no mood for banter, and I'm afraid I started visibly at what seemed to be a lewd suggestion. In this house of ill-repute, at least. Mrs Feather's manner remained inscrutable, so I opted for a gin and tonic, torn between the need to still my nerves and the very real fear of taking the lead out of my precarious pencil.

The funereal silence was punctuated only by the tinkle of ice in my glass, and by the eye-watering scrape of a fork as Sheila chased an errant lump of apple across her plate. I couldn't talk openly to The Madam in front of The Tart, and I couldn't talk to The Tart in front of The Madam. Mrs Feather no doubt considered this agonising hiatus Quality Time – the time for me to size up my adversary – sorry, my victim – or should I say my prize? I turned down the offer of a piece of pie several times, and in the nick of time stopped humming to myself.

I was thinking, 'Where are all the rest of them? How much is all this going to cost?' I had lacked the courage or the foresight to ask this question on the telephone. 'If there's just Sheila, am I supposed to take her to my place? My landlady will dial the three nines! Or to a hotel? I don't have any luggage! Dear God! If there's just Sheila – WILL SHE DO?'

At last, stopping her munching, Sheila sat looking bored. Inviting my scrutiny, I suppose, though I was much too shy and sensitive to her self-esteem to give her more than an accidental glance. From the evidence of my peripheral vision and the odd surreptitious blink, I ascertained that she was pretty, pale, small featured, neatly dressed. A total turn-off. If I could have disinterred some fantasy female buried in a forgotten recess of my subconscious, some fabled Odalisque that might arouse me sufficiently to achieve the calculated coupling I had come in search of, then she would have to be as different as possible from my two lovely sisters, my daft Aunt Gatty and my sainted mother; she would have to be a little wicked, flagrantly sexy and possibly black. This description did not fit Sheila. Despite the evidence of her presence in this House of Shame, she looked VIRGINAL! And Sheila would most definitely NOT DO! But wait! Something was happening...

Mrs Feather had risen and was moving towards the door. Was another customer arriving? More girls? The Police?

'Sheila, dear!' Sheila obeyed the summons and was whispered at. Maybe Sheila was protesting that she wouldn't take me on! Maybe she found me repulsive! Too young. Too short. Too inexperienced. Too thin... I could now see it was against the poor girl's will, but Mrs Feather propelled Sheila into the hall and closed the door on her, then turning the full radiance of her brown chipped smile upon me, she asked silkily, 'I think Raymond would approve, don't you?'

She closed her eyes briefly, and pouted. Her mannerisms were inappropriate to a woman of her seniority, but they were a relic, perhaps, of happier times when she was involved in the business of prostitution at a more grass-roots level. 'Will Sheila be all right for you?'

'YES!' I said, without a pause. What would have happened had I said 'No!'? 'Come back tomorrow and maybe Sally...' And more Apple Pie... And more sidelong glances... I couldn't go through it all again.

'That'll be five pounds,' she said, suddenly businesslike, and she didn't call me 'John' any more, let alone 'John, dear'. (In 1950, £5 was worth about £100 today.)

'Do you want me to pay now? Or...after?'

'Now, if you don't mind.' If I paid the woman now, I wouldn't have to go through the humiliation of having to face her for the Post Mortem. She might insist on hearing all the details, like Stephen, and they might not reflect to any-body's credit...

Fumbling for my cheque-book, I asked 'Do you have a pen?'

She was disgruntled that I didn't have the correct amount in notes, but she had no choice, so she accepted my cheque in the end, flapping it to cool her brow as she led the way up the broad staircase to a door on the first floor. In the room there was the usual amount of furniture, but all I could see was a bed; or rather a sofa-bed, made up and turned down to reveal clean yellow sheets. Massive girders of sunlight dancing with motes plunged through the high windows onto a Turkish carpet, and Sheila had vanished off the face of the earth.

'The bathroom's through there.' Mrs Feather nodded towards a closed door which mercifully explained Sheila's disappearance. She switched on a standard lamp, and seizing fistfuls of chenille in her gnarled and heavily ringed fingers, she heaved the great curtains together to shut out the summer.

'Tell Sheila to pop in and see me before she goes,' she said, then as she was leaving, she shot over her shoulder, 'You won't be disturbed!' and closed the door.

'Disturbed!' The thought had never occurred to me. But now that Mrs Feather had planted in my mind the possibility of (a) casual intruders, or (b) the unwanted attentions of pathetic perverts who 'got their rocks off' watching others, I leapt wildly at the door and double locked it.

Sheila was taking forever behind the closed door. I didn't dare to remove even my jacket till we had talked a little, got to know each other. I approached the bathroom with my knuckles raised and shaking, in preparation for a friendly rap to let her know that she was not alone, when the door was suddenly flung open and Sheila appeared naked except for flesh-coloured panties – her armful of clothes, however, concealing all above the waist except her pointed pink shoulders.

'What are you hanging about for?' She pushed past me to drape her garments over the back of a chair, and with one flick of her thumb she removed her briefs and was between the sheets before I had time to loosen my tie. Her briskness would have dampened the ardour of Casanova.

I slowly undressed to my underpants, which flapped as everything inside them dived for cover. I sat on the end of the bed hanging my head like a prisoner in the condemned cell. 'I'm always a bit shy the first time,' I drivelled.

'I can't wait all night!' Sheila protested. 'I've got to be at "The Pigalle" at ten!' She wiped off her lipstick with a tissue, rolled it into a ball and lobbed it at the wastepaper basket; she missed, but as she leant over I caught a flash of the cleavage between her buttocks and there was the faintest stirring in my Y-Fronts like a wind change on the surface of a lake.

'You're meeting someone else? At "The Pigalle"?'

'I work there, silly! I'm a dancer. I only do this part time, as a favour to Mrs Feather.' Even as she said it, she realised that such self-sacrifice might be hard to credit, so she added, 'And for a bit of pocket-money of course. And it gives me something to do in the afternoons. I don't like sunbathing on the Serpentine.'

'You what?'

'I got a delicate skin. Have you got a French Letter?'

'No.'

'I'm clean. And I'm going to stay that way.'

'I'm sorry. I didn't realise. Does that mean the whole thing's off?' I honestly think I felt relieved.

'I got one in me bag.' She rummaged, slapped the little square envelope on the bedside table, then lay back examining her nails. Tentatively I leant towards her. 'No kissin'!' She sat bolt upright. 'No one kisses me except my boyfriend!'

Her whole demeanour was of quivering outrage that I should presume she was the kind of girl that would let anybody kiss her! Her absence of enthusiasm was not only dispiriting, it was infectious. Reciprocated passion is intoxicating because it enhances self-regard; it doesn't take Einstein to work out that the opposite does the opposite.

There are women to whom lack of fervour in a man is seen as a challenge – to my considerable grief, I knew this only too well. But were I Adonis or Quasimodo, Sheila had made it manifestly clear that I was just another customer, and since she was just a part-time tart doing it for pocket-money, she could establish her part-time virtue by refusing to enjoy it.

I crept into the bed beside her and ran my hands over her neat little body, because I thought that's what you did. She held her head averted with – distaste would be too strong a word, indifference too weak – but her determination to blot out the whole performance was unequivocally grim. I was about to throw in the towel when Sheila turned sharply, and looking me straight in the nipples, she asked, 'Are you in the Guards?'

I thought, 'So Stephen was right! This is where the scions of the great houses hang their bowlers.' Even although we were horizontal she could not have failed to observe that my stature of five feet eight inches would disqualify me from entrance to this elite Corps. Was she trying to flatter me into tumescence? Or was she actually trying to make conversation at last to put me at my ease?

'No,' I said. 'I'm not tall enough.' It came out as if it were my life's ambition to be in the Guards, but with my present preoccupations, explaining my life's ambition seemed superfluous.

Having cracked the ice with this witty exchange, Sheila allowed me to cuddle her for a bit. Then when she saw and understood my problem, she condescended to knead it gently with her fingers. She said one kind thing that almost saved the day... 'Don't worry. It often happens...' Then she ruined it by adding – 'Maybe you should try a chap.'

Anxious to bring all this fumbling to some kind of conclusion, Sheila conceded defeat over her insistence on my wearing a sheath, and between us, with some patience and much persistence, we achieved a perfunctory coupling. Before I had time to say, 'Thank You', Sheila withdrew me like a cork from a bottle and leapt into the bathroom as though on springs. From the amount of water I heard splashing about, she was attempting suicide by drowning.

I lay back to take stock. I had paid for and used another person's body to prove something to myself. Sheila was making her pocket money, and if it hadn't been me it would have been someone else – quicker, maybe, but not necessarily less boring. Eddie, my psychiatrist, had advised me that technical failure at this stage of what he hoped was my recovery might prove to be a serious setback, and he had warned me above all that sex without love was meaningless.

I disagreed with him on both counts. My problem was sex, and romantic love could blossom for me only if I were secure in the knowledge that I could consummate it. Mechanically my body had finally responded to a total stranger, but would it respond if initial failure caused distress or disappointment to someone I knew, let alone loved, or worst of all respected?

As Sheila bounced back into the room I felt a flood of warmth towards her; for allowing me to use her sweet little body, however reluctantly. We had been through something together, and I felt a kind of collusion which was close to desire. I wanted to make love to her slowly, gently, without anxiety, without the necessity of getting it up or of putting it in or even of having a climax if we didn't want to.

'Come here,' I said, feeling proprietorial.

'I gotta get dressed!' She snapped on her panties as fast as she had thumbed them off. Practice makes perfect, I suppose.

'What's the hurry?' I jumped out of bed and embraced her, but she pulled sharply away.

'It's all right for you!' she said. 'I gotta be at "The Pigalle" at ten. I'm gonna be late!' She didn't have to add, 'Because you took so long…'

Now that she was fully dressed, I felt self-conscious in my nakedness, but I couldn't resist turning sideways under the standard lamp so she could see I wasn't a complete waste of space.

'Can I see you again?' I'm still not sure whether I wanted to, or whether I simply wished to reassure her that the shortcomings in my performance were not due to her lack of attractiveness.

'You can always phone Mrs Feather.' She took a little brush from her handbag and fluffed out her hair. 'The afternoon's best for me.'

'Could I take you out, or something? For a meal. We could have a chat. Get to know each other a bit –'

'I work evenings, remember? Anyway, I got a boyfriend.'

'That's it then,' I said, as she smoothed a touch of lipstick on her pert little mouth, appraising the result in her compact mirror.

'See you,' she said, aiming for the door.

'Thanks. Thanks for everything…'

But she was gone. *Post coitum triste*, I got dressed, and Mrs Feather ushered me out into the never-ending sunshine to ponder on the state of my libido.

9 ROMAN CONQUEST
And a Defeat

I WAS OFFERED a leading role in a costume film called *Lady Fair*, which was a trilogy about three legendary beauties: Helen of Troy, Geneviève of Brabant and…I forget who the third beauty was. The three women in this curious package were all to be played by one actress – arguably the most beautiful woman who has ever appeared on the screen – Hedy Lamarr.

The shooting was scheduled to take place in Cinecitta Studios in Rome and on location throughout Italy. I accepted the offer, script unread.

I was to play a young knight called 'Drago' in the Geneviève episode, and all I can remember about this character is that he died in the heroine's arms. 'Drago don't die!' was the immortal line delivered over my expiring form, a line so deathless as to need repeating, not once but many times – 'Drago, don't die… Drago don't die…' Dead.

We were accommodated at the Residence Palace (sic), an uncompromisingly modern but luxurious hotel in Parioli, a chic district in new Rome outside the historic centre, though still just a twenty-minute walk through the Borghese Gardens to the Via Veneto, the Spanish Steps, the Campidoglio, La Dolce Vita.

After sundown in every town throughout Italy between six o'clock and eight o'clock, the young people take to the streets in the ancient ritual of *La Passeggiata*, the evening promenade where old friends can meet and chat, where new acquaintances can be struck up, where a boy can catch the eye of a girl who takes his fancy, or a girl can signal by a blush or a toss of the head how she cares for the boy of her choice. By eight o'clock the streets are empty, as everyone goes home for Mamma's pasta.

At twenty-two years old, after nearly a year of psychoanalysis, celibate but simmering, Rome flaunted its sensuality at me like a painted whore. In the Via Condotti, and elbowing through the crowd milling round the fountain at the base of the Spanish Steps, I could taste the lust like marzipan, cloying, at the back of my tongue; smooth brown beauties loitered in fantasy-inducing undress, lounging, laughing, caressing strangers with their dark, inviting eyes; and where the succulent breasts and slender waists and ripely swelling buttocks stopped, the statues took over, everywhere rejoicing in the beauty of their nakedness, stone drapery flying from the muscular forms with the airy lightness of muslin. The hot earth-colours of the buildings, amber and ochre and cotta, the magnificent salons coyly hiding behind peeling, slatted shutters, their lofty ceilings writhing with more sumptuously painted nudes, reclining, drugged with pleasure ten feet above the dusty chandeliers…even the water in the fountains appeared languid in the searing heat.

And in every square, up every little side street, tables stood set for dinner behind potted hedges of box, the starched napery gleaming and sparkling with silver and glass. You could feel the roasting cobbles through the soles of your shoes – and the smells: olives and fresh bread and vanilla-sweet pastries and strong coffee and black tobacco and garlic and dark heavy perfume and ripe peaches; smells laced with barely discernible tendrils of sweat. Colonies of wiry cats lay splayed in the purple shadows. I was tempted to join them. I wanted to feast on this banquet of the senses forever. Glasgow never seemed further away.

For two weeks I was concussed, and when I came to my senses, I knew I was in love. And like its epithet, my love has lasted a lifetime.

For I was in love with the Eternal City of Rome.

The Stazione Termini is for the newly-arrived, the backpackers, the pickpockets, the touts, the Via Veneto is for the high-class tarts and the International Set, but the Piazza di Spagna is the meeting-place for young Romans.

At the bottom of the swirling flights of steps Vespas quacked around the fountain as though longing to take a swim, flower sellers rearranged their gorgeous stalls and pressed nosegays onto passing lovers, guitars strummed lazily, North African traders spread their hand-made jewellery on Moroccan blankets, and young artists at their easels dashed off charcoal portraits 'while you wait'.

The balustrade was warm against my back as I pretended to read the *Herald Tribune*. I didn't wish to seem as if I was waiting, which I was. For what or for whom I was not sure, but deep in a cunning recess of my brain I knew I was about to throw my analysis to the winds and sample the forbidden fruit that I could sense was burgeoning all around me in the teeming streets. For twelve long months I had succeeded in banishing from my thoughts any possibility of sexual expression with a male, but I am not made of the stuff of martyrs or heroes, and my urges had become too strong to resist.

I am forever grateful to Eddie for opening my eyes to new vistas in the mysterious landscape of human behaviour, for persevering in his belief that I was redeemable; but though I dreaded the consequences of abandoning my struggle,

I knew at the deepest level of my soul that I would never sexually crave a girl the way I craved these dusky youths who sauntered past me with a backward glance.

He was called Aldo. He was young, he was interested. He was a bloke. And I was desperate. My Italian in those days was rudimentary, a stab at Latin leaving the end off the word, a shot at French with an Italian pronunciation, enough to ensure at least that there was no misunderstanding and that we were unequivocally on for sex. He took me to the Borghese Gardens where there are glades and some areas of dense undergrowth. We found a secluded spot and I kissed him.

Suddenly the bushes erupted. Six menacing young thugs burst through the greenery and surrounded us, one brandishing a knife and threatening to use it if I made a noise. It was instantly clear that Aldo was a member of this gang, and that he had lured me to this pre-arranged spot as a victim.

The gang took everything but my clothes. All my money – quite a lot – my pen, my glasses, my watch, even my pocket handkerchief. It was all done in silence, and very quickly, since there were people not so very far away, and a shout might even have brought the Carabinieri.

No doubt from guilt, or to prove his hard-man status, Aldo treated me more roughly than the others did, including the one with the knife, but there was another boy, a handsome youth who seemed to be standing up for me. Through the mists of incomprehension, I thought I understood his whispered phrases like, 'Leave him his glasses, for God's sake. They're no use to us.' Or, 'Who wants a handkerchief? We've got his money, let him go.' And even, 'He's probably a student. Give him back a couple of thousand Lira.'

As the gang surreptitiously dispersed, I caught this youth's arm. In my mongrel, halting pidgin I tried to make him understand. 'You know I have nothing to give you.' This was easy, I turned out my empty pockets, and pointed to my watchless wrist. 'But you are kind. And *sei bello*! You are beautiful. Will you make love with me?'

He looked utterly astounded. Then slowly the skin round his eyes crinkled in a mischievous smile.

'*Va bene*,' he said, slinging an arm over my shoulder.

His name was Renzo, and I recklessly took him back to my hotel. He was quite sharply dressed, we were both of an age and it was early, so the receptionist hardly noticed us. I estimated that he was about eighteen, with the lean body of a ragamuffin, a smooth column of a neck for which I felt an aching infinity of tenderness, and nicotine-stained fingers. We made love till the small hours of the morning, and for me it was, succinctly, like having died and gone to heaven, until he insisted that he must get home before his Mamma missed him.

He agreed to meet me the following Tuesday on the bottom step in the Piazza di Spagna. I waited an hour and a half, but he never turned up. I was devastated as only frustrated young lovers can be, and I wondered about his divided loyalties. If he had told his gang, no doubt they would have disapproved of him forming an attachment to a target. I knew nothing of his life, and any number of contingencies could have arisen to prevent him from keeping our appointment. But he could have left a message at my hotel – Of course, he didn't know my surname…

Renzo was a milestone in my life. After this fleeting experience, I knew that no woman could satisfy my longings as this young gangster had done. It was not with resignation but with an overwhelming sense of peace that I acknowledged to myself that the battle to be what I most emphatically was not, was finally lost.

10 A BRUSH WITH A STAWR
Hedy Lamarr

HEDY LAMARR'S BEAUTY was like music: it inspired emotions even when, as in my case, it kindled no desire. I imagine she was well into her forties at that time, and considered by Hollywood to be over the hill and on the skids. She was tall, which was unexpected in a woman with so fine-boned a face, and it was hard for anyone to look at anything else when she was around, her features were so perfect and symmetrical.

But she had lost the facility for holding a conversation. Whenever she entered company she launched into a monologue, a stream of consciousness which made no sense at all to those not *au fait* with her preoccupations. She had brought with her from Hollywood her 'Grey Lady' who was called Frankie Dawson, and her psychiatrist who didn't seem to be doing her any good.

Frankie had a voice to which the word 'gravelly' would not do justice. 'Bouldery' would be more like it. Satchmo Armstrong's was of the same variety, though Frankie's voice was more *profondo*. The manufacturers of Marlboro and Gilbeys should have given her a pension. She confided in me:

'You see, Jahn, the trouble with Hedy is that everybody treats her like a Big Stawr!' She paused for a drag and a slug. 'But Hedy just wants to be treated like a noymal poyson.'

I had never worked with 'A Big Stawr' and I was grateful to have this nugget of information.

The unit had started filming the 'Geneviève of Brabant' section, but Hedy and I were still on stand-by at the hotel, which was not a penance since we both played tennis and there was a swimming-pool.

We were at lunch some days later, just Hedy and I, and I had been listening patiently to her non-stop drivel for what seemed like an eternity.

'I miss them so much, but I never see their father. Where is it now? Tucson, or some such dump. If he ever sells, I get half. I have my lawyer working on it, sure, in one big silver frame, so I don't have to shuffle them like cards. You think it's expensive? Not for that district. I couldn't ask her. She'd be lost without Buzz. But he's no good for, with all that Schlitzbergen business. I'm supposed – they told me I had costume approval!' Her tone rose from a subterranean rumble to a cry for help. 'How can they stick me in that Ball Gown! I need scarlet! Or lilac to go with my eyes…'

'Hedy!'

'They want to ruin my career. I'll look like Doris Day before she was a virgin! I'm going to walk off the picture. That's what I'm going to do. I'm going to walk off the picture. Walk off it. Just like that. Just leave. Get on a plane tomorrow. Frankie'll fix everything. I'm not sticking around here to have my future flushed down the john…'

'Hedy!' I shouted, quite quietly, and miraculously the flow was stemmed. I remembered Frankie's injunction: '– Treat her like a noymal poyson –'. 'You'll look wonderful in anything!' I assured the reluctant Big Stawr.

'I'm playing one of the most beautiful women in the world, and they want me to look like a Christmas parcel!'

'You are the most beautiful woman in the world, and we haven't even started filming yet. They'll listen, all right, once we start working. Don't walk off the picture! You'll see, everything will turn out fine.'

I had raised my voice because I was sure that if she walked out on us now, the producers would never find a replacement for her, and the film would have to be scrapped.

There was a further, unprecedented pause, while the substance of my interjection seeped somehow into the chaos of her thoughts. She bent her lovely gaze on me without speaking for quite two minutes. She then said in a gentle voice, extremely lucidly – 'Who are you, you little flea, to tell me what to do?' Not what you might expect from a noymal poyson.

I was very young and totally unprepared for any kind of parry or riposte to this lunge from nowhere. I gaped for a moment, then got on with my lasagna. Hedy left the table.

Instead of walking out of the production I learned much later she had tried to get me sacked. For not treating her with enough respect. Our scenes together were not easy since she refused to talk to me; all our communications were therefore through the Director, Edgar Ulmer, who was Austrian by birth and Jewish, like Hedy, which might have led one to expect a warmth of feeling between them based on a shared history and a tribal loyalty, but this was far from the case. Their relationship was bitter and hate-filled and spectacularly stormy.

It was the big day of my death scene. 'Drago, don't die… Drago, don't die…' Remember?

I had just fought a duel to defend Geneviève's honour and lay mortally wounded in a forest glade, a lovely location on the coast near Fregene which had been chosen by Edgar and the Assistant Director in the spring. After the long hot summer the grass had burnt brown and it looked as if an army had marched over it, so they sprayed it a virulent, poison green. It hurt my eyes just to look at it. Hedy's double had galloped up several times, dismounted and thrown herself in a sobbing heap across my body.

It was now time for the double's place to be taken by the Big Stawr who was in a magnificent gown of lilac velvet embroidered with seed pearls and semi-precious stones, a design she had not only approved of, but with threats had demanded. The chippies provided her with a deeply upholstered footstool, so she would be comfortable appearing to squat on the poison-green sward, cradling my head in her voluminous lap encrusted with jewels.

'ACTION!'

'Drago! Don't die!' Hedy dug the fingers of her right hand up to the knuckles in my wig, and wrenched my head away from the camera to bury my face deep in the cleft between her breasts. Most men would willingly give up all thoughts of a career in the cinema to have this experience no fewer than ten times before Edgar's patience broke, but not this man.

'Drago, don't die!' she intoned, her lovely face laid sideways on my wig to fill the screen.

'CUT!'

Edgar lifted his forearm to his face and bit hard upon it for a long moment. Those temperamental Mittel-Europeans!

'Mees Lamarr!' he groaned, when he had removed his savaged limb from between his teeth. 'Ze vay you turn ze boy's head – ve cannot tell if she iss a man, or he iss a vooman. Ve cannot tell if ziss hairy zing you hold in your hendz is an Animal or a Shooman Beenz. Ve cannot tell if ziss Shooman Beenz or ziss Animal iss alive or dead! Und, vot iss more, if ve cannot see his VACE, vee don't CARE!'

He covered his face with his outspread hand and, dangerously, he wiped the cascade of sweat from his brow. 'GOING AGAIN!'

The make-up team finished their primping and scuttled for the safety of the caravan. From what I could glimpse from my recumbent position, Hedy's flawless jaw looked dangerously set.

'ACTION!'

'Drago! Don't die!' The long fingers slowly tightening in my Prince Valiant hairdo, then SNAP! Defiant, Hedy rammed my face once more between her breasts. I was tempted to follow Edgar's example and start chewing.

'CUT!' Edgar rose from his crouching position behind the camera and with one stride across the phosphorescent turf he thrust his face into Hedy's.

'Mees Lamarr! I am zee Director of ziss Fucking Rabbish, unt you vill do vot I say! Ve vil chute ze scene mit a DUBBEL eef you vill not let us ZEE ZE BOY'S VACE!'

Hedy dropped my head like a cabbage, and firmly putting one hand on the collar of her dress, with one savage wrench she ripped the priceless garment from the neck to the navel.

With this gesture, Hedy halted filming for a week. For continuity reasons, the identical material had to be found and the intricate embroidery recreated to make a replica before we could continue.

Thank God I never had to work again with a noymal poyson. I stuck exclusively thereafter to Big Stawrs.

I wish to add this rider in Hedy's defence.

Despite Frankie's insistence Hedy Lamarr was never a noymal poyson. Not only was she considered to be the most beautiful woman in Hollywood, she was one of the patent holders of the idea of 'frequency hopping' communications. This revolutionary concept is now used in everything from mobile phones to military satellites to jam-resistance radar. Neither she nor her co-inventor, composer George Antheil, ever received a penny for their idea. Their patent expired before it became technologically possible to implement it.

Worshipped for her beauty, and a scientific genius as well. Too much for any ordinary mortal to cope with. The constant presence of her psychiatrist should perhaps have alerted us to the fact that she was seriously mentally disturbed. Later, in London, she was arrested for shoplifting. In her teens she had made her first film in Austria, *Extase*, in which she appeared briefly in the nude. In those days this was tantamount to hard porn, and Hedy Lamarr, with her astounding beauty, became notorious overnight. According to 'Satchmo' – Frankie Dawson, who was evidently not employed for her discretion – Hedy's mother, a poor woman, 'sold' her daughter to the highest bidder, forcing her in to a loveless marriage with a millionaire industrialist who turned out to be a sadist. This, Frankie assured me, was the start of Hedy's decline into mental instability. She had escaped from the industrialist, and by the time I worked with her she had tried three other husbands, but none had made her happy.

She had been fawned upon, indulged and exploited ever since she had reached the age of puberty. Her extraordinary intelligence did not encompass wisdom. How could she have learnt about the values that matter, about kindness and acceptance and laughter, in the Dream Factory that is Hollywood? She had been thrust into the limelight at a pitilessly early age, been devoured by rapacious lovers and producers who saw her ravishing beauty as a ticket to success, and who looked elsewhere when she began to grow older.

Beauty and money in moderation are undoubtedly a blessing. In excess, they are surely a curse.

11 ADRIFT
Where do I go from here?

EDDIE KNEW as soon as I walked in, and he came straight to the point.

'Sit down one last time.'

'You know?' I asked him, flabbergasted.

'I've been seeing you three times a week for ten months. It's my business to know.'

'How?'

'If I were your father, I would make you feel guiltier than you do. I would rail at you for spending two months away without a note to let me know how you're getting along, two months without a phone call to say hello and ask after Mirca. You're a thoughtful boy. But I'm not your father, I'm your doctor. These are not omissions. They were deliberate.'

He smiled, to let me know he wasn't angry, just a little sad. 'I'm not going to force you to go on with analysis against your will.'

He knew of course about my affair with Ian, but since starting my sessions with Eddie, I had truly tried to quash any homosexual feelings. I sat down now and told him about Aldo and the gang, about Renzo, but finally I explained that my change of heart was not because of my experience with one boy. For nearly a year, it seemed to me now, I had been fighting to hold back the sea.

'I don't have the strength to fight any more, Eddie.'

I had sorted out my thoughts over the last week since returning from Rome, before confronting this man who had been doing his utmost to save my life. I had great respect and affection for Eddie, but I had made up my mind.

'I've wanted to be "cured" for the wrong reasons. From fear. Fear of what others might think of me, fear of ruining my career. I want a normal life, where I'm accepted as a decent thinking person, not some kind of a freak obsessed with boys, a pervert whose body is just a life-support system for his prick.'

'Just take it easy John. I'm on your side, remember?'

'Sorry, Eddie. I've been worrying about telling you all this, but I want you to know that it's not Analysis, or Jung or you that's failed to make me straight. It's me. And it won't be a tragedy, so long as I can find a loving chap of my own age with a sense of humour and a lovely bum.'

'I thought you wanted children...'

'I can't, that's all. I'd also like to be six feet tall.'

'So what's your life plan?'

'I just want to get on with it. I think I can now, thanks to you. I'm Scots. I'm a Humanist. I'm Left Wing. I'm an Actor. I'm shorter than I'd like to be. There are a lot of labels you can pin on me, but I don't want to be categorised by any one of them.'

'You came to me to change yourself, and now you want to change the world.'

'You've released me from my self-disgust.'

I got ready to go, with sadness in my heart.

He gave me a hug. 'Don't hesitate to ring me at any time. I'll always be here for you.'

'I've learned so much, not only about myself, but about how we all fool ourselves, how afraid we are, where our anger comes from.'

At the door I said, 'Give my love to Mirca.'

'Won't you come and see us – for a social visit?'

'I'll give you a ring.' Even as I said it, I knew I wouldn't. I wanted to put all this anguish behind me, and get on with the business of living.

'My Aunt Gatty's recipe for happiness,' I told him. '"If ye don't get whit you want, want whit ye get!"'

'You don't need me any more.' He smiled. 'Your Aunt Gatty has all the answers.'

I nodded in agreement. 'I think I might just have begun to grow up.'

THREE
A Grown-Up (Of Sorts)

1 A LEARNING CURVE
Mick the Blink at The Old Vic

IN SPITE OF my youthful impatience, at twenty-one I knew that there was still plenty of time to make the Big Time, for I was ambitious in spite of myself. With four films behind me that had failed to make me into an international star, I worked out that if I wanted a career as an actor I would have to consolidate by gaining some experience in the theatre. The film industry in England is too erratic to provide enough work for any but a fortunate few, and even for those lucky ones, film careers are never continuous and often short.

Rachel Roberts was joining the Old Vic company for a season, and she told me that they had not yet cast the line of 'Juvenile' parts, which included Florizel in *A Winter's Tale* and Claudio in *Much Ado About Nothing*. At that time the Old Vic was the precursor to the National Theatre and along with the Stratford Memorial Theatre was the most prestigious theatre company in the country. I applied for the job and was accepted. I was released from my film contract for six months. I learned the most valuable lesson of my professional life there. And I met George.

My less than blazing path across the theatrical firmament began with the cameo part of Octavius in *Julius Caesar*, a stripling in Shakespeare's play, who nonetheless leads his army against Caesar's assassins. Historically he went on to become Rome's first Emperor, Augustus, a wise and humane ruler. Since my small reputation had been achieved, so far, only on the screen – in television and in films – I was eager to show this distinguished company that I was not just a 'Starlet' but a serious actor. I had studied my role, researched it, and was word perfect at the first reading. In spite of Octavius' first appearance as a General commanding his troops, I had decided to play him as a rather bookish academic, giving a hint of the great man to come.

The director of the company, Michael Benthall, had a nervous habit of squeezing his eyes together and was thus affectionately known as 'Mick the Blink'. He had directed the 'Victorian' *Hamlet* of Paul Scofield at Stratford which, when I saw it at the impressionable age of sixteen, clinched my determination to pursue a career in the theatre. Mick the Blink was considered superficial rather than inspired. His productions were always ravishing to the eye, often designed by

Loudon Sainthill (a sumptuous stage decorator in the style of Oliver Messel), but perhaps he lacked the insight of his great contemporary Tyrone Guthrie.

Since *Julius Caesar* was the opening production of the season the set was already in situ on the stage – a pair of gigantic pillars and an endless flight of steps leading up to the flies, dwarfing the human protagonists in Imperial bombast – so we were able to dispense with the unsatisfactory business of navigating through mazes of colour-coded tape, denoting walls, stairs, doors and so forth, which is the usual procedure in a rehearsal room.

Mick the Blink was a fast worker, and on the third day of rehearsals we were 'blocking' the second act – many of us by this time without scripts. It came to my big scene, a confrontation of the armies, one led by Brutus, the other by Octavius. I had twenty actors behind me, and another twenty facing me with their swords at the ready. Not one of these strangers had I had time to get to know beyond the usual pleasantries. Barriers of reserve fall more easily in a theatre company than in other professional situations because of the communicative nature of what we do, which requires mutual trust and emotional honesty, but it takes time to happen, and we had had none. I started my speech: 'Come come, the cause! If arguing make us sweat, The proof of it will turn to redder drops!'

I became aware of a restlessness in the company. It started insidiously, a snort here, a stifled cry there. As I proceeded it became clear that the entire Old Vic Company assembled on stage for the first time that season was suppressing a tidal-wave of laughter. There were tears in their eyes, their chests were heaving, they clung to each other for support. I continued with my speech, my face the colour of a peeled tomato, the world sliding from under my feet.

When I got to the end Mick the Blink shouted, 'Well done everybody. Break for lunch. Back at two. John – can I have a word?'

I felt as if I was in an elevator and the cable had snapped. With an awful prescience, I knew I was about to get the sack.

I could get away with acting on the screen where my photogenic face carried me through, but I had failed the litmus test in front of the most celebrated company in the British Isles. Crushed, humiliated and in despair I faced Mick the Blink in the echoing stalls.

'Michael,' I asked him, 'why did they laugh?'

He blinked three times in rapid succession.

'Because you were very funny.'

His shoulders shook at the memory.

'You're on quite the wrong track. Don't worry, we'll get it right before the opening night.'

It requires a kind of courage, or at least a kind of arrogance to get up in front of other people and show off in a loud voice. At rehearsals sometimes you never know what you are going to sound like until you've tried it. In spite of appearances, actors are sensitive creatures, and just as prone to shyness and self-doubt as everyone else, perhaps even more so, since they set themselves up to be criticised, very frequently in print. Consequently, many actors take a long time to commit themselves to the interpretation of a role, feeling their way gradually like a mole in the dark, before they dare stand up, so to speak, to be counted. My inexperience had made me jump in at the deep end before I had learned to swim.

But Mick said then the most important thing that has ever been said to me throughout my career, advice which I have passed on to future generations when I have been in the position of director.

'You will never be a great actor,' he said, smiling and blinking at the same time, 'unless you are prepared to make a fool of yourself at rehearsals. And you certainly succeeded in doing that.' Seeing my distress, he took me in his arms.

'I'm very proud of you,' he said.

Thereafter the company stopped laughing, and I got good reviews on the opening night.

2 THE FUNNY FARM
Posket, and Nine Thousand Broilers

I HAD BEEN little more than a child when I had plunged headlong onto the stage, and though I continued to enjoy some success, doubts gnawed constantly at my resolve, and prevented any complacency – doubts about the importance, the worthiness, or even the necessity of the theatre as a profession. Was I justified in spending my life as a flibbertigibbet, when volunteers were dying of typhoid in refugee camps, ferrying grain to famine victims and saving babies in war zones under the constant threat of mutilation or death? There were overworked young scientists slaving in laboratories extending the frontiers of knowledge, classrooms choking on despair where young teachers were fighting to kindle a spark in the damp apathy of their deprived students. At frequent intervals I toyed with the idea of abandoning my career, applying to university and studying to be a doctor; then, an alternative presented itself.

A poultry farm in Surrey.

Who could deny that agriculture was at the cutting edge of life? Up with the dawn, the song of the lark, fresh country air. Life and death, and scenery and mud and poo, and at the end of it all food for the starving. Well, the hungry at any rate.

Posket Farm was owned by a fellow contract artist, Peter Reynolds, a young actor of great insouciance who was a bosom buddy of Diana Dors. I hardly knew him, though we had worked together in my second film, a domestic comedy best forgotten, where I had admired his debonair, laddish kind of charm, and his tumbling blonde forelock which turned out to be stuck on. He was not bald, but what hair he had was baby blonde and distinctly dispirited. When he told me of his need for a partner in his farming venture, I leapt into my MGA and raced down to Posket at the first opportunity, striding with him in my newly-purchased wellies round his fifteen acres and metaphorically chewing a straw. There were three gigantic sheds housing nine thousand birds, ranging from day-old chicks to sixteen-week-old capons ready to be packed off to be 'processed': in other words, slaughtered, plucked, gutted and trussed to look appetising on the slab at your local supermarket. We fondled the newly hatched chicks, warm from their overhead infra-red lights, and still smelling sweet from the fresh wood-shavings of their deep litter, and discussed the business arrangements.

'I need four thousand to clear off the building costs of the sheds, and as surety for the next feed delivery. I'm having a swimming pool dug at this moment, as you probably saw at the front of the house on your way in. Come summer, this place'll be the Beverley Hills of Guildford.'

I hardly heard, let alone made sense of, the statistics he started to reel off.

'It guarantees us twenty per cent of the net total. If we can keep up five hundred a month, that's one thousand units at the going rate not including damaged birds which should be removed before delivery every two weeks, of birds up to sixteen weeks, by weight of course, anything over being added to the gross, where justified, giving us forty per cent clear profit, minus the processing charge which varies depending on the numbers delivered.'

I nodded dumbly and lightly squeezed a handful of chicks before setting them down to career off into the middle of the canary-yellow mob of fluff. It glowed under the heating lamp like a puddle of overpopulated custard.

'We have a contract with Sainsbury's, which I'll show you before you decide.'

'And the gatehouse is mine, if I come in with you?'

'All yours, Johnny. Plus you'll make a profit. Plus you don't have to be here. Even if I'm filming, I'm living here, so I'm on constant call, and I've put Derek on full time since the last batch arrived.'

'I'll only be able to make Sundays at least till the spring.' I was working fourteen hours a day at the Old Vic, from Monday to Saturday, rehearsing during the day and playing at night.

'No problem!'

Blinded by my enthusiasm for the Farmer's Life, and reckoning that occupation of the gatehouse was sufficient reward for my investment, without taking any professional advice, I decided to sink every penny I had into Posket Farm.

'Hi, Pete!'

Peter rose from his crouching position to greet the silhouette in the doorway of the shed. I could tell by the newcomer's voice that he wasn't Derek, the poultryman I had met earlier, who was well cast as a farmer's lad.

'Vince!' Peter advanced and hugged him. 'I wasn't expecting you. This is Johnny Fraser. He's thinking of coming in with me on the farm.'

I approached, and Peter introduced me. 'This is my brother, Vince.'

I shook his hand. I reckoned he was in his early twenties and extremely handsome, though running to fat.

'How's Ursula?'

'Fine. She's inside talking to Mum.'

'Mum's out is she? Is that wise?'

I could make nothing of this. We ambled back towards the homestead and removed our wellies in the porch. Peter ushered us both into the drawing room.

'Excuse the sparseness of the decor,' he explained; 'we still have some decorating to do, so most of the furniture's in store. Make youselves comfortable. Vince, help Johnny to a drink. Shan't be long.'

It was a large bow-windowed room covered wall-to-wall in deep-pile lilac carpeting, and it was empty save for a gigantic white leather sofa, a well-stocked cocktail bar in one corner, and a music-centre in the other, with stacks of LPs littered around it.

'What'll you have, Johnny?'

'Do you have whisky?'

He nodded. 'White Heather, Chivas Regal, Bell's…'

'Bell's please. Just a small one, and same again with soda. No ice.'

I could hear raised voices coming from the back of the house, culminating in a woman's angry screeching followed by a barked order. I tried examining the sofa for hidden meanings but as Vince handed me my tumbler the size of a paddling-pool, I could no longer avoid his eye.

'It's nothing,' he said, sitting beside me with his own drink cupped in both hands. 'It's just Mum. She's in a bit of a state at the moment. I think the move's upset her. Cheers!'

'Cheers!'

Outside in the corridor, Peter was in command. His voice was steady and hardly raised at all, but the woman's shrieking had subsided to a low mumbling, the kind of miserable grizzling that children go in for when they can't get their own way.

'So, when did you all move in?' I asked.

'Oh, I don't live here. Thank God. My wife and I bought a farm in Forest Green – just along the road.'

My first impression of Vince in the semi-darkness of the chicken shed had been of a young man, no older than myself, though unhealthily overweight. Sitting side by side, I now got quite another impression. The tone of his voice was pompous, middle-aged. Perhaps he was Peter's older brother…

'Ursula was born in Surrey. She comes from a close-knit family. Quite convenient, really.'

As we talked, I caught a glimpse of the back of his neck and the tips of his ears. They were quite black, as if he had anointed them with boot polish. I was about to mention it, when I hesitated. Perhaps there was a kind of skin ailment that needed treatment with this filthy substance? His shirt collar looked like a mechanic's rag.

'Are you in chickens, too?'

'We have a few layers, that's all. Sixty head of Aberdeen Angus. A hundred acres of arable. Mixed, in fact. And you?'

'Oh, I'm just an actor, like Peter. But I'm keen to – widen my interests…'

'No doubt about it, intensive farming is the way forward, and there's a huge demand for economically-produced poultry. Pete's got his head screwed on… You could do a lot worse than go in with him, that's a fact. A lot worse.'

Not only was the skin round the nape of his neck an oily black colour, but his mop of curly hair had been painted as if for a pantomime; it was greasy with a thick silver unguent that made his head look like a battered tin helmet.

Peter escorted an elderly woman into the room, and I was relieved to note that his mother seemed to have pulled herself together.

'Sorry to leave you like that.' He gestured with his head towards the hall. 'Mother's having a bit of a wobbly I'm afraid.' So the old woman on his arm was not his mother. 'She asks to be excused. Moving house is quite traumatic at her age. Ursula – this is Johnny Fraser, a colleague of mine. Johnny – this is Vince's wife, Ursula.'

I was flabbergasted. When we were all sat on the sofa looking the same way as if travelling in a railway carriage the conversation was sticky till Peter decided to throw himself on the floor and I felt free to follow suit. I could then get a clear view of Vince and Ursula, which revealed the facts, superficially at least, of their unusual marriage. It was not till much later in our relationship, when I had sunk my life savings into Posket Farm, that Peter told me the rest of the story. But from my viewpoint on the purple carpet, this is what I saw.

On the left, a perfectly pleasant, ordinary looking woman of at least sixty-five, thin, white-haired with no lipstick and the merest dusting of powder; on the right, a fat young man of twenty-two, his head like a Christmas Tree decoration sprayed with silver from a can. Could it be that Vince – aware of the incongruity of their pairing and of the vast disparity in their ages – thought that silver spray-paint on his youthful curls would convince the world that he was a pensioner? Surely there would be a downside to this equation. What was most bizarre of all was that I wasn't expected to notice anything out of the ordinary.

We passed the time pleasantly enough till it was time for me to go.

'You ought to see the lodge,' Peter said as I made my goodbyes. The gatehouse had been dangled as bait for my investment, a two-bedroomed cottage which was a little dilapidated, though structurally sound. Once across the threshold, I fell in love with it. There was an open fireplace in each of the two reception rooms, a boxed-in staircase, a mullioned dormer window in the sitting room…and I couldn't wait to get started with a paint-brush and rolls of paper for the attic-bedrooms. My dream of doing something useful with my life was within my grasp. I was twenty-one years old, and I was about to become a farmer! The circumstance that I might continue my highly enjoyable and so far extremely profitable life as a flibbertigibbet was an even greater inducement.

Standing in the doorway as dusk crept up on us, I agreed to hand over six thousand pounds to Peter in return for my immediate tenancy of Posket Farm Lodge, and a stake in his poultry farm. I could see a new life stretching ahead of me, with one foot in the floating clouds of showbusiness, but the other firmly rooted in chicken shit.

'I'll instruct my lawyers on Monday,' I said. 'Grand' is not an adequate description of how I felt. I had broken free from my frivolous fetters and was taking a confident step into the real world.

I had three happy months decorating and furnishing my little house, with the help of friends who would join me for the weekend and hold the ladders. I learnt about automatic drinkers and high-protein feed and coccidiosis and fowl pest. Deep litter chickens, though running loose, are in severely congested conditions and need a lot of surveillance. The height of a broiler's ambition is to get onto his back with his feet in the air and move as quickly as possible to that free range in the sky. When I wasn't decorating, I spent Sundays chasing after drugs to put in the drinking-water, weeding out corpses and de-beaking the worst of the cannibals, for when they're not catching all the diseases they're prone to, broilers like to peck each other's bums till their insides drop out.

Peter, Derek and I had just finished clearing the pungent deep-litter cake from the floor of a small shed, in preparation for the arrival the following day of a new batch of day-old chicks. They came by post in cheeping cardboard boxes. Vince was calling round with his tractor in the morning to remove the litter which he could mix with manure and spread on his fields before ploughing.

'I may have to go to America for a while,' Peter said. 'There's nothing happening for me here.'

I was completely taken aback by the casual, throw-away tone in his voice. I could not imagine how the farm could function without him.

'How do you mean? Who's going to run the business?'

Derek was locking up and was no longer within hearing distance.

'You'll be down at weekends –'

'Peter. You're not suggesting Derek can manage all week on his own. He's a good pair of hands, but there are decisions to be made, cheques to be signed, traders to be dealt with.'

'I have to go, Johnny. Di rang last night.' Diana Dors had been summoned to Hollywood to discuss some project (which never came to fruition), she was ensconced in a rented villa, no doubt feeling lonely, and was evidently throwing out invitations to all her mates who were daft enough to believe her enticing tales of MOVIES being made and ROLES to be filled…

'When?'

'Next week.'

'Next WEEK! That's the dress rehearsal for *Winter's Tale*!'

'Di says there's a whole bunch of films being made with parts for English actors. I've never been to Hollywood, and I want to give it a try. She has the house – it won't cost me a cent – just the fare. And she's got the introductions. She's lined up her agent. It's the chance of a lifetime, you must see that, Johnny.'

I could see that his mind was made up.

'You're leaving me with a terrible responsibility, Peter. What if you get a part? You could be away for months.'

'Vince will keep an eye on things. Don't make problems before they arise.'

Over a drink in the lilac lounge I asked him, 'What about your mother?'

Mrs Reynolds – I never called her anything else, nor would I want to – had been the source of the uproar I had heard on my first visit to the farm some months before. She was a paranoid schizophrenic who was frequently violent, but she mostly kept to her room. I was never sure whether this was entirely her choice, for I had seen Peter lock her in more than once. I had met her when she was let out to cook large quantities of stodgy food, of which, out of politeness, I had to partake on several occasions, but she always treated me with suspicion bordering on hostility. She had a white birthmark on her nose which was difficult not to stare at or indeed not to try to wipe off, for it looked exactly as if she had just finished baking a cake and had left a smear of flour across her face by accident.

'She'll be fine. Vince will pop over most days to see she's okay.'

In my mounting panic, I drank more than was good for me and found myself straying where angels fear to tread.

'Is Ursula very rich?'

'Quite rich.' He smiled, and following my drift he slowly shook his head. 'Vince isn't interested in firm flesh. He likes old tortoises. He's turned on by snowy locks and sagging tits. It's handy that the old ones are often rich, that's all. But it's not the money that appeals to him. For some reason known only to himself, Vince wants to fuck his Granny.'

Peter left for Hollywood on Friday, and on Sunday just after dawn on a misty October morning, I was wakened by a heavy knocking on the front door of the lodge. It was the first of the creditors waving his bounced cheque at me and threatening to sue. Throughout the day there were others, who must have heard through local gossip that Peter had taken off for America; they were convinced that any chances of receiving payment had disappeared for good.

From Monday to Saturday in the evening I wrestled with the role of Claudio in *Much Ado About Nothing*. Claudio makes every entrance with his friend, a character called Don Pedro. Being short, I am resigned on occasions to looking taller actors straight in the zip, but I get depressed when I see daylight through their legs. Our Don Pedro was a mere tissue's thickness short of seven feet high. He should have been in the circus. So I got out the scissors and the newspapers…you've heard it all before. Gordon Briggs, a fellow Scot, an acquaintance and a critic wrote, 'John Fraser plays Claudio as if he is about to jump.' When I was making the film of J B Priestley's *The Good Companions* I confessed to the make-up man that I was wearing 'elevators' in my shoes. He said: 'You think you wear lifts? If you look very closely at Richard Todd, you'll see his toes peeping through his flies.'

Except for Wednesday and Saturday afternoons when we were onstage for the matinee, from ten in the morning till six every day I was rehearsing the part of Florizel in *A Winter's Tale*; since there is so much enforced 'resting' in our profession, you will rarely hear an actor complaining of overwork, but by the end of the week I was exhausted. As the curtain fell on Saturday night, I switched to farmer mode, leapt into my MGA and sped through the night with all possible haste to my dear little gatehouse and my suicidal chickens.

With the dawn on Sundays came the dismal procession of creditors. Everything, it transpired, had been bought on the never-never. Buildings, equipment, stock, litter, feed. The poultry feed and broiler pellets salesman threatened to stop deliveries altogether if at least part of his bill were not paid. How could I let nine thousand chickens starve to death? As I signed the cheque, my heart was in my boots. Although I was on a film contract, it had been suspended while I was at the Old Vic, and I was on an Equity minimum kind of salary. At this rate, I was afraid the next knock on the door would be the rozzers to cart me off to the slammer.

Vince's white Cadillac swept through the gates of Posket and lurched to a halt.

'Vince!' I cried. 'Thank God you're here.' In spite of my repeated phone calls, answered exclusively by Ursula or a Filippina maid, till now I had had no success in persuading him to meet me for an urgent talk.

'No panic!' he said holding up his chubby hands as if to ward off trouble. He knew the state of things. Both he and Peter must have known the debts could not be ignored forever.

'This is not my problem, get that straight for a start. I have my own farm to run. But here's my advice for what it's worth. The only bugger you have to worry about is the feed supplier. Contact the processors, tell them you want to sell off the older birds, whether they've reached maximum weight or not, so you can afford to pay for the feed for the younger birds.'

'We'll lose hand over fist! There's no profit in selling underweight chickens, and we're still getting deliveries of chicks! Five hundred through the post last week. It's insanity! He must have ordered them for months ahead at regular intervals. I haven't got the kind of money we need to bale us out of this. Have you spoken to him?'

'Last night.'

'So?'

'He's up for a western with Richard Widmark. He wants to hold on for a week or so just in case. If he gets the part your worries will be over.'

'And if he doesn't?'

'Don't be such a pessimist.'

'Give me Di Dors' phone number in Hollywood. I have to speak to Peter about this.' He wrote it out for me, and turned to go. 'Your mother's been throwing lighted newspapers from her bedroom window. I imagine she thinks of them as distress signals. I've tried to speak to her, but she won't let me in. She keeps calling for Peter. I'm afraid she's going to set the house on fire.'

Vince slumped over the bonnet of his car.

'If it's not one thing it's another.' He gave me the semblance of a pat on the shoulder, and muttered, 'I'll top up her medication'. Then he trudged up to the house and let himself in the back door.

To minimise the poultricide I had to do as Vince suggested – sell off the fatter birds to pay for feed to keep the younger ones alive. It would have saved us money to slaughter the lot, but I could not bring myself to expedite such a draconian measure. I made several phone calls to Di Dors' house in Hollywood, but I could not move Peter to take our plight seriously while the possibility of stardom in the movies was in the offing, no matter how utterly remote were his chances. He showed signs of the self-destructive behaviour that was to kill him some years later, and he seemed quite content to take me with him.

Vince refused to help physically or financially – 'It's pointless sending good money after bad' – so in a last ditch attempt to bring Peter to his senses I thought I would try to get him connected with his mother telephonically. Her flaming newspaper distress flares had diminished, which I hoped was an indication that under Vince's augmented medication her state of mind had become more amenable and perhaps less hostile to me personally.

It was a bright morning in December when I was wakened by an almighty banging which I recognised as someone having an altercation with the dustbins up at the farmhouse. It was the middle of the night in sunny California, but desperate situations require desperate remedies, and I leapt from my bed hoping to seize the moment, buttonhole the chronically bewildered Mrs Reynolds, risk waking up Diana in Coldwater Canyon and make Peter speak to his mother on the telephone.

The clattering continued as I approached the back door of the farmhouse at a jaunty pace, with a demeanour that I hoped exuded optimism and good will.

At my approach Peter's mother looked up from the dustbin and squinted at me over the smudge on her nose, like a naughty child caught stealing from the fridge.

'Good morning, Mrs Reynolds. Having a clear out?'

She was surrounded by a sea of saucepans, oven dishes, cake tins, and was banging them in turn against the rim of the corrugated zinc bin.

'I don't like spiders,' she muttered. 'Hate them.' Bang! 'Hate Spiders!' Bang! BANG!

'Heard from Peter at all?'

'What's it got to do with you? You got any complaints, ask a Policeman.' Bang! BANG!

'I thought I might try and give him a ring, and you could speak to him! Wouldn't that be nice? And you could let him know that we're in a spot of bother here, and it might be best if he flew home as soon as poss–'

'BRABAZON!' she shrieked at me. 'INTERFLOT BRABAZON!' She picked up a ribbed iron frying pan and hurled it at my head. It fell short by a mile, but it was followed by a tornado of pots and pans and lids and casserole dishes and a beautifully moulded fish-kettle that hit me on the head.

'THEY'LL BE COMIN' ROUND THE MOUNTAINS IN PINK PYJAMAS! FARRINGDON YOUR FRIENDLY STATION!'

I left her to it.

Perhaps the telephone wasn't such a good idea.

The next time I tried to ring Diana in Hollywood the phone had been disconnected.

Eventually Vince sent a telegram:

'MOTHER SET THE HOUSE ON FIRE. DESPERATELY ILL. COME HOME BEFORE TOO LATE.'

It was Christmas Eve. The last of the chickens had gone to the processors only the day before, and the great sheds that for months had echoed with the cries of broilers gouging out each other's backsides and the still-sanguine chirrup of the day-olds blissfully unaware of the short and brutish existence that was in store for them, lay empty and silent as the grave.

I had paid Derek off with the last money in my bank account. A thick blanket of utter desolation lay over the farm, pierced only by the baleful light from Peter's mother's bedroom window, where the occupant, in voluntary imprisonment, emerged only to eat and replenish her store of matches. The distress flares continued unabated.

My little lodge was festive with ivy tacked to the beams and frosted with glitter like Vince's hair, with red and white candles guttering in the draught from the mullioned windows, and a cheery fire filling the room with smoke. I was not alone, but that's for another chapter.

There was a knock on the door and Peter stood shrugging on the doorstep. I gave him a drink, and we sat and stared into the flames.

'So sorry. So dreadfully sorry. If I'd got "Bart" we'd have been clear to start again.'

'Bart?'

'In *Gunman's Creek*. With Richard Widmark. They called me back twice. I was set to test –'

I was curiously unmoved by his evident heartbreak.

'What happened?'

'They decided to cast an American. A weedy little unknown called Montgomery Clift.'

I took a deep breath. 'And the farm?'

'I owe quarter of a million. It's all mortgaged up to the hilt. I'm bankrupt, that's the truth of it. We have to be out by the 15th of January. The Receivers won't wait… I'm sorry, Johnny. You did your best.'

'And my investment?'

'You'll get it back. Every penny of it. No matter how long it takes. You have my word on that –'

'That was my life's savings, Peter. The peanuts I make at the Old Vic goes on rent for my London flat. Otherwise I'm penniless. The gatehouse is my home, my security. It was a commitment for life –'

'You're only twenty-one, for Christ's sake. Your life hasn't even started. You'll make it back in no time.'

'Six thousand pounds – and my home… How am I ever going to make that back?'

'Just give me time –'

I knew then I would never see my money again. I could sue him, put him in prison for fraud, but you can't get blood from a stone. For Peter, a shot at Hollywood was a fantasy, a desperate attempt to snatch at success in America as the downwards skid of his career accelerated over here.

'Vince was no help,' I said. 'He could have tided us over –'

'Don't talk to me about that little cunt! I picked him up from the gutter. I gave him everything, a home, my name, an education, a proper start in life, and he does this to me.'

'You mean Vince is not your brother?'

'I adopted him! Oh, it's all legal now. I picked him up in The Red Lion in the Old Kent Road when he was fourteen. He was on the game then – or would have been if I hadn't rescued him. You can hardly believe how beautiful he was… I couldn't see beyond that. He was a wicked little bugger then, but I thought I could change all that. Give him a chance – a future. I was crazy about him and I thought there was still time… Now he only likes old women.'

His face crumpled and he hung his head and sobbed, deep wracking sobs of despair.

I did my best with whisky and half-hearted hugs to ease his misery, and as the clock struck midnight he smiled wryly through his tears and wished me Happy Christmas.

'Happy Christmas, Peter,' I responded, as his forlorn figure set off up the drive to celebrate with his mad mother.

Two years later Peter Reynolds emigrated to Australia and enjoyed a brief stint in one of their soaps before setting alight his mews house in a Sydney suburb and burning himself to death.

3 TAKING THE PLUNGE
George

I WAS GARBED in white and gold and tucking into my buck rabbit in the canteen under the stage at the Old Vic. The costume, designed by Peter Rice, regularly drew gasps from the audience when, playing Florizel, I escorted the lovely Zena Walker down the colonnade of the Palace of Sicilia to find Paul Rogers as Leontes brooding on his throne, the entire stage covered with his peacock cloak and festooned with cobwebs. Heroic bulls adorned the staircase, but their nostrils had stopped smoking after twenty years since Perdita had been taken as an infant to the pagan wastes of Bohemia... We were doing it Minoan, and offstage I was sharing my table with two shepherdesses, Mopsa and Dorcas played by Rosemary Harris and Rachel Roberts, who were partaking respectively of a cheese salad and a baked potato with savoury mince.

A youth appeared at the bottom of the concrete stairs which led to this Gourmet diner in the bowels of the Waterloo Road, bearing a winged object supposed to be some mythic serpent, greened for age and gilded in patches to make it look ancient and alluring. He stood there, seeking vainly for someone to relieve him of his fanciful artefact and our eyes met for just an instant.

My heart stopped beating.

Then, with a shrug, he proceeded to the counter to order an omelette and chips in a strong cockney accent. Thus did George enter my life, forever. For better or for worse.

He was a sculptor who had just qualified as an art teacher, and he was helping a colleague in the prop department temporarily till he found a more permanent post, but he appeared to us, in his jeans and splattered T-shirt, to be a scruffy and probably penniless young stage hand. If I had made an overture of friendship to this 'Piece of Rough Trade' the company would have known instantly that I was making a play for him, as George was so evidently a Steaming Hot Cup of Tea.

Since I had accepted that my orientation was immutable, my problem was how to have a sex-life without getting found out. That the practice of homosexuality was against the law was the least of my worries. Film stars are figures of fantasy, and few fantasies will survive the knowledge that the love-object is a raving poof.

It has taken nearly seventy years of movies for Ian McKellen and Rupert Everett to be accepted as openly gay, and though neither is effeminate, they are often cast as homosexuals.

Before the first world war, the essential epithet for any bachelor was 'Gay'. 'A Bachelor Gay Am I...' goes the song. This, I believe, is the origin of the euphemism.

The public perceives homosexuals as individuals without commitments, without responsibilities, with no wives to support or children to educate, who spend their pink pounds on self-indulgence and their every leisure moment in the pursuit of sexual gratification. The word 'gay' does nothing to dispel this illusion, but it's better than the alternatives.

At the Old Vic in 1954, I was a leading actor, with forty colleagues in the company to choose from as my friends, forty young men and women whose hopes and aspirations I shared. If I had been female, or if George had been a girl, everyone would have blessed a relationship based on mutual attraction. As it was, it took months before we found a way round this social impasse.

At the Christmas party we met and talked for the first time – on such occasions, fraternising between players and workers was encouraged. My film contract had enabled me to buy a flashy, acid-green MGA with white upholstery. My contemporaries, eking out a living on their pittances, may have been put out by this vulgarity, but I was never aware of any resentment. At the end of the evening, I offered George a lift, and he accepted.

So I embarked on my double-life, and George was my big secret.

We set up home together in the most glamorous flat in London, the top floor of a sixteenth-century clap-board farmhouse abutting on Hampstead Heath called 'Wyldes'. Gene Kelly had been the previous occupant of this spectacular apartment. The bedrooms had the original Elizabethan beams, and the gigantic main room, which had been added in the nineteenth century, had four double bay windows, two open fireplaces, a grand piano and a studio window the size of the Brompton Oratory's.

We lived there happily for five years. We shared the last two with a Bush Baby, called Gosh, because he always looked so surprised. I acquired him to console me during my convalescence.

I had returned from India suffering not from Delhi Belly, or from Dysentery or from Malaria, but from the much more lasting and disagreeable effects of –

The Jaipur Jab.

4 THE JAIPUR JAB
A Broken Jaw on The Wind Cannot Read

UNDER AN ANCIENT Tamarind a group of men squatted, rhythmically chanting to the beat of a bass tabor round a Holy Man holding a picture of Ganesh the God with the head of an elephant in one hand and a flaming saucer in the other. His emaciated black torso was smeared with ash, his matted hair stuck out in gorgon ringlets and his face was dusted with red and yellow and orange. The chanting reached a crescendo, the men barking and lurching to the beat till it stopped in a shout; and there was silence while the Sadhu set down his picture against the tree and placed the flame in front of it. He picked up a fluted cake of cow dung and, crumbling it like a papadum, he fed the pieces into a tiny fire that barely glowed between his haunches. He bent his wiry body double and blew the fire into life. Some people at the front of the crowd gave him gifts which he added to the pile at his side: a wrinkled apple, a few nuts, some tired corn-cakes, a policeman's whistle.

A blazered youth in glasses, his hair swept up and tied with orange chiffon in a straggly top-knot that made him look as if he were balancing a squashed tangerine on his head, introduced himself.

'My name is Paranjeet Singh. I am honoured to know you. You must meet the Sahdu.' He clicked his tongue against his teeth. 'He is quite a fellow to reckon with. He claims to speak English, though I cannot vouch for the authenticity of his proud boast.'

The Holy Man's withered body was slung between his legs like a papoose between two poles. He was palming seeds to his lips and spitting out the husks so that for the first time we saw that he had three gleaming teeth in his upper jaw and two in his lower which when he closed his mouth fitted perfectly together like a Chinese Puzzle. He had a bone through his nose and a black bag under each eye the size of an over-ripe plum.

Paranjeet addressed him in Gujerati, and the old man peered at us warily from under his dusty eyebrows. He swung his scarecrow physique to an upright position, the rags round his loins suspended on the rim of his pelvis. He swayed towards us on his gnarled feet and brought his palms together like a prayer, in greeting. In the darkness beyond the fire all we could see of his face was the bone through his nose, but we knew he was smiling for we caught a momentary flash of the Chinese Puzzle.

'Good morning!' he said, loud and clear, though in surprisingly treble tones, then he repeated the greeting.

'Good morning,' Zareen and I said as one, and the Chinese Puzzle came out to stay. He shuffled back into the firelight motioning to us to follow, and though we put polite questions to him and attempted conversation, all he would venture over his shoulder was 'Good morning!' over and over again, interspersed with phrases in his own language.

Chuckling and wobbling his head in our direction, to our dismay the Sadhu started to interfere with himself. He plunged his hand into the depths of his greasy loincloth and from some unmentionable cranny or fold in the filthy garment he produced a very flat, rather damp packet of ten Woodbine cigarettes. As a new crowd had convened to watch the Sadhu 'talking' with the strangers, and as his 'proud boast' of speaking English was in danger of being exposed as inaccurate, to save the Sadhu's face I felt constrained to accept the proffered cigarette. It was scant comfort to see the Holy Man put a limp fag between his own lips, for apart from being both squashed and bent, I could see by the flame from his match that the cigarettes were also lightly steaming. We puffed at each other in a strained silence while the onlookers murmured their approval. With a flash of inspiration I delved into my pocket and offered him my half-full packet of Benson and Hedges. The Sadhu accepted it with diffident grace and proceeded to interfere with himself once more as his fingers explored his groin for his secret repository. We raised our hands again in *namaste* and said, 'Good morning', but as we parted I couldn't help wincing at the thought of those cardboard corners.

I finished relating this account of my last night's adventure to the small company round the dinner table, and the lovely Japanese actress Yoko Tani leant over and kissed me on the cheek.

I was on location in Jaipur for *The Wind Cannot Read* with Yoko, Dirk Bogarde and a Welshman called Ronald Lewis, hailed at that time as a great actor in the making. He had tiny eyes, inexpressive like a bear's, a jaw like the bumper of a truck and a dangerous quality, for the good reason that he was. Extremely dangerous. I found out later that he had thrown his live-in girlfriend out of a first floor window, breaking her skull and several ribs; he had attacked David McCallum when filming in Australia and beaten him up. Both David and I may be perfectly proportioned, but we are neither of us – let us search for the appropriate word here – big. In other words, Ronnie Lewis was a bruiser and a bully.

Later he became an alcoholic, booked a room for himself under a false name in a boarding house in Brighton, locked the door and killed himself.

The unit was staying in the Rambagh Palace, one of the Maharajah of Jaipur's homes which had recently been converted for commercial use. It was a wonderfully serene oasis at the heart of the Pink City bustling with taxis and luridly painted trucks and rickshaws and camel-carts, an elegant garden hotel, all creamy cloisters and minarets, the East meets West architecture so charmingly suited to the colonial life. I was twenty-three years old and reeling from the Subcontinental experience, and since my role in the film was subsidiary, I had plenty of free time to reel.

There was a young Sikh adviser on the film, and we became good friends. Gurbachin had a mongoose called Rikki that he took with him everywhere on a lead; Rikki was highly intelligent and full of fun, and I fell completely under his spell.

I also befriended one of the junior receptionists in the hotel, a lovely Parsee girl called Zareen, while making enquiries about the possibility of borrowing a bicycle to explore without the need to pinpoint a destination, and then order a car or a rickshaw in the approved manner. She had not only obtained a bicycle for me (belonging to a member of the staff), she had suggested she might accompany me on her own machine so that she could be my guide on her afternoons off. Zareen was friendly but completely unflirtatious, and I felt we could trust one another. Speaking the language, she revealed to me an India I would never have found on my own: the bazaar, where she introduced me to the stallholders, guided me in choosing my purchases and haggled on my behalf; the buried city of Amber, now reclaimed by the jungle and swarming with apes, which we discovered together as if we were the first to set eyes on its wonders since The Great Moghul had led his caravan on to Fatehpur Sikri. She took me to her home where I met her family, and we ate orange segments sprinkled with salt in a room with walls so blue it was like sitting on a cloud.

'Who do you think you're kidding?' Ronnie hated India. He hated the heat and the multitude and the poverty and the erratic plumbing, and he was blind to the beauty on every side. He spent his free time by the pool drinking Pimms or brandy sours, and by the evening he was often morose. He could 'haud 'is boattle', as my Aunt Gatty would put it. He didn't slur his words or bang into things or fall over; his drunkenness was dogged and depressed.

There were only Yoko, Ronnie and myself left seated at our table. Dirk and the other members of the unit had retired since they were on early call. I can't believe Ronnie would have behaved as he did had there been other men around to remonstrate with or stop him. But there was only a fragile little Japanese lotus blossom. And me. This was temptation too strong to resist.

'I should have hit you last night when you were going on about "Zareen and I did this" and "Zareen and I did that". Are you trying to make us believe she's your girlfriend? A pansy-boy like you?'

Yoko dropped her fork. She lived in Paris and was quite westernised, though she often wore a kimono and always looked ravishing.

'Ronnie! Prease!' she remonstrated.

'You keep out of this!' The other diners stopped eating and turned to listen. 'You're a nasty little bum-boy. That's what you are. Right?'

Physically I am the least aggressive of men. During my military service, as an officer cadet I was forced to box; before going into the ring and afterwards I felt sick, but I had to acquit myself well or jeopardise my commission. Adrenalin was my substitute for courage. I have never hit anyone in anger. I certainly did not feel anger towards Ronnie on this occasion. I was shattered and overwhelmed with dread.

'Please don't make a scene…' I murmured.

'Come outside and I'll thrash the fucking daylights out of you –'

'Ronnie! John! Prease! Prease don't quarrerr…'

'This is ridiculous,' I protested.

'You're yellow as well!' He was shouting by this time, getting into his stride. 'I should have belted you last night. Yellow and a fucking pansy-boy!' He lurched to his feet, knocking over his chair. Everyone in the dining room was staring, appalled. I stood up – I had no choice – and said, 'We'll talk about this outside.'

We left the dining-room together.

The terrace was furnished with wicker chairs and tables and cooled by gently whirling fans; below was a lawn kept emerald-green with sprinklers. The flower beds were ablaze with dahlias and poinsettia, and the evening air was fragrant with tuberoses and jasmine. A flight of green parrots alighted in a jacaranda as the scarlet crescent that was the last of the sun slipped over the horizon.

Ronnie tore off his jacket, getting one arm stuck in the sleeve which he pumped at furiously till he finally ripped his arm free.

'Come on you yellow fucking pansy bastard. I'll show you what a man can do to a fucking Nance!'

Why didn't I say something witty like, 'May you die of cancer, you piece of pus!' and take to my heels? If I had locked myself in my room he would have broken down the door, but the staff might have been able to restrain him or call the police. It was cowardice alone that made me stay and fight. The diners were now assembled on the terrace immobilised by horror and too afraid of the Welshman's rabid fury to restrain him. The fear of their contempt forced me to go through with this primaeval contest.

As if in a dream I removed my jacket and tie; in those days, so soon after Partition and 'Home Rule', dressing for dinner was *de rigueur*. I unstrapped my watch and laid all my belongings in a little heap on the grass. I put up my fists and prepared to circle my adversary as I had done in my bouts in front of the colonel.

But the factor that I had failed to take into account in this struggle was that my opponent was insane. Sexual jealousy and envy and resentment boiled in his brain, already inflamed with drink, to make an already miserable and angry man demented. As soon as I was facing him he charged me like a maddened bull at the matador's cape and with one swing of his fist he felled me and broke my jaw. Not one other blow was exchanged. The diners, galvanised at last by his savagery, came to my rescue, preventing him from killing me.

I was not aware at the time that he had broken my jaw, only that I was bleeding profusely and that I had spat out a molar into the palm of my hand. The cameraman couldn't shoot on me for a week, so the company had to alter the schedule. Filming is not like school or the army. There is no one to say, 'Bad Boy! Go to the bottom of the class!', no commanding officer to court-martial wrongdoers. The producer wants to finish the film, so he will go to any length to smooth oil on the waters.

Ronnie never apologised, and when I showed him the molar he had knocked out, he said, 'I was aiming for the front ones.' To the rest of the crew he maintained, 'The little Nance had it coming to him!'

Though I was in pain, I refused to be seen by a local dentist, preferring to wait for my imminent return to the UK.

Back home in London, when the root of the broken off molar was removed, it was discovered that a hole had been punched in my antrim, the fragile bone partition which separates your mouth from your sinus. After the extraction, my sinus became pathologically infected, and I had to undergo two operations to repair the damage, spending over three weeks in hospital.

I was urged by my agent and by many of my colleagues to sue for damages.

A court case would have attracted enormous publicity, dragging Yoko, Dirk and others into the witness box, and with the repetition of Ronnie's taunts, cruelly highlighting my sexual nature and revealing my feebleness. I was assured, with the medical evidence of my injury, that I would receive a substantial sum. But I was not prepared to throw away my reputation for vengeance and a few thousand pounds.

I have never hated anyone. But when Ronnie Lewis killed himself, I felt not a twinge of sorrow or regret.

5 NOCTURNAL HIGH JINKS
Gosh Meets The Famous Pianist

GETTING TO KNOW Gurbachin's mongoose Rikki had been such a joyous experience, that I decided I wanted to keep a wild animal for myself. Unusual pets are sometimes mere fashion accessories, to be paraded for the press to gain an exotic reputation for their owners, but this was far from my own scenario. Journalists and photographers were never allowed across my threshold, since the large apartment I now lived in was shared by my lover, and we had to keep our domestic situation secret.

In my early years I had considered studying to become a vet. Throughout my life, at various times I have been the happy owner of a rabbit, three dogs and several cats. I had looked after one litter of twelve puppies and several litters of kittens. I had failed to achieve the ownership of a horse, but I had tended nine thousand chickens on Posket Farm, and the idea of looking after a beguiling animal that could also teach me something became irresistible.

Importing a mongoose from India proved to be an impossible task because of the bureaucratic problems involved, so on my return to London from Delhi, having persuaded George that what we needed to transform our life into an idyll was a *herpestes edwarsi*, we made our way to Harrod's Department Store which in those days had a pet department on the top floor.

Our flat on Hampstead Heath was huge, with three bedrooms and a box-room, and we felt sure that we could accommodate a small, non-domesticated animal there and give it a rewarding life.

We were en route to the mongooses when we were stopped in our tracks at another cage. The creature, though nocturnal, was awake. Gerald Durrell calls it by its Swahili name, Golago, but in English it is known as a Bush Baby. Bush Babies are primates, related to humans in the chain of evolution, but more closely related to lemurs and sloths. Because they live and feed at night, they have huge spooky eyes. The phenomenon of large eyes in animals is known to evoke a sympathetic response in humans – they appear to us to be sentimental and to need protection. George and I were particularly vulnerable to these signals, since we had no immediate prospect of becoming parents. Our latent paternal longings were aggravated beyond endurance by the sight of the Bush Baby. The very name suggests 'Child Substitute'. It had a turned up nose like a Disney cartoon and prehensile fingers that looked capable of playing miniature concertos, and it looked lost and frightened. They are timid creatures, acrobatic, intelligent and bewitching. They can also be ferocious at times, as all wild creatures have to be if they are to survive surrounded by enemies.

So instead of a mongoose we bought a Bush Baby and called him 'Gosh'. If we had found a mate for him, which we were already contemplating, we would have called her 'Golly'. They look so surprised.

A fully-grown Bush Baby standing on his hind legs measures approximately nine inches from his head to his toes, and his tail measures about the same again. They crouch in repose, and in this position they are about the size of a capuchin monkey or a large rat, depending on how you are disposed to think of animals.

Gosh lived in a tea-cosy during the day – a woollen tea-cosy to keep him warm. At night we let him loose in our main room, with two fireplaces and a studio window overlooking the Heath, which we hoped would remind him of the rain forest and make him feel at home.

We had to cover the fireplaces with wire netting or he would have been straight up one or other of them like a trout up a stream.

In the morning the hunt would begin. He rarely slept in the same place twice. He would often make use of a glove or a scarf or a discarded sock, then find some untried hiding place behind a book in the bookshelves, or behind a painting, where he would wrap himself up in his purloined bedding and wedge himself tightly in. Picture frames at crazy angles, displaced books or ornaments tipped over usually betrayed his presence, but he was adept at finding his way into the table drawer by the back way leaving no clue to his whereabouts, making us fear he had escaped onto the Heath forever. He once succeeded in getting right inside the piano, but the reverberations from the finely tuned strings I think unsettled him, for he never tried it again.

His principal diet was mealworms, which anglers use for bait. Mealworms are about half-an-inch long, and vigorously wriggly. Gosh would select the wriggliest after a breathless moment of teeth-watering choice, then pick it up between his thumb and forefinger and pop it into his mouth with an almost audible 'Mmmmmm!', sucking his fingers as he withdrew them. He also had a sweet tooth. Glacé cherries were his undoing. He would abandon all other pursuits and come flying from the farthest chandelier at the merest sniff of a glacé cherry.

When night was falling, and the lump in the tea-cosy started to stir, I would open his cage and make myself comfortable in an easy chair. Noise didn't bother him. I could have the Emperor Concerto playing, and he didn't seem to notice. But the smallest movement sent him flying back to his tea-cosy. In the first few weeks, if I swallowed, the constriction of my throat was enough to make him jump. After a month or two I could move about the room freely without upsetting him if I walked smoothly and made no sudden movements.

He never walked anywhere. His progress consisted of a series of sudden springs from one landing-spot to the next. A golago's life in the wild is arboreal, and he leapt distances of over six feet with ease – from the table to the book-case to the picture-rail to the piano.

One aspect of his behaviour puzzled me. When he was planning to make a long leap, measuring the distance and the effort required to reach his destination, he appeared abstractedly to doodle with his willy. Since this solecism did not occur on one chance occasion but on a regular basis, I examined his performance more closely and discovered that he was not idly masturbating as I had seen monkeys do, but peeing on his hands. He would land in the coal-scuttle, eyeing the picture-rail. Fumble fumble. Piss piss. BOING!

Skywards.

Little black hand-prints all along the wall. Was this, I wondered, like someone spitting on their hands to strengthen their grip? Like in a Tug-o'-War? I consulted the celebrated zoologist, George Cansdale (the host of an animal programme on television), who explained that for these creatures pissing on their hands before leaping was territory demarcation – just as dogs mark lamp-posts.

Gosh also did big jobs in mid-flight. Since the 'jobs' invariably consisted of dry round pellets, this habit was not as unpleasant as it sounds, and the detritus was easily dealt with. It is, however, not conducive of concentration when immersed in a book or a script to be peppered from above with golago-poo.

Gosh was soon tame enough to sit on my shoulder examining my ear with his cold little fingers, but he rarely allowed me to pick him up. Every morning, once I had found his sleeping place, I would move him to the comfort and the security of the tea-cosy in his cage. If he was deeply asleep after an active night this was easy. If, on the other hand, he was wide awake and in no mood to be trifled with, he could be savage. He frequently bit me to the bone. I never wore gloves, since I hoped that in time he would accept that he was safe in my grasp, but he never did.

I was working on a television play with the late, much loved, eccentric actress Beatrix Lehmann. She was a passionate animal-lover, who had famously tamed both a sparrow and a spider. The spider came up the plug-hole in the bath when she whistled and sucked milk from her finger. We had been rehearsing for a week before I discovered that she was the owner of a Bush Baby.

Hers was a female whom she called 'Mrs Bush The Famous Pianist'. We could not believe our good fortune. We neither of us knew the first thing about the mating habits or the female oestrus of the golago, but we decided to introduce our animals, even if it were just for companionship, and not necessarily for reproduction.

Bea suggested that I should bring Gosh over in his cage to her house in Islington for several consecutive evenings, so that Gosh and Mrs Bush The Famous Pianist could get to know each other through the bars – a sort of betrothal period during which they might find out if they were suited to each other, before taking things any further.

Mrs Bush was every inch a lady, and much tamer than the ferocious Gosh. She never bit anyone; she never peed on her hands, and when she leapt she did so sedately, remembering to point her toes. She was plumper than my male, and she squirmed inside her fluffy pelt like a naked hooker luxuriating in an expensive mink. Bea was a wonderful cook, and she often used to let Mrs Bush roam freely among her guests when she was entertaining, sometimes to their consternation.

One evening before we had embarked on the process of golago rapprochement, Bea invited me to a rather grand dinner. Everyone had admired Mrs Bush while we had been sitting in the comfort of the sitting room, watching The Famous Pianist swing coquettishly on the bars of the coffee table, and lollop across the carpet in her most fetching manner, but the atmosphere changed completely once we were seated round the dinner table; for it was no longer possible, beneath the napery, to keep a precise track of Mrs Bush's movements.

We had started on the soup – it was bright summer I remember, and Bea had concocted a delicious gazpacho – when the gentleman on my right, Sir Robert Irving (the renowned conductor of the orchestra at The Royal Opera House in Covent Garden), stopped with his spoon halfway to his mouth and spluttered between clenched teeth: 'Bea, dearest. Mrs Bush The Famous Pianist has just gone up my trousers.'

Bea purred, 'Don't worry, Robert dear, she's just exploring!' Then, turning to the assembled company, who by this time were looking distinctly uneasy, she explained – 'She just loves dark corners! They live in hollow trees, you see, so she finds fresh nooks and crannies completely irresistible!'

Sir Robert dropped his spoon in his soup with a clatter and started to lose colour. 'She's climbing up my leg!' he hissed.

'She won't hurt you Robert! Don't be a baby!'

'She has very cold hands!' He started to shiver.

'Pianists always have cold hands! It's part of their mystique! Don't move or you'll give her a fright. Hollow trees don't move, after all, do they? And who knows what Mrs Bush might do if you frighten her?!'

Since Bea was determined to treat the episode lightly, the guests, including myself, felt it it would be impolite to cause a fuss, so we all endeavoured to carry on taking our soup, regardless of Sir Robert's winces, which were reaching a crescendo along with his mutterings of 'Oh My God!'

'*Courage, mon brave!*' Bea urged him, to no avail.

'CHRIST!' shouted Sir Robert, and we could no longer ignore his plight. 'SHE'S INSIDE MY UNDERPANTS!'

'Just keep calm, my dear!' Bea cried. 'Panic won't save the day! I keep telling you if you frighten her she might bite!' Then looking round the table at the array of anxious faces, and with a gracious inclination of the head acknowledging what seemed to Bea our wholehearted approval of her superhuman restraint and her eminent good sense, she coaxed the conductor with wheedling tones – 'Very slowly, dear Robert – and I mean very slowly – for all Bush Babies are terrified of sharp movements – simply terrified – for your own good, you understand – VERY slowly – Undo your flies!'

By this time, the guests had swivelled in their chairs and were craning their necks to look under the table, holding the damask cloth high above their heads, and peering with unblinking concentration into the darkness and straight at Sir Robert's crotch.

With a trembling thumb and forefinger Sir Robert inched the zip on his fly down as far as it would go. With an audible 'Phaw!' of relief, Mrs Bush's head popped out from his Y-Fronts, then with both sets of elegant fingers she parted his flies as if she were peeping through the curtains before taking her final call.

She squirmed out onto his lap, then turned to look back down the long dark tunnel of his trouser-leg up which she had so bravely ventured, and considered for a moment. With a shrug she dismissed the idea of returning whence she had come, and instead hopped prettily to the floor.

Bea, reckoning that enough was enough, fondly popped Mrs Bush back into her cage.

Sir Robert, still trembling, adjusted his clothing, the table cloth shrouded our knees once more, and the rest of the meal proceeded as if nothing untoward had happened. But I couldn't help noticing that Sir Robert had lost his appetite.

I arrived at Bea's house in Islington for the Big Night with Gosh tucked up in his tea-cosy at the back of his cage. No sooner had it been set on the floor next to Mrs Bush's cage than The Famous Pianist was out of her nesting-box in a twinkling, holding onto the bars with both hands – each little finger extended as if she were sipping a cup of afternoon tea from the finest bone china. Her wide eyes were wider than ever with astonishment, and she bobbed and ducked and squinted through her legs, trying every angle to get a peek at the cause of this extraordinary new development in her hitherto humdrum existence.

She could smell golago.

She showed not a sign of fear, just frustrated curiosity, like a nosy neighbour trying to get a glimpse of the new tenants who have moved in next door. Mrs Bush was on home ground, but after the journey across London and all the strange new noises and smells, Gosh huddled resolutely in his tea-cosy for the entire evening without stirring. Bea suggested that the next time she should bring Mrs Bush to my flat, and see if relations improved.

She did, and they didn't.

In Hampstead, with the two cages facing each other and all but touching, Mrs Bush was out and about instantly, evidently quite desperate to discover what delightful potential awaited her inside all that wool.

The bulge acted dead.

The only thing to emerge from the situation was that Gosh was a die-hard misogynist.

On the third evening there was no further progress. Mrs Bush was her usual sweet self, all of a dither and anxious to please. The utter stillness of the tea-cosy was beginning to look ominous. Bea and I decided to throw caution to the winds, so we opened both cage doors simultaneously.

And waited.

Mrs Bush was out of her cage before you could say 'The Famous Pianist'. She stood at the door to Gosh's cage, her head inclined at a tender angle towards the tea-cosy, stilling the beating of her heart with fluttering fingers. She waited with increasing impatience, but she was too polite to enter his premises without an invitation. I swear I heard her clear her throat.

The lump looked not only dead but decomposing.

'Ah well!' Mrs Bush seemed to shrug and tip-toed across the threshold into Gosh's cage. She approached the tea-cosy, her fingers now clenched into a fist over her thundering heart, and stood very close, watching the woolly mound with an utterly vulnerable expression on her pretty face.

Nothing.

She stretched out one dainty hand towards the opening of the tea-cosy, then lifting the top side of it delicately and painfully slowly ever higher into the air, she peered voraciously inside.

She started visibly at what she saw; but undeterred, she devoured the contents of this unpromising looking little woollen bag for several seconds, with growing wonder.

Suddenly, with one bound, she was inside the tea-cosy and had pulled down the flap. Where once the tea-cosy had been a dromedary with one hump, it was now a bactrian camel with two. This state of affairs lasted for a mere moment, before the whole outline of the bag erupted with some mortal struggle inside it. Mrs Bush emerged first, piping with terror, metaphorically adjusting the orange-blossom in her hair. She leapt high for the first time in her cosseted life, emitting a fusillade of pellets from her rear end, and landed with a skid on top of the door to Gosh's cage. Her embonpoint was palpitating with the horror of it all.

All her illusions shattered, her dreams of love and companionship lying in pieces about her dainty feet, Mrs Bush The Famous Pianist waddled sadly to her nesting-box, and Bea clanged her cage-door shut.

Gosh charged out from his woollen cave with his fangs bared in fury, his grey-brown pelt suddenly thick and dark as each hair stood on end. He seldom made a noise, but he hooted strangely now, and it was clear that the sound denoted neither desire nor pleasure. He hadn't damaged Mrs Bush, just frightened the living daylights out of her, and he had spoiled forever his chances of becoming a father.

We never repeated the experiment, as Bea was mortally afraid that Gosh might put paid to Mrs Bush's promising career on the concert platform.

After two years of trying to tame Gosh, I finally accepted that no matter how much care and attention you are prepared to lavish on a wild animal, they are not suited to domestic life. He was bewitching, but he bit me savagely and often. He thrived physically and he appeared to be perfectly happy, but he was wild and I could no longer cope with him.

George Cansdale had a private zoo, and when I had consulted him about Gosh's behaviour, he had expressed a lively interest in him, so I handed him over to the eminent zoologist with mixed feelings.

I felt a little like a father who has only himself to blame when his child turns out badly.

6 THE IDOL OF THE ODEONS
Dirk Bogarde

NOËL COWARD was passing the Odeon Leicester Square when he glanced up at the billboard and read –

MICHAEL REDGRAVE and DIRK BOGARDE
in
THE SEA SHALL NOT HAVE THEM

He turned to his companion, and in the bored, clipped syllables that had made his delivery famous, said: 'I don't see why not. Everyone else has.'

This is wicked and funny and doubtless apocryphal; and as far as the protagonists are concerned, it is very wide of the mark.

Dirk Bogarde was so garlanded with good fortune he had no right or reason to be bitter. His uncommon good looks had launched him on a career which made him 'The Idol of the Odeons', but it rankled that his one Hollywood film, a lavish biopic on the life of Liszt called *Song Without End*, had been a catastrophic flop. This setback, however, for which he blamed everything and everyone but himself, failed to dash his hopes of international stardom. But you mentioned Laurence Harvey, Richard Burton, Richard Harris, Michael Caine, Sean Connery and latterly Anthony Hopkins at your peril. He maintained that his contract with The Rank Organisation had bound him to a treadmill of British films, which prevented him from achieving the worldwide success which was his due, and for which, by Hollywood standards, he was grossly underpaid.

> O wad some Pow'r the giftie gie us
> To see oursels as others see us! (Rabbie Burns)

He was prodigiously talented in many directions: he was a gifted artist and a skilled restorer of oil paintings, he had a visual flair which would have assured him a success as an interior decorator or a landscape gardener, and above all he was a born writer, as his volumes of autobiography show. He was never at ease on the stage – he moved stiffly and his voice was reedy – but he was a consummate film actor.

But he could not accept, could not understand, and could not see when he watched his own performances, that he was effeminate.

There have been plenty of homosexual film stars, starting with Rudolph Valentino, but their lack of *cojones* didn't show on the screen.

But Dirk wanted only to be a leading man.

The English were so thrilled to have a home-grown Star to adulate that they overlooked his camp mannerisms, but in the world outside people laughed at his too-perfect coiffure and groaned at his tantrums which represented rage.

In interviews he would confess with mock-humility how he wore pads even in his vests because his shoulders were too narrow, or he would laugh about the contoured stockings he wore to fatten his calves in *A Tale of Two Cities*. He would describe how the make-up girl applied pancake to his neck to disguise his weak jaw and admit that he insisted on being photographed on one side of his face because the other side was less photogenic. He sounded like Marilyn Monroe.

Can you imagine Bob Hoskins giving away his beauty secrets?

But his bitterness was also the result of a lifetime spent concealing his homosexuality.

In the Fifties, the tall, handsome, virile and quintessentially English actor Antony Forwood divorced the squeaky-voiced and irresistible film star Glynis Johns, his wife of some years and the mother of their son, to move in with Dirk and be his 'Manager'. Now *there* is a love story worthy of Dirk's pen, but it is a story he was too cowardly to write. In seven volumes of autobiography, he never once acknowledges that their relationship was other than a business arrangement. He always refers to Tony as 'Forwood', making him sound like a butler. I am certain that even within the privacy of the bedroom, 'Forwood' was Dirk's most affectionate name for his 'manager', for no one else ever called him anything but Tony.

The choice of such a distant form of address, with its overtones of public school and the army, was an indication of the extent of Dirk's denial. Their relationship lasted fifty years until Tony's death, and they were closer than most married couples.

After two months in India filming *The Wind Cannot Read*, I became friends with Dirk and Tony, and on our return to England I was invited to one of their famous Sunday lunches. He was a dazzling host, for whom entertaining was almost as rewarding as acting. Being an inspired interior-decorator induces itchy feet, and once the curtains were up, and the 'Oohs!' and 'Ahs!' of his friends had died away, Dirk was always on the lookout for another challenge. I visited all three of his homes in England before he and 'Forwood' moved to Provence where he settled down at last.

The first was in Chalfont St Giles and the second in Beaconsfield, both within easy reach of London and near Pinewood Studios where the Rank Organisation, to which Dirk was on contract, had its headquarters. I was flattered to be invited to lunch and interested to meet his illustrious guests – Rex Harrison and Kay Kendall; the Boxes (Sydney and Muriel, film producers); George Cukor, the legendary Hollywood director; Basil Dearden and his beautiful wife Melissa Stribling; and last but not least, the incomparable Judy Garland.

Another guest, the thirties musical star Jessie Mathews, was a sort of in-joke, I suppose – and as jokes are frequently wont to do, it misfired. She not only sang 'Over My Shoulder' to Judy, but piling Pelion on the Ossa of embarassment, she insisted on high-kicking her way round the table showing her knickers, which barely concealed an uncharted moonscape of cellulite.

After lunch, Dirk led a crocodile of the younger guests, or those too polite to refuse his suggestion of a 'constitutional', over a stile and across the fields, for which wellies, I remember, were provided. We were accompanied on this jaunt by a friendly mastiff whose name I forget.

As we squelched through the mud Dirk explained to me.

'When I was first put under contract to Rank, I had a little flat in Ebury Street,' he said. 'I was lonely, working all week in the studios. I hadn't been in London long enough to make friends, so I used to invite some of the kids round at the weekend. We'd have bacon and eggs, baked beans, that sort of thing. The make-up girl, the second assistant, the chippy and his girl-friend.'

After our tense, show-bizzy lunch, short on stimulating conversation and with all the Stars competing to dazzle and confound the others, I warmed to the thought of this unpretentious friendly bunch. I was just waiting for him to lament the loss of these simple pleasures, to complain at the irksome responsibilities of being a public figure...

'One day,' Dirk continued, 'I looked round at these insignificant people with whom I was sharing my precious, precious leisure – and I thought – "If you're going to be a Film Star, ducky, you better start behaving like one. Get yourself some proper friends!"'

He laughed in amazement to think that he could ever have been so naive as to mix with ordinary mortals.

'I've never looked back!' he said, as Judy took his arm and cuddled up.

Not for the first time I thought: 'I'll never make a Film Star.'

But it was in his last house before they left for France, a stunning Elizabethan manor outside Guildford, that he finally dropped his defences.

Dirk was not comfortable with gay couples in mixed company. As far as the business was concerned I was still in the closet, and I too preferred discretion. As did George, who resented any suggestion that he might be perceived as my appendage, and he would have refused point blank to appear with me either in public or 'in society', even if I had asked him for his company on these occasions (which I never did). In private of course we were inseparable, and with Dirk and Tony I had made no secret of my domestic situation, so George and I were invited over for a light informal supper where we were the only guests.

It was a balmy evening in August, and while Tony and George were deep in conversation about Leighton House and the Pre-Raphaelites or something elevating and suitable for a summer evening with the stars, Dirk led me out through the French windows with a glass of wine apiece to show me round the estate.

Candour is often callous and sometimes cruel, and what I consider to be my refreshing honesty and lack of cant is frequently described by my acquaintances as 'gross tactlessness'. It is often triggered by a dislike of small talk and a moderate amount of alcohol.

We had come to the end of the herbaceous border, when I stopped and asked Dirk –

'Do you and Tony still make love?'

I was in my twenties at this time, and both Dirk and Tony, though supremely handsome men, seemed to me settled and middle-aged. I might just as easily have asked the same question of a married heterosexual. It was the duration of physical attraction that interested me, not whether the expression of it was gay or straight.

It was abundantly clear that their relationship was deep and strong, but there was never the slightest inappropriate gesture between them – inappropriate, that is, between heterosexual men. No brush of a hand, no touch on the shoulder. Even their conversation was guarded, so I felt the need to know.

Dirk smiled – enigmatically, I think you would describe it.

'We've been together a long time,' he said. 'Now, we're like brothers.'

The celibacy he implied seemed to me a desperate and a joyless option. When away from George my randiness had already caused problems. I had jeopardised the life we had built together for a nearly terminal dose of Grand Passion with Frank my Puerto Rican lover in New York, whom I had met while appearing as 'Dorian Gray' in a Television Playhouse. (George C Scott, playing Lord

Henry Wooton, was fine when he wasn't tired and emotional. Then, plate glass windows nothwithstanding, he was inclined to rearrange the furniture.) Charles Russell and Lance Hamilton were 'over there' running Noël Coward's business affairs, and since 'The Master' was in Jamaica, they suggested that if I was discreet and didn't tell a soul I could stay in Noël's pied-à-terre in East 55th Street: two grand pianos groaning with framed photographs of Princess Margaret, Lord Mountbatten, The Queen Mum and Marlene Dietrich, all signed to 'Darling Noël'. New York for the first time was pretty heady stuff, and in all the feverish excitement I lost my head. Frank was criminally sexy, with no mind worth mentioning. I brought him briefly to England, and left George. When Frank was drafted for military service after four months, and had to return to America, I wept with relief, acknowledging that I had made a dreadful mistake, and begged George to forgive me. He did, and we started again.

'What do you do for sex?' I asked Dirk succinctly. 'Do you have casual affairs?'

'God, no,' he said. 'How could I possibly in my position? Everyone knows me. I can't go anywhere without being recognised. There's blackmail...the *News of the World*. I would be ruined...' He shook his head sadly. 'Completely...utterly out of the question...'

'Do you reckon it's worth it?' I asked him in wonder. 'Money, fame, all the rest of it. If you have to live like a monk?'

He held out his hands as if to embrace his whole estate, the long low farmhouse with its mullioned windows peeping out from under breakers of climbing roses, the immaculate lawns that led down to a little wood of great oaks and silver birch...

'Don't you think it's worth it?' he said. 'For all this?'

'No!' I thought. 'A thousand times no!' But I smiled, and nodded wisely.

'Let me show you something,' he said, leading the way indoors once more.

He took me up the sweeping staircase to the first floor, past the master bedroom, then up a steep, narrow stair to a large wooden trapdoor upon which he braced his hands like Atlas supporting the world before he eased it up with a groan from the hinges to let us in.

We entered a loft which spread over the length and breadth of the whole house, with dormer windows set into the eaves so that the space was light and airy. In the middle, set high upon a plinth, was a Harley Davidson motorbike. Golden shafts of light from the dying sun caught the tangle of metal and made it glitter; the fuel tank was scarlet and sleek – a turkey oiled for the oven, spewing out its eviscerated intestines, the slipstream turning them silver as they caught in the wind.

The unwieldy contraption had been hoisted up the outside of the building with a crane. A whole window frame must have been removed; and here it stood high above the ground, safely out of reach of the demanding tarmac, immobile forever, the ultimate trophy for a man who had never learned to drive a car, let alone to control a powerful motorbike.

'Isn't it magnificent?' he asked me. His eyes were moist with immortal longings.

I could only agree.

The vast machine froze ready to pounce from its dais straight at the wall ahead of it, and framed within its meaty, flashing handlebars, high on this wall which housed the chimneys, was hung a gigantic, a heroic-sized picture, removed from the marquee outside a cinema advertising Dirk's film *The Singer Not The Song*.

It was a photograph of Dirk Bogarde clad from head to foot in gleaming black leather; in which his booted legs were planted astride, the bulge in his groin was thrust into the light and a lascivious sneer twisted his sensual lips.

Some poor deluded critic had commiserated with Dirk after the opening of this film. 'They forced poor Dirk Bogarde into tight black-leather, a Marlon Brando gimmick which was incongruous and caused hoots of derision.'

Poor Dirk my eye. Forced, was he? I could hear the crack as Dirk twisted the designer's arm. 'Black leather, all black leather and nothing but black leather! Or I don't do the picture.'

And here was the proof of it.

And this image of himself was the shrine at which he worshipped.

'This is my playroom,' he said, his voice hushed and thick with emotion.

He scrambled up onto the platform and straddled the machine. With effortless expertise he flicked the clutch and kick-started the engine.

The planes of chrome on the fat exhaust refracted rainbow splinters across the ceiling: it was like something off a rocket at Cape Canaveral. With a roar that reverberated in your bowels, a jetstream like the blast from a furnace filled the loft with acrid fumes, as the gouged black rubber on the back wheel, which was supported by a rigid clamp, spun in space at a hundred miles an hour.

Dirk rode the thunder and gazed up at the leather-clad icon of himself filling the wall in front of him, his expression like the rapture on the face of a mediaeval saint in awful contemplation of a vision of Our Lord.

After ten minutes of this bedlam, Dirk switched off the engine. The silence was intense, broken only by the swish of the driving wheel as it continued on its ghostly journey, till Dirk jabbed on the brake and it reluctantly shuddered to a halt.

Like a conductor after leading his orchestra through a long and passionate piece of music, Dirk slumped over the handlebars. Then slowly he gathered himself up, dismounted from the motorbike and slid off the platform to join me on the floor of the loft.

Wiping beads of sweat from his brow with the heel of his hand he said, 'Now you know.'

We never spoke of it again.

Thirty years later, when Tony's terminal cancer finally forced them to abandon their adored farmhouse in Provence, Dirk gave as the principal reason for his return: 'I don't drive. I couldn't stay on there without my chauffeur.'

Noël Coward, Terence Rattigan, Ivor Novello, Anthony Asquith, Cecil Beaton and too many others to mention of Dirk's generation in both the cinema and the theatre were famously gay and hardly discreet, but they didn't write five books and give interviews in which they shouted from the rooftops that the accusations of homosexuality levelled at them were lies from beginning to end.

Everyone can understand Dirk's secrecy when he was at the height of his fame as a sex-symbol. One can even indulge his ludicrous claims of affairs with Capucine and Judy Garland. But what I found hard to stomach were his protestations that he was heterosexual, long after the laws against homosexuality had been repealed and when the prevailing moral climate had become more tolerant. He was old and huffy and no one cared who he fancied any more because no one fancied him any more. What sort of dream-world did he live in? A wonderland sustained by doting fans who are loyal unto death only if their pathetic fantasies are never exposed to the harsh light of the truth?

Dirk's life with 'Forwood' had been so 'respectable' – not even the *Sun* could dig up a rent boy in South America – their love for each other so profound and so enduring, it would have been a glorious day for the pursuit of understanding and for the promotion of tolerance if he had screwed up the courage somewhere in the interminable volumes of so-called autobiography and self-analysis, in all the acres of print he turned out about himself, to make one dignified allusion to his true nature and the mainspring of his being.

Self-love is no substitute for self-respect.

A good man shines through his memoirs, but Dirk's incandescent prose is the cloak for a curmudgeon; uncensored, he was full of umbrage and dudgeon.

One Wednesday he was quoted in the press, protesting that when he died he wanted his ashes strewn anywhere in the world except in England. He never forgave his native land for showering him with all the success he had ever deserved. And more.

The following Thursday, the country he despised gave him a knighthood.

I used to fantasise that Dirk and John Osborne would have made a perfect couple. Both enormously gifted, both vastly rewarded with fame and riches, yet each twisted into a pointless ball of bitterness.

And what use is talent, or even genius, for God's sake, if you have to live a lie and deny love?

7 TWO STABS IN THE DARK
The Hit Parade and Hollywood

THE ROYAL ALBERT HALL
POP CONCERT
LITA ROSA DENNIS LOTIS LONNIE DONEGAN JOHN FRASER

AS A RESULT of appearing in a lavish musical version of J B Priestley's classic *The Good Companions* (with the sublime Celia Johnson as Miss Trant and Eric Portman as Jess Oakroyd), I was offered a recording contract, and for a short while I rejoiced in the madness of being a Pop Singer. Two of my records made the Top Ten.

I appeared on *The Six Five Special* and *Cool For Cats*, and I sang live with Joe Loss and his Orchestra, an appearance which plumbed unsounded depths of awfulness. By this time I had acquired some confidence as an actor, but as a singer I was still a rank amateur, and appearing live in front of an audience of millions was one of the most terrifying experiences of my life. I froze like a rabbit caught in headlights and sang off key. Fortunately I had a Fan Club which cheered me to the echo no matter what I did or how I did it.

My apogee was the concert at the Albert Hall. I shared the platform not only with those billed above, but also with a chubby Cliff Richard and a toothsome Tommy Steele.

My big hit single was *Why Don't They Understand?*, a song aimed squarely at the teeny boppers.

I didn't pursue my pop career partly because I was getting lots of film offers – in quick succession I had made *The Dambusters*, *The Wind Cannot Read*, *Touch and Go* and *The Good Companions*, along with four forgettable films – but mostly because I didn't have what it takes to get out there in front of the baying mob and sell myself.

Which is why I got cold feet about Hollywood.

While I was in Los Angeles promoting *The Good Companions*, I was approached by Ross Hunter, the American producer of romantic comedies like *Pillow Talk*, with Doris Day and Rock Hudson; although he did not have a specific role in mind, he asked me if I would consider signing an exclusive contract with him. This was common practice in Hollywood at that time, and if I agreed to sign with him, he promised he would make me a star. He had certainly succeeded with Rock Hudson. And look what happened to him... It was only after his tragic death from AIDS in 1985 that anyone – even in the gay community – realised the full extent of the studio cover-up to keep the secret of his sexuality from his adoring public. Even his marriage, which was a sham, had been arranged by the studio. At this time, of course, no one in the business, let alone Ross Hunter, knew that I was gay.

I felt safe in London, with George, and surrounded by friends with whom I had no need to pretend. London is an international and a cosmopolitan city, the centre of government, of finance, of university education, of museums, of libraries, of galleries, of science, of medicine, of industry, of commerce, of music, of theatre, of sport, of import and export, right on the threshold of Europe. In this epicentre of civilisation, actors are pretty small beer. I wanted to be a success without attracting too much of the limelight, for I knew I could never cope with the constant anxiety that living a lie would entail.

I was prepared to be discreet, but I would not sacrifice my personal happiness for fame and a kidney-shaped swimming pool.

Hollywood is the movie capital of the world, and that's all it is. Actors there eat the movies, sleep the movies, breathe the movies. You are as successful as your last movie, and if that is a flop, you're on your way to outer Siberia. Professionally and socially. Big stars mix with other big stars, and little stars mix with little stars, and bit players mix with bit players, for everyone is afraid that failure is contagious. Honesty and spontaneity are poisoned by money and the worship of success. Once you sign on for The Dream Factory, if you fail, you might as well be dead. For The Dream Factory is all there is.

I have never seen so many beautiful girls. By the poolsides, at reception desks, waiting on tables. To say nothing of the beautiful men, serving in gas stations – like Rock Hudson – by the poolsides, at reception desks, waiting on tables. They were all impossibly bronzed and perfectly toothed and TALL. I had never felt more Glaswegian.

So I thanked Ross Hunter for his offer and said no. These days it's possible to work in 'Hollywood Films', which are not made exclusively in Los Angeles but on location round the world, and continue to live in Europe, but I didn't have that option then.

Considering the odds, I would almost certainly never have made the big time anyway. And as it turns out, thank God, I have never at any time since had the slightest twinge of regret.

Above: The family in the halcyon days before Daddy hit the bottle. Chris, Daddy, Jean; Gatty, me, Mummy.

Left: A shy highland girl from the Western Isles – my mother on the eve of her wedding.

Right: Me and The Philosopher, my cloth-eared, great and good Aunt Gatty.

I

Above left: With my cousin Moira, 1938. The Big Chief and his Mighty Squaw. Such nonchalance, such insouciance, such bare-faced effrontery. We were about to dodge inside the wigwam for another session of naked 'sudgery'.

Above right: Aunt Gatty made all my kilts for my growth. When I was fourteen, my last kilt started under my armpits and reached below the knee. Perfect for the mature Sean Connery. I never grew to fit it.

Below left: 1948. National Service. My first leave, with my sisters Jean and Chris, outside our new council flat in Battlefield.

Below right: Playing my new role as a Subaltern in The Royal Corps of Signals, while acquiring a Tasmanian accent.

II

Above left: My first love affair. Ian Hornton. Doctor of medicine, later an eye-specialist. Classical pianist, cabaret entertainer, athlete. Ian was more of a star than I ever was.

Above right: My first TV role, as David Balfour in the BBC adaptation of *Kidnapped* (1952). Like him, I seemed to be on my way...

Below left: 1952. Octavius in *Julius Caesar* at the Old Vic, with John Neville as Mark Antony. Everybody laughed at the first rehearsal, and I learnt a hard lesson.

Below right: 1954. Hoppy Hopgood in *The Dambusters*. In a huge cast, I passed as one of the lads.

III

Above left: With George, my first long-term relationship (fifteen years).

Above right: With Gosh the Impaler. When he was fractious, he would bite me to the bone with his sabre sharp incisors.

Below left: With Janette Scott, recording the title song from *The Good Companions*. Despite a dazzling cast – Celia Johnson, Eric Portman and others – the lavish all-singing all-dancing musical was a dismal flop. But it started my recording career. My single 'Why don't they understand?' made the Top Ten. I sang in the *Six-Five Special*, in *Cool for Cats*, and in concert at The Albert Hall.

Below right: At the premiere of *The Good Companions* with my sister, Jean Allan. Squeezing her little brother's hand, you can see by her knuckles how nervous she was.

Above: With Dirk Bogarde, filming *The Wind Cannot Read* (1958) in a desert in Rajastan.

Left: Playing The Country Squire, with Rhodesian Ridgebacks, Shaka and Fred, at Rout's Green Farm in Buckinghamshire.

Right: 1960. *Tunes of Glory*. One of the few times in my career I played a Scot. I used my mother's West-Highland accent, and everybody thought I was Irish.

Above: With Peter Finch in *The Trials of Oscar Wilde*. We were in a race with another film on the same subject, with Robert Morley as Oscar, and we finished ours in six weeks.

Left: With Richard Burton and Shirley Anne Field at Elstree Studios. Shirley Anne was my friend, and I had been in Richard's *Henry V* at The Old Vic. He asked to be introduced…

Right: 1961. King Alfonso in *El Cid*. Shot in Spain and Italy. Eight months of undiluted joy.

Above: El Cid again. Being directed by Anthony Mann, while Sophia Loren looks on. The air around Anthony was always blue. He was a rough diamond, of the old Hollywood school.

Below: Peter Sellers, Dany Robin and me at the Cannes Film Festival with *The Waltz of the Toreadors* (1962). Just before my idyll with Dany in the Forêt de Rambouillet.

Photographer unknown

Photographer unknown (Associated British Pictures)

Above: With my Fan Club in Hull. I was grateful to these sturdy Yorkshire lasses for making me look like a six-footer.

Below: 1963. *Tamahine*, with Dennis Price, Nancy Kwan and Derek Nimmo. Dennis had yet to meet up with his treble-toned nemesis…

Above: 1965. With Catherine Deneuve in *Repulsion*. Roman Polanski directed the film at the studios in Bray and on location among the traffic in South Kensington. He was a genius, she was a cold fish. It's all about depression and madness. Not my jolliest experience.

Left: The Russian Firebird. Off the Richter Scale.

Right: Rod, about the time I first met him in Johannesburg. I helped him escape from the Apartheid regime.

IX

Above left: Hedy Lamarr. A Noymal Poyson posing as a Big Stawr.

Above right: Bette Davis. She may have been a dragon, but she was still an Empress.

Below: 1968. With Big V (Vanessa Redgrave) in *Isadora*. A talent to match her prodigious height.

X

Above: In my one-man show about J M Barrie, *The Man Who Wrote Peter Pan*. I played all over the world, and finished with a platform in the Olivier at The National.

Left: In *Strike a Light* at the Piccadilly Theatre. A wonderful experience, in a fabulous musical. But – like the Oscar Wilde film – there were two shows on the same theme. The other (*The Matchgirls*) had opened first, and though both had wonderful reviews, neither lasted long.

Right: 1970. My Charlize Theron moment, playing John Wilkes, the famously ugly eighteenth-century wit, roué and reformer, in *The People's Jack*, a musical for Granada TV.

Above: 1963. In Soweto, with Andrew Ray. Few white South Africans dared venture there, but as entertainers, our vagabond image protected us.

Left: Suzan Farmer and I, staying with Mrs Okongwu, in her mud-compound in Nnewe, Nigeria. Wilfred Thesiger would have been proud of us.

Right: Making friends with the deer in Hiyajima, a beautiful island with the oldest Noh stage in Japan, built on stilts in the sea.

Above: The London Shakespeare Group *Twelfth Night* Company in Beijing. Between Edward Hardwicke and me is 'Swallow', our interpreter.

Below: In Tiananmen Square. Our photo call stopped the tanks in their tracks. Amongst the crowd are Edward Hardwicke, Edward Petherbridge, Sarah Porter, Emily Richard, Gary Raymond, Suzan Farmer, Simon Gipps Kent, and me.

XIII

Above: The Japanese version of a Pyjama Party. Hotels supply guests daily with crisply laundered cotton kimonos. In Shinjuku, Tokyo, with the *Macbeth* company: Howard Harrison (Company Manager and Lighting expert); Gareth Armstrong (Ross and a witch); me (Director, Duncan, Porter); Richard Heffer (the eponymous); Hilary Drake (Lady M); Phil Bowen (Banquo); his wife Stefanie (Designer); Mark Greenstreet (Malcolm).

Middle: LSG *Twelfth Night* curtain call, Fukuoka. Edward Petherbridge (Feste), me (Director, Malvolio), Suzan Farmer (Olivia), Simon Gipps Kent (Sebastian), Emily Richard (Viola), Gary Raymond (Orsino), Sarah Porter (Maria).

Below: Rod with Al (Dante Alighieri) our cat. When we found him in a drain, his Persian coat was so matted after months of neglect that he had to be shaved. In spite of his traumas, his sweet nature was indestructible.

XIV

Above left: My Shylock was described by our presenter in Sweden, who I like to think meant it as a compliment, as 'Pathetic!'

Above right: With Rob Edwards as the Prince in *Hamlet*. I was Polonius. Lying under the arras, dead, in Jogjakarta, a cockroach the size of a salami crawled up my leg. I almost resurrected.

Below left: Gianluca, one of Ossi's gang (see page 241). He's a Bandierista, an expert flag-juggler, who performs at festivals, both at home and abroad.

Below right: By the pool in Scopeto.

Above: With Rod in Scopeto. We've survived twenty-seven years together.

Below: My seventieth birthday. Meeting at Florian's in St Mark's Square, Venice, before taking a launch to the Cipriani for dinner, as guests of Anne and Jim McMeehan Roberts. (I gave Anne away at her wedding to Jim.) With Rod and Gareth Armstrong. I must have done something right...

XVI

8 CLASH OF TITANS
Alec and Johnny in Tunes Of Glory

ALEC GUINNESS leapt to stardom in his first film playing the small part of Herbert Pocket in David Lean's *Great Expectations*. John Mills was an established star when he played the leading role of Pip and he was not pleased when the newcomer stole his thunder.

Years later, when Ronald Neame was casting *Tunes of Glory*, which had two equally spectacular leading men's roles, he offered the part of the Colonel to Alec Guinness and the other part of Jock Sinclair to John Mills. After *Kind Hearts and Coronets* Alec was a bigger name than Mills, and he said he would play in the film if the roles were reversed. Alec wanted to play Jock Sinclair, the Major, a rough diamond promoted from the ranks who is the arch enemy of the Colonel, a product of public school and Sandhurst. John Mills agreed to swap parts. Alec won the battle for the top of the bill, though Mills was heard assuring colleagues that the billing was alphabetical, since G comes before M.

Since *Tunes of Glory* was set in a highland regiment, everybody had to wear kilts. Alec was self-conscious about the pallor of his legs, so he applied 'Man Tan' liberally to the sections of his legs beween the bottom edge of his kilt and the top of his stockings. 'Man Tan' had just been invented: once applied to the skin and left for a few hours it turns the complexion imperviously ruddy. This was designed to produce the effect of prolonged exposure to the sun without the use of make up, although it fools none but the colour blind since the resulting hue is like nothing so much as a tangerine with a hectic flush. Armed, or legged, with his new tan, Alec strode about as if his knees were blushing. To me it conjured up images of Major Jock Sinclair spreadeagled on the battlements of the castle, coyly lifting up his kilt to let the sun caress his hairy legs.

Alec became so distinguished that people forget that he had come to prominence not simply as an actor of limitless versatility, but also as a comedian: *Kind Hearts and Coronets, The Lavender Hill Mob, The Card, The Man in the White Suit.* Unlike Peter Sellers, in private Alec was wickedly and waspishly funny. Not till *The Bridge on The River Kwai* was he perceived in a 'serious' light...

I played a piper in the film; I was grateful for the time I had spent in the band when I was at school, for, although I never learned the bagpipes, I needed no instruction to imitate the apoplectic 'Puff' required when miming to the playback. Susannah York was my sweetheart – her first film – and she has proved over the years to be indestructible.

Having got John Mills' role plus top billing, Alec's superior position was doubly established, and the enmity the characters have for each other in the script was not hard for the two stars to simulate. Being gentlemen, both subsequently knighted, they behaved with impeccable manners both on set and off it, though their relationship was not cordial and their only discernible contest ended in a draw.

It was a magnificent ball at Stirling Castle, built at Pinewood Studios. The ladies wore ball gowns with a tartan sash over one shoulder. The soldiers were in full dress uniform, while civilians wore velvet, silver-buttoned tunics frothing with lace at the throat and at the wrists, some with a pheasant's claw mounted in silver and studded with jewels pinned to the kilt, with more jewels glinting in a dagger, or 'Skean-dhu', thrust down one stocking.

Alec, as Jock Sinclair, leads the eightsome reel. Throughout the story he has been relentlessly reproved by the Colonel for boisterous and un-officer-like behaviour in the mess. John Mills as the Colonel enters the scene at the top of a staircase, witnesses Jock whooping and whirling the dancers into a frenzy, watches in disbelief for a moment, then goes insane. (He later shoots himself.)

It is not the kind of scene that can be rehearsed at full pitch; John Mills had merely sketched it in till the camera started rolling. When he shouted 'Stop the dancing!' on the first take, everyone on the set, actors, extras and the film crew were struck dumb. It was an electrifying outburst. It was a wide shot with Alec and the dancers in the foreground, and John Mills in splendid isolation at the top of the stairs at the back. At the end of the first take there was spontaneous and deserved applause for John Mills' performance, then there was the usual confab between the director and the cameraman before Ronnie Neame sadly shook his head and we heard the dreaded words 'Going again!'

There was a groan of disappointment, and Johnny Mills looked crestfallen.

'He'll never be able to repeat it!' we muttered among ourselves.

'No good?' John Mills asked the director.

'Not you Johnny,' Neame assured him. 'Bloody marvellous. Keep it up. It's a tricky one. Marks, I'm afraid. Can we have a bigger mark for Mr Guinness?'

As the chippy hammered a slat into the floor so that Alec could feel his mark even if he couldn't see it, Ronnie Neame had a word with him. 'Absolutely crucial these marks, Alec.'

'Sorry Ronnie.'

'Are you happy with that?' Neame tapped the slat with his toe.

Alec said, 'It won't happen again.'

But it did. And again, And again. And again. And again! We went to six takes before Alec managed to hit his mark. John Mills' voice was hoarse by the time they got it in the can, but his performance remained fresh and thrilling throughout. It was an object lesson in professionalism and restraint.

It is not easy when whirling around at twenty miles an hour to stop dead on a strip of wood three centimetres long, but I could see by the slitty way the Colonel regarded Jock that John Mills thought it should have been five takes easier than that.

9 THE CASTING COUCH
Jimmy Woolf

THE SEAL on my status as an actor was set when I was invited to appear at the London Palladium in *The Night of a Hundred Stars*, which was an annual event for charity performed by everybody who was anybody in the business. It began at midnight after all the other theatres had closed, so that there were as many artistes in the audience as there were on the stage, and the resulting mutual-admiration and in-joke atmosphere would have been nauseating to an older or a more cynical performer.

No one did what they were famous for doing. Comics would play Hamlet, and Hamlets would play the banjo. John Mills and Laurence Olivier did The Tramp routine – 'We're a Coupla Swells' – from *Easter Parade*. Laurence Harvey and Simone Signoret sang a duet. The second half of the show was comprised of a night club scene with a bona fide Cabaret Artiste – Judy Garland, Frank Sinatra, Lena Horne, Tom Jones – preceded by a walk-down of celebrities who had flown in to justify the boast of 'A Hundred Stars': Liz Taylor, Cary Grant, Ethel Merman, Burt Lancaster. It was a Big Night. I appeared in it four times, but always as part of a chorus line composed of young hopefuls: Peter O'Toole, Sean Connery, Jeremy Brett, Gordon Jackson, Roger Moore. We rehearsed about half-a-dozen times, and did a passable version of 'Tea for Two' with top-hats and canes one year, 'There is Nothing Like a Dame' from *South Pacific* another, stripped to the waist with glycerined pectorals and little Barbara Windsor flaunting her assets.

The presenters of this spectacular entertainment were Charles Russell and Lance Hamilton. They had managed Noël Coward's estate for some years, but they were also involved in property, and they ended up multimillionaires. They invited me to tea at one of their residences – I think it was in Islington, or it may have been Belgravia, for they moved house so often getting rich that it was confusing. Their invitation reeked of intrigue. Their manner was often conspiratorial and the opposite of above board.

Over doughnuts and a chocolate cake they made me a proposition. The most illustrious independent film producer in the country at that time was Jimmy Woolf. *Room At The Top*, which had launched Laurence Harvey into international stardom, had been made by his company Romulus Films which Jimmy ran with his brother John. Romulus had a string of award-winning classic films to their credit, including *The African Queen* with Humphrey Bogart and Katharine Hepburn, and *Moulin Rouge* starring Jose Ferrer and Zsa Zsa Gabor. Jimmy was now planning to make *Lawrence of Arabia*, with David Lean directing.

According to Charles and Lance, Jimmy had taken a serious shine to me.

It was well known in the business that Jimmy was in love with Laurence Harvey. He had put his protégé into film after film, all of which had flopped, until he bought the film rights to John Braine's sensational best-seller, contracted the great Simone Signoret to play opposite Harvey, and finally made his lover a star. But Harvey kept marrying to further his career. Larry's whoredom was so blatant it was disarming. As a teenager, fresh from South Africa, he started out living with Hermione Baddeley, a brilliantly talented but grotesquely blowsy star of intimate revue who was more than twice his age. Then he married Margaret Leighton – old enough to be his mother, but a woman of style and one of the best actresses of her generation. When this marriage was over, he married Joan Cohn, the widow of the Managing Director of Columbia Studios, who had taken over her late husband's job and was now a millionairess with all the power of the Hollywood Studios at her command. And throughout all these career marriages, he still managed to string Jimmy Woolf along – though, not surprisingly, Jimmy's constancy wavered.

He had tried Terence Stamp. I cannot imagine he got very far. He had tried Albert Finney. He must have got nowhere at all. Now he wanted to try me. At any rate, he had asked Charles and Lance to introduce me to him.

'Chocolate cake?'

'Thanks.'

Charles passed me a Crown Derby plate with a tiny linen napkin and a little two-pronged pastry fork.

'Treat him badly, John,' Charles advised me, pouring the china tea through a silver strainer. 'No good being nice to him. He likes to be treated badly.'

I had no idea how to start treating anyone badly.

'I pretend for a living,' I said to my advisers rather pompously, 'and I could pretend for five minutes in my private life. But I couldn't keep it up. If he doesn't like me as I am, too bad.'

Charles and Lance exchanged a withering look.

'He hasn't cast Lawrence in *Lawrence of Arabia* yet. They want someone young – someone new.'

Lance added, passing my tea – 'And he likes to be treated badly.'

'Don't say we didn't warn you.'

I spent sleepless nights worrying: not simply over the terrifying prospect of going through some nameless sexual practices with a man I knew by report to be no Apollo – although I worried about that too – but I was fretting over the bigger issue of prostitution, of selling my body for professional gain, something I had never had to do. I spoke to George.

'If Jimmy Woolf wants me to go to bed with him I know it'll be a disaster. I'll probably be worse off than I was before. But if *Lawrence of Arabia* is on offer, I'm going to at least TRY to be a whore for a part like that. What do you think?'

The answer was quite a lot. None of it conducive of self-esteem. It was a long night. The first nail in my coffin.

Jimmy Woolf lived alone in a suite of rooms in Grosvenor House on Park Lane. When I got to know him well, I would ring the bell of his suite and he would let me in, clad only in a dressing-gown. The first time he greeted me in such *déshabille*, I was prepared for the worst, but nothing happened.

I was invited to dinner two or three times a week for two years. Every time he was in his dressing-gown. And every time he would disappear into the bedroom and hold an inaudible conversation with someone he informed me later was his doctor who came daily to give him an injection of Vitamin B12. I believed him then. I don't now.

Who was this doctor? I never saw him. Of course, Grosvenor House being a hotel, every room has a door giving direct access to the public corridor without going through any of the other rooms. Was Jimmy talking to himself? Why did his vitamin injection always coincide to the minute with my arrival? Was it a vitamin injection at all?

He lived in the middle of a hectic social whirl and I met galaxies of stars at his apartment. I felt for that brief period as if I had wormed my way into the very core of the Golden Apple. I had starred in six films, but by Hollywood standards I was small time. Because of their host's known proclivities, I was sometimes treated like just another in a long line of 'Jimmy's Pashes'. This was hard to take, and harder to forgive.

A memorable transgressor in this respect was Martita Hunt. A distinguished character actress, Martita was bursting with self-importance. Alec Guinness wrote about her sympathetically in his memoirs, but you can only talk as you find. She looked like a sheep, so she had decided from an early age to be a character, which was tiring for the company she kept. She would stand on her head to illustrate a story, or grab the flowers from a vase and stuff them up her skirt, and everyone had to laugh uproariously.

I had just been to see Rouben Mamoulian for the role of the young gigolo in the film of Tennessee Williams' *The Roman Spring of Mrs Stone*. The unknown Warren Beatty got the part… For every job you get you miss ten. 'Heat' and 'kitchens' come to mind.

Martita was a close friend of Vivien Leigh who was to play Mrs Stone.

'She's too young,' I opined, since I had read the book.

'What do you mean too young?' Martita, who had been happily hanging on a door, dropped to the carpet and glared at me.

'The point that Tennessee Williams makes in his book is that Mrs Stone feels liberated sexually by the menopause. She is no longer able to conceive a child, so she feels free to screw around. Vivien Leigh looks too young to be menopausal.'

It was as if I had lit a fire in her knickers.

'You stupid boy! You know nothing! How can you understand a woman's psychology?'

'I'm not making any claims to understanding a woman's psychology, I'm just telling you what Tennessee Williams wrote!'

'Oh, take him away!' she commanded the room at large. 'He is quite insufferable!'

Was Martita Hunt menopausal herself and resentful of the implications of this, which were Tennessee Williams' conclusions and not mine? Or did she consider it bad manners to refer to the possibilities of sex as recreation, and indeed to the inexorable passage of time itself? Or was she put out that I was not deferential, that I spoke to her like an adult, and did not behave myself like Jimmy's shame-faced piece of fluff? Silly cow.

Jimmy Woolf was a bold and gifted producer but fundamentally a pernicious man. He was one of those power-driven gamblers who breed in the film industry like termites in rotten timber. In his profession he was astute, but in life he lacked any wisdom. He harboured grievances, vowed revenge, wreaked retribution and plotted spiteful deceptions to wound and to score points off his adversaries, as if it made some sort of sense. I've seen him throw a plate at a waiter in uncontrolled fury because his steak was overdone – then, contrite, slip him a tenner to make amends. He had baleful blue eyes and an ingratiating manner which utterly belied his steely will. He was always kind to me. He was barely fifty when he died of a drugs overdose. It was almost certainly an accident, since he took a lot of drugs, a fact of which I was only fully aware after his death. I should feel shame in betraying someone who cannot defend himself, but he died without heirs so long ago there is no sense in penning polite platitudes.

I didn't even try to treat Jimmy badly, which is no doubt the reason, thank God, that I didn't arouse him sexually. He lavished presents on me: a Cartier watch, gold cufflinks, a Fabergé gold cigarette case with a ruby clasp, and finally the down payment for my Aston Martin. I felt guilty accepting these gifts for nothing in return. But clearly not guilty enough…

According to Charles and Lance I should have flung them in his face demanding more. In the two years or so of our acquaintance he would often croon to me about how desirable I was, almost as if by saying it he might believe it and something in him might respond, but it never did. All that time hob-nobbing with Liz and Monty and Marlon and Judy, being lavishly entertained at glittering parties and grand suppers, I played out the charade of being Jimmy's latest Pash, which did not automatically brand me as 'queer' since he was known to like normal men. I put a brave face on this situation because I was ambitious. Towards the end, there was also the very real prospect of *Lawrence of Arabia* ahead. And I held onto my self-respect because I knew, even if no one else did, that I wasn't sleeping with him.

Jimmy arranged for me to meet David Lean in the Park Lane Hotel, which is not in Park Lane at all, but in Piccadilly. He was a formidable man who seemed to me to be playing the part of a Great Film Director exceedingly well. He was seeing very few people, and although he was polite I knew he was unimpressed by my modest demeanour and my stature, even though Lawrence was in real life a short man. I guessed he was looking for Star Quality in an actor, a dash of flamboyance mixed and stirred with the cold Threat of Danger.

The good old T of D. I could act all that, but I couldn't claim that these were my salient characteristics – that I knocked you in the eye with my panache or made your hair stand on end like a lavatory brush with my gimlet gaze.

I was proved right when Peter O'Toole was cast in the end. The rest is history.

But I got a consolation prize.

10 BAFTA NOMINATION
The Trials of Oscar Wilde

SINCE DAVID LEAN didn't want me for Lawrence, Jimmy let me know that Warwick Films, who were making *The Trials of Oscar Wilde* with Peter Finch as Oscar, had still not found the young man to play Lord Alfred Douglas – 'Bosie' – although they had tested no fewer than six actors for the part.

My agent felt strongly that it would be disastrous for my career to play a homosexual since I was one, so I was apprehensive. But the role of Bosie was sensational, and if I got it I had no intention of playing him with a lisp and a wiggle, so I begged the company to consider me.

They sent me two scenes through the post, with a letter explaining that they were doing no more film-tests. If I prepared an audition, however, they would see me.

This was not only unprecedented, it did not bode well. If they were not prepared to spend the measly amount of money, in film terms, to test me on celluloid, they clearly had little faith that I could play the part as they wanted it to be played. I had a track record of which I was not ashamed, and I could easily have taken umbrage at this treatment of me as if I were a beginner. But I wanted the role so badly I swallowed my pride.

I rehearsed my scenes at home as if for a play. Many fine screen actors learn their lines only sketchily, believing that uncertainty gives the impression of spontaneity. This may be true with contemporary, ultra-real, semi-improvised scripts, but with stylish, period drama, I believe you can only attain the appearance of spontaneity if you are so certain of the lines you can do anything with them. Then no extraneous interruption can possibly throw you.

At my own expense and on my own initiative, I went to Monty Berman's, the favoured theatrical and film costumier at the time, and from their vast stock of genuine period costumes I chose a beautifully cut Edwardian suit which flattered my figure. Since my hair is mouse coloured, I dusted it with gold, but subtly, so that I didn't look like a chorus boy from an Ivor Novello operetta. I packed my props – a bread-knife, a large leather-bound book, and a pile of papers – into a holdall, and after a good-natured exchange with a startled cabby, I took a taxi to South Audley Street and gave the performance of my life.

What followed had never happened to me before and it has never happened since. The production team did not say as they invariably do, 'Thank you. We'll let you know', or 'We'll call your agent.' There were four of them: Cubby Broccoli, Irving Allen (Producers), John Redway (Casting) and Ken Hughes (Director). They asked me to wait while they retired to the next room. They were gone for no more than a few minutes, and when they came back Ken Hughes said, 'Thank you John. You've got the part.'

This was one of the happiest moments of my life.

Apart from Peter Finch as Wilde, they had Yvonne Mitchell as Constance his wife, Lionel Jeffries as Lord Queensberry – Bosie's father – and Nigel Patrick and James Mason as Defence and Prosecuting Counsels respectively. No expense was spared on sets and costumes, though we made the film in six weeks working seven days a week, since 20th Century Fox were making a film on the same subject at the same time and it was a race to see who could finish first.

Much of Ken Hughes' script was based on authenticated fact, and in one scene Lord Queensberry calls Bosie a pervert and slaps his face. Bosie turns on his father, saying that he is going to kill him and threatening that he is about to buy a gun for this purpose. This Bosie actually did, firing it off in the Café Royal where the bullet shattered the glass ceiling, missing his father by miles but causing a considerable stir in fashionable circles. The Queensberries were all mad.

The script called for a close up of me threatening parricide after my father has slapped my face. Ken was satisfied by the first take but I was not. I knew I could do better so I begged a re-take. Ken's brow furrowed as he consulted his watch. We had to get six minutes in the can every day or we should fall badly behind in the race against the clock – a race which engendered an atmosphere of co-operation and trust on the set which I have never experienced in any other film that I have worked on.

'Okay,' Ken said wearily, knowing I would not have claimed that I could improve on the take if I had not felt strongly that I would be able to deliver something extra.

Lionel Jeffries, who was standing behind the camera to cue me, stepped forward.

'John!' he said urgently. 'Would it help if I really thumped you?'

He had pulled his punch on the long shot to avoid hospitalising me and torpedoing the picture.

'No,' I said, patting his shoulder. 'Thanks all the same.'

Ken shouted, 'Roll it!' In the short pause for the camera to gain speed, before the director would shout 'Action!', I had second thoughts.

'Yes!' I hissed at Lionel. 'Hit me!'

Without a moment's hesitation Lionel advanced and delivered such a slap to my face it set my head spinning. It brought tears to my eyes and I saw stars. My pupils dilated, my breathing became spasmodic, the fury in my whole demeanour was unfeigned. I didn't have to act. I had to fight to keep calm. I said my lines simply, too simply, with a venom the more lethal because it was not expressed.

'Leave me alone. Or I will buy a gun. And before God I swear I will kill you without compunction.'

CUT. First Ken embraced me with tears in his eyes. Then I hugged Lionel. We both had tears in ours.

Actors' emotions are close to the surface. Because we can call on them so readily, we are accused of being shallow and insincere and dubbed sentimental 'Luvvies'. Ought our children to be torn from us before we weep? Or our lives be threatened before we rage? 'Deep', 'shallow' – these are English concepts. I have lived half the year in Italy for over thirty years, and Italians weep and rage on a daily basis and no one ever calls them shallow.

The Fox film opened in the West End the day Ken finished editing ours. Robert Morley, an actor of great charm and wit, played Wilde. Oscar had both these qualitites in abundance, but Morley was fifteen years too old and absurdly fat. Wilde was overweight, but he was tall and attractive with a glorious voice. This is attested to by his contemporaries. John Neville played Bosie. Ralph Richardson played Carson, the prosecuting counsel, and he was spellbinding as always, but the film was shot with a very small budget in black and white, and after a week or two in London and the provinces, it sank without trace.

Our version was in wide-screen colour, with sumptuous sets and costumes. It had an impetus that reached right out of the screen into the stalls, bred of panic and the urgency with which it had been shot. It was hailed as a triumph.

Both Peter Finch and I were nominated by The British Film Academy Award for Best Actor. I didn't win, of course. It would have been unseemly if I had, since my fellow nominees were: Alec Guinness, John Mills, Laurence Olivier and Peter Finch. 'Finchy' won. A darling man and a great actor, particularly on the screen. The drink got him in the end. Like Richard Burton, Ian Hendry, Robert Stephens, and too many others to be counted.

FOUR

A Precarious Foothold

1 THE FRENCH CONNECTION
Dany Robin and The Waltz of the Toreadors

PETER SELLERS was the living confirmation of the cliché that Funny Men are depressives, for in private he was a joyless man. But he was touched with genius. In the film of *The Waltz of the Toreadors* by Jean Anouilh he played the General, a vainglorious randy old goat, and his comic timing and his acute perception of human foibles made you cry as well as laugh, which only great comedians can do.

I was playing the General's secretary in our film which we were making on location at Leeds Castle and in Pinewood Studios. Sophia Loren, with whom I had yet to work in *El Cid*, was working on the other side of London at Elstree.

Peter had just split up with his wife and the mother of his two children. He was living in the Dorchester, and like half the civilised world he had fallen in love with Sophia. With his phenomenal success, he had taken to playing the Film Star with a vengeance. Almost overnight, it seemed, he had lost two stones in weight, which probably contributed to his premature death from a heart attack some years later. He became vain about his appearance, which had never been his strong suit; he would pose for still photographs smouldering over one shoulder like a heart-throb, when all his life he had been a fat, mother-ridden wimp, thoroughly spoilt and a bit of a cry-baby.

He loved toys. He had three cars at a time, including a 'Roller' and a DB4 Aston Martin, and he would change them almost on a monthly basis. He always had the newest camera, tape recorder, miniature television or cine-camera, which he would show off to the dumbly sycophantic extras like the rich kid to the orphans in the snow on Christmas morning. In short, he had never grown up. Which of course was at the root of his genius.

And it was also the reason why he behaved like a love-sick teenager. Sophia was happily married to the producer Carlo Ponti, who was her Svengali – a father-figure much older than Sophia, a foot shorter and as bald as an egg; and despite her sexual allure she was known to be chaste and unavailable for casual affairs. Perhaps this fanned the flames of Peter's ardour.

In his caravan, while we were waiting for the lamps and the reflectors to be positioned and the camera track to be laid, he would regale me about the nights he had spent gazing up at the cracks between the curtains of her apartment when he had been refused entry for the umpteenth time. Or how he had bought all the red roses from the florist's in Park Lane, and had had them delivered to the Elstree Studios with stray blooms spilling from the windows of his Rolls Royce. Just like in the Movies.

In our own movie, meanwhile, the General's secretary (me) falls in love with the General's mistress. She was played by Dany Robin, a French actress of incomparable beauty and wit who was the paramount star of her generation in her native country. She had triumphed briefly in Hollywood opposite Kirk Douglas in *Act of Love* directed by Edward Dmytryk, but her accent made her difficult to cast in America. At a not so very subliminal level, before I even met Dany, her boy's name intrigued me.

But she was not remotely boyish. She was forthright, funny, clever, completely uncoquettish, older than me by ten years and so in my eyes, womanly. She was warm and open and quite devastating. She was married, so I felt safe to develop a schoolboy crush.

We had love scenes together, and she responded to my kisses with enthusiasm, but within the requirements of the script. But those requirements were wide in scope. Galloping on horseback, I had to kidnap her from a train moving at fifty miles an hour. I prided myself on my horsemanship, so I did all but one shot in the sequence without a stunt double. It was easy because Dany was watching me. To win Dany's approval I would have done the last shot as well – the most dangerous one – snatching her from the racing train and flinging her in front of me across the pummel of my saddle. Happily it was forbidden by the insurance company.

Then I had to rescue her from drowning in an ornamental lake in the magnificent landscaped grounds of Leeds Castle. It was November by this time. The logic of filming invariably dictates that beach, swimming and drowning episodes and any other scenes requiring total immersion al fresco must be shot when the artistes are most likely to catch pneumonia. This anomaly is all to do with 'Scheduling', where there are important factors to be considered, like money, compared with which the actors' comfort is of no importance.

Dany was in corsets, petticoats and furbelows, and I was in the uniform of a subaltern in the Grénadiers d'Algérie. We were both cocooned in thermal underwear from head to toe, not primarily for our health or for our comfort, but yet again at the insistence of the insurance company. In our caravans, the wardrobe department had laid out warm bathtowels and dressing-gowns and slippers and brandy and hot-water bottles, as well as several changes of clothing. We spent the whole day in and out of the lake in sub-zero temperatures, towelling, and changing, and shivering and getting pissed on cognac. It was a day of almost undiluted joy. And in the course of it, the make-believe became reality, and I began to fall in love.

In truth, I was as immature and foolish as Peter Sellers. Where could this feeling for Dany lead?

I had been living with George for four years, and we were totally committed to one another. We had disagreements, principally over my fear of journalists or anyone in the business discovering that I was sharing my life with a man. He never answered the telephone. There were no answering machines in those days. And we were never seen together on the sort of occasions where the Press might be in attendance. At airports, we walked separately, and met up on board the plane. But we were mostly happy together. Or as happy, as I saw it, as two men could ever be.

Was this feeling for Dany the onset of another of my experiments, doomed yet again to failure and disappointment? For both parties? I had spent nearly a year and a great deal of money in Analysis and was getting on with my double life as best I could.

But perhaps I was changing? Nothing in the whole wide world need be inscribed on tablets of stone. There might still be hope for me…

Dany was married to a film star, Georges Marschal. 'He must be thick!' I told myself, for he had no pretensions at all to being an actor; he was pure beefcake, appearing as Achilles or Jason in muscleman biopics made in Italy on shoestring budgets. But they had two children, Chantal and Daniel. Dany had shown me photographs, father and mother with their two beautiful children like something out of a story book, taken at their Château in the middle of a forest not far from Paris. Both Dany and Georges, like me, had come from a poor background, and had created their rural idyll entirely by dint of their own efforts. Did this romantic picture of family life make my profound but confused passion for Dany safer? Or more hazardous?

Le Château de Guiche is in the depths of the Forêt de Rambouillet, yet only half-an-hour's drive from the Arc de Triomphe. Its perfectly regular façade can be seen as you leave the Autoroute N 12, behind cast-iron gates which open onto a rectangular pond where swans symmetrically preen in their own reflections.

There was a private zoo composed of over a hundred small animals: badgers, otters, stoats, some gazelles, capuchin monkeys, countless rabbits, guinea pigs and gerbils, herons, flamingos and other exotic birds, plus the swans on the pond, six peahens and four peacocks that wandered the grounds shrieking like ganders on crack...

They also had a stable with six horses and a groom to look after them. The horses were *trotteurs*, since they were used primarily for stag hunting, and in *La Chasse* the trot is the only permissible gait.

She had invited me while we were sitting on our folding chairs behind the flats of the ballroom set, waiting for our call onto the set of *The Waltz of the Toreadors*.

'Georges is on location in Greenland,' she confided. 'He's playing Gunnar in some Icelandic Saga. Would you like to come to Rambouillet during our break?'

We had a week off while they filmed all the family scenes, with Peter, Maggie Leighton, Prunella Scales and Cyril Cusack.

To say I flushed would not describe my reaction. I thought the blood would spout from my ears.

'Are you serious?'

'Does that mean you'll come?'

Perhaps all she felt for me was affection without the taint of desire. If so, why had she invited me to her home during the one period in the whole of their lives that her husband was away at the North Pole?

Taking a mighty breath I nodded, for I did not trust myself to speak. George would make the furniture fly, but I was prepared to suffer his rage.

I went.

'I've never hunted in my life, except in a film, without a fox. They cut in shots of the fox running afterwards.'

'Fox hunting is a participant sport with many casualties – even deaths, every season. But stag hunting is not dangerous. It is mediaeval – a spectator sport. The hunt-followers have to stay on the bridle paths which have been cut through the forest for this purpose.'

'Is it true the stag is killed with a sword?'

'Oh, yes! It is a noble beast, and it dies a noble death!'

'Why is it more noble to die by a sword than by a bullet?'

'We must hold onto our ancient rituals, they are our continuity, our recognition of where we come from, they give our lives meaning. It is just something you feel in your bones. You think it is cruel, I know.'

'I don't think it's kind.'

She leant over and cupped my cheek in her hand.

'We love all our animals. You can see that. We truly love them, and we are never cruel to them. But it is not cruel to die. We all have to die. The wild deer have a wonderful life in the forest. They have enough food, they mate and they have their young, they are as free as the air. In nature, they will begin to die slowly of an agonising old age, or they will be savaged by a rival stag and left for days and days to die. With *La Chasse*, they spend the last day of their happy and fulfilled lives fleeing through the trees to be brought to bay and killed quickly in such a panoply of sound and excitement that there is no place for pain. They are in shock, and everyone knows that shock is an anaesthetic. Pain is only suffered in tranquillity. What a wonderful way to die! We are not sentimental about animals like the English.'

'Scottish.'

'Sorry, Scottish. Aren't the Scottish sentimental about animals?'

'On the evidence I would have to say no. Our chief export is Death. Stags and pheasants. And Whisky. And you might even call Whisky a slow death. I have problems with killing animals for fun.'

'It is the chase which is for fun, not the death. No hunter takes part in the sport to revel in the bloodshed at the end of it. By far the greatest majority don't even see the death of the quarry.'

'And you think the fun of the chase justifies terrifying an animal to the point of exhaustion and then killing it?'

'It is a prey's survival mechanism to flee! They flee at the slightest suggestion of danger, often imaginary. Fleeing is what they do when they're not eating or mating. They are professional flee-ers. It's not terror they feel. They have no intimations of mortality! They cannot imagine death! It's their nature to get away, and get away, and get away, till finally, in shock, painlessly they are dispatched! Serving the stag is very beautiful. It is also tragic, and it stirs ancient emotions which need stirring. If only everyone could hunt, as all our forefathers did. It's in our genes. Perhaps there would be less war, less violence, less cruelty to one another. You will see. The hunt leaves one feeling sad, and full of wonder, and at peace.' She smiled. 'I know you were in doubt before you came. But you're here, and you've brought your lovely outfit, and you can't wait to show it off.'

'As Mae West said, if I have to choose between two evils, I'll opt for the one I haven't tried.'

The livery of the Brissac hunt-followers is dove-grey. The huntsmen are in forest green and they wear tricorn hats. The women without exception wear skirts that sweep the ground. Most, therefore, ride side-saddle, though it is permissible for them to wear breeches underneath, with the skirt split to the waist so that they can ride astride.

Dany was straight out of *L'Aigle à deux têtes*. She always rode astride, so that her long limbs were caressed in dove-grey moleskin breeches and her skirt billowed like a crinoline when she walked. At her throat an emerald pin secured her creamy Thai-silk stock. Her miniature tricorn made her face a Valentine, and when she lowered her veil, donned her elbow-length gloves and flexed her crop before mounting, it was hard to believe that someone in the shadows was not going to pipe up with: 'ACTION!'

The Meet took place in a clearing in the forest. I was introduced first to the Duke who greeted me with an abstracted air, then later I caught him looking me up and down, searching slyly for glaring solecisms. I was then introduced to several of Dany's friends. With my bowler buckling my ears at the side, I was heartily shaking the ladies' hands, when out of the corner of my eye I spied how French hunters greet the fair sex. With a flourish the hat is removed from the head with the right hand and tucked under the left arm. The gentleman then delicately raises the lady's gloved right hand from the horizontal – an inch or two, no more – as in a dance. He then bows his head over the hand without bringing it into contact with his lips – he doesn't even smack the air with them – all the while murmuring something excessively polite that in this case certainly was not '*Enchanté*'.

I thought, 'This is like an initiation ceremony in Papua New Guinea!'

Screwing my hat even tighter over my ears, I crushed fluttering little velvet-clad fingers in my manly grip. A damsel left massaging one hand with the other after our introduction turned to her companion as I passed and spat, '*Les Anglais!*'

'*Ecossais!*' I corrected her.

It was a soft morning in November with no nip in the air. Swathes of mist draped the branches, which were still dappled with ochre and gold like beaten bronze.

The hunt ceremony began with the catechism, conducted in mediaeval French in the style of the epic poem *Le Chanson de Roland*.

The Duke mounted his sleek black gelding just as the stag hounds – magnificent animals blazoned with the same motley of tan-black-and-white as fox hounds, only the size of Great Danes – appeared through the mist, yoked together and restrained by the grooms. The Duke, with a flick of his glove to command silence, reached above him to break a twig from the branch of a kingly oak. Snapping the twig in two, he placed one half over the other to form a cross; then laying his left hand solemnly against his heart he intoned a mediaeval prayer to Saint Hubert, the Patron Saint of *La Chasse*. When he crossed himself and kissed his thumb, the French horns played a fanfare that set the misty morning ablaze.

Horses plunged, savage commands, '*Assez! En Bas!*', hounds ululating, an urgent shout, hoarse cries as the rabble scrambled to make way for the Duke's horse which danced a hornpipe with frustration, as his master restrained him from charging off into the forest at a gallop. A lifetime's training never to break from the extended trot was forgotten for a brief moment in the delirium of the 'Off!'

So at last the Hunt had started; a phalanx of huntsmen hobby-horsed past us, their Sherwood Green livery slashed with the gold of their trumpets; veiled women in ghostly grey habits wielding crops as long as an angler's rod clung to the flanks of their gleaming steeds like puppets flung against a gong.

At every intersection, by listening to the music of the hunters, we gleaned information; sometimes it was contradictory, sometimes we sped off north, only to have to retrace our steps and branch off to the east, but gradually we closed in, and reined in our horses at the junction of five paths.

A faint crashing of the undergrowth, and far away along the wide avenue, the Lord of the Forest broke cover for a fleeting moment, his antlers raking the last leaves from the trees, then there was nothing but the sound of his hooves pounding on the peaty floor, pounding, pounding nearer, and the cracking of branches.

He was almost upon us. His harsh winter coat was stained black with sweat and his lolling tongue slung froth at the sky, his huge eyes were dark with fear and the thundering gasps from his labouring lungs were borne off on the wind as he smashed again into the wood and was gone.

We reined in at the top of a treeless hill. A thick wall of rushes grew tall around the edges of a little lake. The stag had taken to the water, as hunted animals frequently do when their strength is giving out and there is nowhere else to run. In his panic his efforts to gallop or to swim dug him deeper into the mud. The pack of hounds ran round and round the perimeter of the lake howling and yelping with frustration, looking for a break in the defences.

Two of the leading hounds finally crashed through the reeds and started swimming towards the afflicted deer. The dogs were now at a disadvantage. There is no doubt that their instinct was to tear out the throat of their quarry, but with their feet in the water, they did not have the purchase to carry out their intention. They snapped ineffectually, and continued to howl, but the stag still had enough strength left to ram them with his antlers, hurling the smaller of the two squealing into the air.

It is at this moment that the huntsman is supposed to ride up with his mighty sword held high, a sword tempered in the furnaces of Toledo and blessed by Saint Hubert, the hunters' intermediary with God, and offering a prayer of thanksgiving, cleanly deliver the *coup de grâce*.

That was not, however, how it happened. Just as I would take no pleasure in describing the process of slaughtering an animal in an abattoir, so I will stop my account of the kill here. The mess was so absolute, they had to shoot the stag in the end.

Dany was not disturbed, as I was, just upset that I had not seen a clean and noble kill and a dignified death. She assured me that this *debâcle* was as rare as it was unfortunate. I wanted to believe her, and I certainly did not hold her responsible for a hideously botched climax to a memorable day.

In the evening, after a healing bath, we sat in the drawing room which was panelled with walnut the colour of wild honey in front of a blazing log fire drinking Dany's favourite apéritif, Negroni, composed of equal parts of gin and Campari, bitter-sweet and strong.

I heard Albinoni's *Adagio* for the first time. I'd never heard Beethoven or Mozart till I was fifteen, when Spotty Calder played me some 'Good Bits' with his wooden needles. So Albinoni is pretty hot stuff, considering.

Both coming as we did from poor backgrounds, our friendship had been born of our childlike amazement at the change in our fortunes, no matter how short-lived our success in the film business might turn out to be. By this time I loved her more than I had ever loved a woman, but there was an ineffable ache at the heart of it. She had a husband whom I believe she loved, two heart-stoppingly beautiful children who were the very centre of her being, and a life which was as near perfection as any I had yet come across. She would never relinquish it. Nor did I expect her to. And this impasse both soured and sweetened our last night together.

For Dany loved me too in a way. She was so used to deflecting male advances that she knew without my telling her that the worship she could spy in my eye was not lust in hiding. Having spent four nights under the same roof with never so much as a tap on her bedroom door must have made that clear.

So after supper when she led me to her bed like a heathen sacrifice roped with yokes of flowers, it was not a prelude to the Kama Sutra, but to the tender expression of a hopeless love, a love which had no future except in my remembering it, with an ache in my heart, forever.

2 COUNTRY SQUIRE
Playing at Film Stars

ROUT'S GREEN FARMHOUSE was like a Christmas card, a genuine Elizabethan Gingerbread Cottage with thatched roof, mullioned windows, inglenooks and oak-beamed ceilings at eye-level. Children and dwarfs didn't have to duck to avoid fracturing their skulls, and it was a really comfortable house once you were in bed or sitting down. Upstairs, when manoeuvring the ancient planked floors, you had to clamp your hands to the walls as if you were rounding the Cape in a force ten gale... American guests called it 'Just dorling!' I would have preferred something less 'dorling' like a Georgian manor house, but the setting of Rout's Green Farm was so lovely, it was within reach of London and the studios, the amount of land was just right, and there was a little house at the gate that would be ideal for the servants.

I had by this time made twelve films and had recovered from the financial debacle of Posket Farm. I updated my acid green MGA to a blue Aston Martin, George had a shooting brake (as estate cars were called in those days), and we had bought a farm in Buckinghamshire, with an orchard and ten acres where I planned to keep horses. This dramatic change in our domestic arrangements can be laid firmly at the door of Dirk Bogarde and Dany Robin. I had been a guest in Dirk's gorgeous houses at Chalfont St Giles, Beaconsfield, and then in Surrey, and I had thought then – 'Oh, this is how you do it!' My visit to Rambouillet had tempered my resolve to live like a FILM STAR while I had the chance. If you come from a council estate in Glasgow, why not?

We installed Brian and Mary in the gatehouse to act as gardener and housekeeper. Brian had been a steward in the RAF, so as well as his gardening duties we got him to serve at table when we had guests. We bought him a white jacket and relegated his wife Mary to the kitchen to break the plates and burn the pastry to her heart's content, while Brian played the spoons and tipped the vegetables into people's laps regularly as he butled. Every time we entertained I was a nervous wreck.

When I wasn't working I spent my life hiding from Brian, who kept asking me what he ought to do on the land, and I quickly ran out of ideas. After six months the situation had brought me to my knees. I conceded defeat, and acknowledged that I did not have the balls to handle servants. I wrote them glowing references they didn't deserve and packed them off to some poor suckers in Wiltshire.

At the farm we had two magnificent Rhodesian Ridgebacks, who produced a litter of eleven puppies; we also had three cats and countless kittens, a flock of white pigeons, and a herd of jersey cows in the field till the stable was built and I could buy a horse. We had *The Horse and Hound* delivered weekly, and I drove round the country trying out various mounts till I fell in love with a four-year-old chestnut mare and arranged for her to be boxed from Oxfordshire.

We entertained discreetly, inviting only people who could be trusted not to blow our cover: Luchino Visconti, with his entourage; Tab Hunter and Tom Tryon; Elaine Stritch; Dirk and Tony Forwood; Pat and Derek Nimmo; Peter Finch and his lovely South African wife, Yolande (his second). Finchy always drank too much, which meant they had to stay the night.

That chestnut mare was the first and last horse I never bought. I had already sent the cheque when I was offered a job I couldn't refuse. It meant being out of the country for six months, so the mare's owners kindly tore up the cheque, and I remained forever horseless.

3 THE IMMORTALS
Sophia and Chuck on El Cid

I WAS TO PLAY the part of Alfonso, King of Spain, in one of the greatest historical epics ever seen on the screen, *El Cid*. The stars were Charlton Heston and Sophia Loren.

Rodrigo Diaz ('El Cid') was a kingmaker, a warrior, a statesman and a passionate advocate of tolerance for the Moorish Emirs who had settled in the south; in eleventh-century Spain he was a hero of almost divine stature, and he remains a paragon for all time. In Samuel Bronston, a producer cast in the mould of Cecil B de Mille, we had the mad scientist, who instead of wanting to destroy the world was determined to create it, a mediaeval world authentic to the last gyve and bodkin. He wooed and won the co-operation of the Spanish government at the highest level to make a film that would blazon the splendours of Spain to the world, capturing forever on celluloid the cathedrals and the great castles of Zaragossa, Valladolid and Belmonte, the snow-capped mountains and the sweeping plains and the breathtaking pageantry of the mediaeval court of Alfonso The Sixth (me!). El Cid was the prophet of integration, and at this watershed in Spanish history some nine hundred years ago, he led the way for a great Christian kingdom to embrace the culture and respect the code of honour of Islam alongside its own.

This was in the days before computer graphics and image augmentation. Everything and everybody up there on that gigantic screen was real. For the Battle for Valencia, the entire Spanish army was put at our disposal. Seven thousand men: the number of hoplites in Alexander the Great's army when he conquered the Persians. These were not film extras but conscripted soldiers, and their tented camp covered an area of four square miles. They fed themselves from their billy-cans over cooking fires. All seven thousand were fitted out every morning before dawn with chain mail and armour and helmets which had been made to authentic designs in a factory requisitioned for the purpose. There were a thousand army horses, and their tented stables stretched for three miles along the littoral.

The horses were tacked in old iron bridles and bucket stirrups and were schooled for three months before filming the Battle for Valencia. They had to be taught to respond to hand-reining with the left hand, since the right was used for wielding a broadsword, and not to flinch as these weapons were swung past their eyes. Quite quickly they learned to bear with wild shouting and the clashes of battle all round them, but the test of their bravery, which took them weeks to pass, was the sight of dead horses lying at their feet. They were dummies of course, but made to look like the real thing, and the horses were terrified of them.

I was assigned a magnificent four-year-old stallion, the best horse in Spain because I was playing the King. Chuck Heston's had to be pure white, and white horses are all aged, so he had three to be on the safe side – in case of injury. They were beautiful, but they were old.

Through no fault of his own, my Olympian steed was called 'Tex'; I would not have changed it, for even the noblest name could never have been worthy of him. He was a dark bay, about sixteen hands, a total miracle of equine engineering with the deep, deep neck of the entero and a smallish Arab head with kind eyes and vulval nostrils. Every night the grooms knotted up his mane with ribbons so that by morning his curls rippled from behind his ears, cascading over his burnished coat like an advertisement for shampoo. I rode him every day for the six months it took to complete the film, and every morning without fail he tried to throw me. Each skirmish was a test to ensure that I was up to his standards and prepared to take him on. After ten minutes of savage bucking and rearing, a lather of sweat would break out on his massive neck, he would stamp with one hoof, toss his head, and stand quivering with indignation, then he would give one mighty snort and concede not defeat but acceptance. Once I had won this battle for supremacy he was as good as gold; but first he had to work off the fizz of resentment that such a strong animal must feel at having to restrain his power and curb his will to his rider's.

Young as he was, Tex taught me *haute école*. I had seen the Lipizzaner Stallions of Vienna prance on television, but one day Tex appeared to do it of his own free will. I was schooling him in the *manège* and he suddenly started this deep, plunging, balletic gait. I must have inadvertently tapped his flanks in the position to give him the signal. I cried out to the groom, who explained in detail the aids Tex thought I had given him till I could deliver them with assurance, and thereafter, when I came onto the set aboard my prancing steed, caparisoned to the ground in scarlet and gold, executing the *piaffe* and the *levade* with effortless ease, I cut a fine figure as King Alfonso the Sixth of Spain. Everyone thought I was the Horseman of the Year. Is it any wonder I loved my horse so slavishly?

Bucephalus was just another nag compared with Tex, and riding him was like flying a tornado.

In England stallions are kept only for stud purposes – you could never ride out on one, since mares abound, and they are often in season. The opposite pertains in Spain where uncut stallions are common, and mares are kept out of their way. In spite of these problems, I wanted to buy my horse, but my ambition was thwarted. The Supreme Commander of the Spanish Army, for his contribution of the seven thousand soldiers under his command, was presented with Tex as his reward at the end of shooting. It was with a heavy heart that I bade farewell for the last time to my wondrous steed.

As well as the soldiers and the horses, a fishing fleet of two hundred boats was painted black and fitted with black sails for Bin Abdullah's Armada. There were siege towers and gigantic catapults and scaling ladders and all the contraptions and engines of a mediaeval war.

The fishing village of Peñiscola south of Barcelona stood high on a rock at the end of a golden beach five miles long. It looked much as it must have done for hundreds of years, but for our film it was to serve as the city of Valencia, so any anachronisms in the architecture were covered in mud-cast false walls, the tiled roofs were concealed under thatch and the windows were screened with Moorish arches. The result was the biggest film set in film history, rich and authentic and as big as a small city.

Before filming started I was flown to Florence to be fitted for my fifteen costumes. The designer Veniero Colasanti was Italian and would not trust any but his own countrymen to realise his exquisite designs. All the materials were coloured with vegetable dyes because mineral dyes are too strong and vivid for that period in history. The vegetable dyes gave the authentic colours, which were soft and primary, and when the cast was finally assembled in the foreground, with the thousands of extras behind, the scene was like a living tapestry or a fresco by Gozzoli or Giotto. Except for Sophia, who looked as if she was on her way to a fancy dress party.

The designer begged her to leave off her bra, and eschew all but the subtlest make-up, to no avail. In the film her mighty and wonderful breasts are accentuated in twentieth-century buttresses of lingerie, and her lovely face is painted like a fairground effigy. This was the style then. Like Liz Taylor in *Cleopatra*.

'We're not making a documentary about Spain in the eleventh century!' she protested. 'This is a movie – for the public. And I'm going to look as beautiful as possible, Veniero, so there!' and she kissed the designer who remained unmollified.

Meanwhile Sophia on her golden palomino and Charlton Heston on his pure white warhorse were riding through the gates of the castle in Valladolid like heroes from legend. Not only were they rich and famous and beautiful, above all they were BIG. Tall and in perfect proportion, with strong features. They were both born to be Film Stars. Their beauty and their size would disqualify them from the real world. Sophia can't bear to be photographed in profile, but it is a mercy she hasn't had her nose altered. I wouldn't swear that she is a stranger to the surgeon's knife, but her nose is as God made it. The whole package is beautifully wrapped, and it contains a warm and earthy woman.

The Director, Anthony Mann, was all but illiterate. His work included death-less classics like *God's Little Acre*, *The Glenn Miller Story* and several Westerns, but he had the constitution of an ox and a flair for the operatic which amounted to genius. There was one shot in the film which exhibited both these qualities, and it took a week to shoot.

It was the master shot for the Battle for Valencia. There were four cameras set up at strategic points: the battlements at the top of the town; below the castle walls; the gates of the city; and half-a-mile along the beach. Anthony had four Assistant Directors on the end of walkie-talkies, plus his very own Assistant Director by his side who bore the brunt of his spectacularly lurid and disgusting tongue.

'Move the f...ing Yourmires!'

The word he was seeking, and never in six months got right, was 'Emirs'. These Emirs were the Muslim Princes befriended by El Cid, and against the muted and vegetable-dyed Spaniards they glowed like exotic butterflies in their dazzling silks and jewelled scimitars. 'Tell the mother f...ing cock-suckers to SHIFT ASS!'

Since I was not involved in this master shot, I had asked the Assistant Director if I could watch its progress from the position of the main camera. Anthony Mann was friends with no one as far as I could see, but he had suffered my company over a few meals without turning nasty, so by his reckoning we were on good terms. He allowed me the privilege of joining the camera crew on the shooting platform provided I kept silent and remained invisible.

The camera was mounted on a platform on the battlements at the very top of the town, commanding an eagle's eye view over three hundred and sixty degrees. After three days of lining up the soldiers and the horses and the ships at sea, we were ready to go for a take. With every day the expletives had become more resounding, combining graphic depictions of sexual degradation with sacrilegious imagery till there was serious concern that Anthony might be arrested and charged with blasphemy in this still devoutly Catholic country. The last commands had been relayed over all the walkie-talkies and the shouting was over. The camera had been loaded with a double magazine to take enough film for this monumental shot which was to last perhaps eight minutes without a break.

'ACTION!'

It begins on a fluttering flag at the top of a pole at the top of a tower at the top of the town. The camera moves slowly down to discover a group of Arab horsemen, all in black, being addressed by their leader Ibn Abdullah. Valencia is now held by the Moors, but El Cid is all set to capture the city for King Alfonso (me!). The black-clad Arabs charge off on their trusty steeds and the camera follows their progress through the town, a town bustling with activity as people go about their business: women hastily shopping at the street market; a young girl carrying water from the well; a farrier shoeing a mule; a baby at a mother's breast; another mother snatching her child to safety as the riders thunder by. Following the horsemen, the camera passes over the walls of the town: out at sea, the fleet of ships all painted black, their black sails fat with a rising wind, is drawing near the shore. The camera skims over this sinister armada onto the foreshore, where five thousand foot soldiers and two thousand archers are advancing along the beach to the beat of drums. One thousand horseman lead this army, their shields held before them, making of their tightly-packed ranks a monolithic reptile undulating towards the city, their lances like its dorsal crest, jagged against the sky. A mighty catapult the length of a tennis court is dragged like an outsize hobby horse behind a phalanx of helmeted soldiers, while siege towers five storeys high, with solid wooden wheels the size of the paddles on a Mississippi Gambler, swaying and creaking in protest, are being heaved by Herculean teams slowly but inexorably towards the walls.

'CUT! PRINT IT! GOING AGAIN!'

It was an incredible and thrilling shot, but Anthony wanted to improve on it. Which meant we had to finish for the day and start again on the morrow, for it took five or six hours to set it up; the ships had to sail back out to sea; the machinery of war had to be taken back to the original marks; the horses and the troops had to be fed, in that order, and all repositioned; the film changed in the camera, the lights refocused on the foreground, and the reflectors adjusted with the sun.

Anthony was well pleased that he had one shot, at least, in the can.

'That was a Jesus c...nt-suckin' mother f...in' SHIT SANDWICH!!' he said, clearly delighted.

While we were filming in the studios in Madrid I shared an apartment with Gary Raymond, who played my brother Sancho. He became my lifelong friend. Gary is quite ludicrously handsome, but since he was engaged to be married to the English actress Delena Kidd, he did not succumb to the advances of one of the most spectacularly sexy and beautiful women in the world. Ursula Andress.

She was staying in the same apartment block and we all met one day in the lift. The moment she squeezed in beside us with her Afghan hound on a leash, I was aware that I was in the presence of greatness. At that time she had never made a film. She was in Madrid accompanying her then-husband, John Derek. Her gorgeousness is only the beginning: she has a Hungarian accent and a husky timbre to her voice which puts you in a good mood straight away. She has a keen sense of humour, and a slightly sheepish, 'naughty girl found out' quality which is irresistible. It was clear she had taken a simply massive shine to Gary. We went to the monastery of Escorial and over the mountains to Toledo in a threesome because Gary was determined to stay true to his beloved at home. I was not in the least surprised when a year or so later Ursula Andress sprang all-but-naked from the sea to instant stardom in the first James Bond film, *Dr No*.

During my six months in Spain, I took a teacher and learned Spanish, which stood me in very good stead. Since I could speak on behalf of the British delegation, talk with journalists, and translate when necessary, I was invited to three Film Festivals: San Sebastian in northern Spain, Acapulco in Mexico, and Cartagena in Colombia.

And thereby hangs a tale.

4 ESCAPE FROM JAWS
Islas Rosarias

A PELICAN, like a battered holdall with pockets flapping, struggled to keep airborne in the thermals above the harbour in Cartagena on the Caribbean coast of Colombia. The camera was pointed at the cobalt sky striated with the masts of the fishing fleet, and as the bird finally keeled over and flopped into the sea, I followed it and zoomed in to the splashdown, and waited. Nothing. Perhaps it was a champion underwater swimmer. Or perhaps it had died. 'Cut!' I said for myself.

Old Cartagena is a Spanish colonial jewel untouched by the twentieth century, but the film I was making was a documentary about the slum city which has grown up outside its ancient walls. It comprises a bustling market, with boats arriving all day piled to the gunnels with bananas or coconuts, with tapioca and sweet potatoes, and fishing smacks full of exotic fish and piles of squid. The squid fishermen are boys with leather lungs, who dive deep and long without the luxury of canisters; they seek out the cephalopods in their underwater lairs, and offer themselves up to their lethal embrace, and while the squid are engaged in trying to squeeze the life out of them, the boys retrieve a dagger from their belts and stab the squid to death. For fun, these fishermen and market folk like to gamble and many keep fighting cocks. Cockpits are improvised out of upturned crates built up into a teetering amphitheatre where the betting waxes ferocious.

With my Bolex 16mm cine camera, I had embarked on a pilot for a series which I hoped to make about 'The Outsiders'. It was a subject that I estimated would have scope – perhaps too wide a scope – for other projects. Since the major companies all have their own documentary teams and I was a freelance and an amateur, on my return to the UK I got nowhere. Even cut and edited, with an illuminating commentary and evocative music, the film was rejected by Granada and the BBC. No doubt because it wasn't good enough. But I had fun trying.

After winning my spurs as a Spanish-speaking representative of the British Film Industry at San Sebastian and Acapulco, I had been invited to Cartagena in South America, and now that the Festival there was over, I was playing at being a Movie Director.

George, who was a professional photographer among other things, had flown out at my request to assist me, and we spent a month among these market traders and fisher folk attempting to capture their colourful life on film.

The best restaurant in Cartagena was run by a Frenchman, a Monsieur Hulot lookalike called Pierre Daguet. He was also a painter. He was pear-shaped with sparse grey hair worn long under his Panama straw hat, which he rarely removed even when serving table. Apart from the restaurant, he owned a coral island, an hour and a half by motor launch way out into the Caribbean among the Islas Rosarias, and he invited George and me to stay with him for a long weekend.

I have never undertaken a long sea journey in such a tiny craft. It was frightening to be so low in the water at the mercy of the powerful swells and currents of a great ocean, often with a wall of water heaving above one's head.

We arrived at Pierre's jetty to be greeted by his houseboy, Diego, a lad of about eighteen, who was charming and extremely good-looking, which made us wonder about Pierre, who was not married. But perhaps he was a 'looksist' like me. Along with brains and wit, I profoundly appreciate beauty in both sexes. Diego was accompanied by a pack of friendly dogs, the leader of which was a schnauzer the size of a donkey called 'Moustache'.

The house was built of coral, and it had a palm-thatch roof which swept the ground. You had to part it like hair to go indoors. It was cool inside, sparsely furnished but comfortable, and it was built with an interior courtyard which Pierre used as a studio. He often brought students from the mainland for Painting Holidays. His seascapes were skilful, but bland. His other passion was skin-diving, which was high on our agenda for the next three days.

On our first evening on a coral island, I was browsing through Pierre's book-shelves, which contained several volumes on the flora and fauna, the history and general information about this part of the world. With growing dismay I noted the frequency of the references to sharks.

'...these shark infested waters...'

'...a high incidence, among the local population, of maiming, loss of limbs, or death by sharks...'

'...ferocious killer sharks, which can be twelve feet long...'

'...out over the barrier reef, the sharks were as big and as fast as a train, but with double rows of razor sharp teeth instead of bumpers...'

There was a photograph of one author standing beside a swordfish bigger than himself, still in flippers, with his mask pushed up over his forehead. Underneath, the caption read: 'Whenever the sharks came near me, I landed the buggers one on the nose with my fist!'

Jacques Cousteau recommended shouting very loud at them under water.

When Pierre came in from the shower with a sarong tucked around his ample girth, bearing a tray with glasses and a bottle of whisky, I brought the subject up, and he failed to allay my fears.

'Shout at zem underwater? Oh Mon Dieu! Non! Non! Zat ees no good at all! Ze sharks around 'ere, ze sharks in ze Islas Rosarias, zey are all deaf!'

'DEAF?' I queried.

'Yes, deaf! Ze islanders feesh wiz dynamite. It's illegal, of course, but who's to stop zem? Zey catch plenty feesh. Boom Boom! Every day. Deaf sharks. Non, non! Your best protection is Zees!' He held up a mask and a snorkel. 'Swimmers on ze surface are in danger. Predators always go after moving targets. Movement triggers zeir brain, first to chase, zen to keel. But when you wear a mask you can see ze shark, and zat ees your best defence. You stay steel! You don't move away! You stay very steel! And ze shark leaves you alone!'

'Thanks,' I said, taking the proffered whisky and knocking it back in one.

'One zeeng I must warn you. And zees ees very important. Zere ees a time to be fright! Oh yes. Ze time to be fright ees zees! Eef I keel a BEEG FEESH! Maybe ze shark, he smells blood. I don't know. I don't know about smelling blood under-water. But sure to say is zees! Eef I keel a BEEG FEESH, his death-zroes make beeg vibrations, and even to a deaf shark, he feels zees beeg vibrations, and to heem zey are like a beeg shout, saying "Deener-Time! Come and get it!" How you say – "Grub's up!"' He nodded, gravely serious. 'Zees ees time to be fright!'

George and I spent an hour in the lagoon getting used to our snorkels, our flippers and our harpoon guns. We weren't using cylinders. If you had to dive to spear a fish, you held your breath while you were down, and spat to clear your snorkel when you resurfaced. With refraction and the drag of the water, my harpooning was not so much erratic as risible, but I was not discouraged.

One part of the lagoon became a mangrove swamp, and straying into it by mistake, I was both bewitched and repelled by the network of spreading roots which turned the sea-bed into a marine cathedral, glowing all the colours of the rainbow in the milky shafts of sunlight as a million sea-anemones that clung to the warty tree-roots pulsed and suckled at the muck in a parody of fledgelings in a nest.

We met Pierre on the jetty at the appointed time, and Diego paddled us out in a canoe to the edge of the lagoon where the motor launch was moored to a buoy. Pierre started up the engine as we all climbed aboard, Diego hitched the canoe to the stern and we were off.

'Now we go over ze Barrier Reef', Pierre explained. 'Eet ees beautiful, but dongjeroose! We are no longer in ze safety of ze lagoon. So. Please remember. Eef I keel a BEEG FEESH –'

'YES PIERRE!' I'm afraid I shouted at him. 'I haven't forgotten.'

In his wet-suit, clutching his harpoon to his chest, he looked like a Marine Commando about to storm an Embassy. He lowered his mask, cried '*Bon Chance!*' over his shoulder, and snatching with his jaws at his snorkel like a terrier pouncing on a rat, he jumped overboard and was gone.

George and I looked at each other, took a very deep breath and followed him.

When we had adjusted our masks and snorkels, what met our eyes was a dream landscape of awe-inspiring savagery and majesty. Visibility was not only perfect, it was magnified, and we could see clearly for miles. It was as if we had grown wings and were flying far out over a magical mountain range. Where the reef shelved away there were towering forests of weed in countless varieties, interspersed with thickets of multi-coloured, luminescent coral, and cliffs of golden honey-combed pumice. Shoals of parrot fish, striped purple and orange and emerald, meandered past us within touching distance, and a cloud of angel-fish far below us wafted as one through whirling tendrils, like a cape of sequins being flicked by some underwater soubrette. Time stood still. I have never seen anything to rival this sight, and I was more than a little scared, which no doubt heightened the experience for me.

I have no idea how long I hung suspended in this fantasy, but George had returned to the boat, and I was dogging Pierre's flippers, watching him swoop through the crystal towards a target, fire his gun and miss, the line taut and quivering for a second, then curling back on itself and dancing in the current till he reeled it in.

Then it happened. He speared a fish the size of a rottweiller. To me it looked like Moby Dick. The BEEG FEESH started to thrash about with demonic ferocity, spouting blood into the ocean like a fireman's hose.

I could feel the vibration in my ears and I could smell the blood like bread from a bakery. I didn't scan the underwater horizons for approaching express-trains, serrated jaws agape. I stood up, saw the empty canoe some yards off and got into it.

When the excitement was over, and Pierre's tuna was decked, we had time to re-cap.

'Mon Dieu! You were out of ze water in a flesh! You fright of sharks?' Pierre snapped off his mask and unzipped his suit…

'Dead right,' I said. 'As soon as I saw your BEEG FEESH, I got into the canoe.'

'Diego was in the canoe?' he asked me.

'No. Diego was on the launch, but he hauled me in.'

Pierre frowned, and thumped his heel into the bleeding leviathan which gasped on the deck in the throes of diminishing contortions, its scales flashing heliotrope in the afternoon sun.

'Zat ees not posseebull,' he murmured.

'What is not possible?' I asked him.

'Nobuddy can get into ze canoe from ze water, unless zere is someone in ze canoe to balance your weight. When ze canoe is empty, eet turns over. Eet capsizes! Oop-la!'

When we got back to the island, we took the canoe into the lagoon and none of us succeeded in getting into it from the water. It turned over every time.

It had been as I had suspected. Terror had given me strength. Terror had inspired me to stand bolt upright in the water and get into the canoe.

Like our Saviour on Galilee, I had walked upon the water.

5 THE RUSSIAN FIREBIRD
Rudy

RUDOLF NUREYEV leapt onto the stage of the Covent Garden Opera House in 1962, and with one *grande jetée* it was as if a volcano had erupted in the petrified forest of the Royal Ballet.

The year before, on 17th June, 1961, members of The Kirov Company were about to board their plane to London, to continue their tour after a triumphant season at the Paris Opéra, when it was announced that their leading male dancer would have to leave the company and return immediately to Moscow. The reason given was that he was expected to dance in a Gala performance at the Kremlin.

The Soviet authorities had been alerted to Nureyev's longing for international recognition, and to his probable intentions of remaining in London at the end of the tour, so they cooked up this story to keep him within their grasp. They were desperate to thwart a high-profile defection, which they perceived as an act of intolerable humiliation.

If Rudy returned to Moscow, this chance in a lifetime of escape to the West would be gone for good. He would be a prisoner in the Soviet Union till the end of his days.

He had only a few minutes to make up his mind.

Suddenly, he fought his way like a tiger through the phalanx of Soviet security guards (a force that surrounded the company specifically to prevent such attempts to escape), leapt the barrier at Le Bourget airport, and threw himself into the arms of the French Gendarmerie, demanding political asylum.

He was the first famous Russian dancer to seek asylum in the West. Later, there were others, including Makarova and Baryshnikov, but the sensation caused by Rudy's defection was never equalled.

His daring and violent bid for freedom made banner headlines throughout the world. Overnight he was a celebrity from Helsinki to Patagonia.

His story was the stuff of legend. Born into poverty near Irkutsk – he was actually born on a train – he was dancing professionally by the age of fifteen, and at eighteen was already being acclaimed as a phenomenon at the Kirov. The vastness of the Soviet Republic, however, was too constricting for his boundless ambition. He wanted to conquer the world.

He had the power and the grace of a panther. He was tall for a dancer, and though his frame was muscular, he was lithe and loose-limbed from his training at the barre. The savage aspect of his Tartar's face, with its high cheekbones and sensual mouth, combined with the head-butt intensity of his gaze before he smiled – a smile to melt the poles – made him, even at first glance, unforgettable.

To audiences in the West, the Bolshoi and particularly the Kirov style was a revelation. Grace and precision reigned unchallenged at the Royal Ballet. But instead of this studied elegance, these Russians sought for wild and wonderful spontaneity: with their rocket-fuelled leaps, they sometimes even fell over, but they brought such danger onstage with them that accidents were viewed as part of the excitement.

By consensus, Rudolf Nureyev, the Russian Firebird, or the Soviet Sputnik as he was sometimes referred to since the Russians had now launched their exploration of space, was the greatest male dancer the world had seen since Nijinsky.

But before he even took a step he was A Star.

He was twenty-four years old and at the peak of his extraordinary beauty when we met.

It was due to my agent that we were brought together.

And it was due also to him that we were driven apart.

In the whole theatrical profession, I am aware of no other actor besides myself who has stayed with the same agent throughout his entire life. This was, of course, due to loyalty, but also due to laziness, or lack of self-esteem. Actors change agents whenever their ambitions are frustrated, which is usually frequently. Sometimes a fresh approach brings results, but I believed that if my career was faltering it was due to other factors – competition, looks, age, talent, personality, luck...

I signed up with Jimmy Fraser – no relation, sadly, for he was a huge success – when I was nineteen, and I stayed with him till the day he died. Not that long ago. And although I have given up acting, I am still with the firm he founded. They get commission on my residuals.

Jimmy Fraser managed a formidable list of Stars – Richard Harris, Terry Stamp, Julie Christie and Maggie Smith among them. He was very tall, which may have been the reason for his decision, when he was in his thirties, to give up show-dancing and take up Personal Representation. His snakey hips could outswivel Elvis', but this talent alone was not a firm enough basis on which to found a career. And his height precluded all attempts by choreographers to fit him into a chorus line. He was always a sunflower wafting in a field of daisies.

Besides, he had the gift of the gab, an almost clairvoyant gift for spotting talent, and a shit-hot business brain.

He trained wisps of specially grown hair over the top of his bald head in the approved Arthur Scargill manner, he had a gravelly voice from smoking endless cigarillos, and he flubbered when he spoke as a result of a weak 'R' and too much to drink. His propensity for claret latterly put him out of commission entirely, after lunch.

He was universally popular, extrovert and noisy, with a great big heart and a thick Glasgow accent. Since we shared our surname and our provenance, people used to wonder if he was my father.

An unlikely possibility, since he was as camp as a long row of very frilly tents.

He had an irresistible penchant for mischief. Or perhaps, for granting your wildest dreams. Which can sometimes amount to the same thing.

'Would you like to come?' he asked me.

I had popped into his office in Regent Street to sign the insurance forms for a film I was about to start called *Fury at Smuggler's Bay*, playing opposite a French atomic sex-kitten called Michèle Mercier. More trouble.

'Tell me again.'

I was playing for time, and trying to collect my thoughts, which were racing out of control.

'It's my fiftieth birthday on Sunday. In the evening, I'm having a little celebration. Just friends, nice and intimate. I've discovered a Chinese restaurant in Docklands called "The Golden Dragon". The food's fabulous – Cantonese cuisine – and they have partitions, so they're like private rooms. I've booked a table for ten. Alan Bates is coming with Julie Christie, there's Douglas and Maggie Attwood, Terry and Jean. And wait for it. Svetlana Beriosova's bringing Rudy.'

There was then only one 'Rudy'.

'He saw you in *The Wind Cannot Read*.'

Jimmy put on a swooning face and clutched at his heart.

'When he heard I represented you, he begged me! He made me promise "to arrange I meet Fraser"!'

Since Rudy was known to the world as 'Nureyev', perhaps he thought that all distinguished folk should be called by their surnames.

By this time Rudolf Nureyev was the biggest star there had ever been. He was lusted after by a large percentage of the female population of the civilised world.

To homosexuals, he was considered the most beautiful and the most coveted object of desire since time began. His sex-appeal was the equivalent of Marilyn Monroe's for red-blooded heterosexual males. Or Ava Gardner would perhaps be closer to the mark. And he had 'begged', if I had heard Jimmy correctly. And made him promise 'to arrange I meet Fraser'!

I was living happily with George in Hampstead, but at that time it would have been unthinkable for me to appear with my lover in public. I was, however – no matter how you beat about the bush – definitely spoken for. Should I therefore have hesitated to accept an introduction – posing as an unattached and open-for-anything person – to the most famously randy and indiscriminately promiscuous tyke in London? Who had 'begged' Jimmy, and made him promise 'to arrange I meet Fraser'?

Having escaped from the repression of the Soviet Union, it was rumoured that Rudy was behaving as if he were determined to drain the cup of western decadence to the dregs. I later discovered that those rumours had been bred of envy and wishful-thinking. He had no doubt had a few affairs, but the insatiable sexual appetite for countless different partners, which was attributed to him, was a vicious calumny and totally without foundation. There simply were not the opportunities for him to lead such a predatory existence. And with his unquenchable passion and commitment to The Dance, with the hours and hours of punishing practice and rehearsal, plus appearing in public almost every night, to accommodate sex-mania in this schedule he would have to have been superhuman.

Which, of course, he was.

Drugs were not in common use then; but even if they had been, he would never have been tempted by psychotropic substances. He drank only wine, and that sparingly, because his body was a temple. Sex was his only indulgence. He estimated that sex would have no ill-effect on his dancing.

Which is ironic in the light of his terrible death from AIDS thirty years later.

He had seen me in a film, and he had evidently been attracted by what he saw. I could not believe it was my talent he was interested in. Nor my mind nor my wit nor my personality. Going by his reputation, I guessed what he was after. Succinctly…

Sex.

By this time, I sneered to myself, he had probably had all the dancers in the company who were butch enough for his tastes.

Like Dirk Bogarde, Rudy was too famous to troll the streets or the bars where homosexuals met surreptitiously to find partners. There was the ever present threat of blackmail, and the even greater danger of having an unscrupulous 'pick-up' sell his story to *The News of the World*.

The safest kind of lover for Rudy would be someone who, like himself, had a reputation to protect. Someone also in the public eye.

Like me.

Jimmy's projected birthday party was to be not just a social gathering. It was a set-up. An opportunity for Rudy and me to size each other up to see if we were ready to take the risks.

Jimmy knew this.

I knew this.

I said yes.

It was my duty to take pity on Rudy.

I'm only human!

Oh! The tyranny of the tackle!

It's a male thing!

Life is not a dress rehearsal!

Tough… Poor George.

He'll never know.

I hope.

Let's see…

'The Golden Dragon' was truly tacky, with strip-lights and wallpaper with a 'Postcards from the Seaside' motif, and pink and purple oilcloth tablecovers. Among the bottles of condiments and soy sauce, in the centre of each table there was a little vase containing a single, dispirited, but nonetheless real carnation.

You couldn't help but admire Jimmy's self-confidence, inflicting this hideous venue on such distinguished company. But Jimmy always had a finger on the pulse. He knew that slumming was the new chic. It was rather like the thirties in New York, when belles in their satin gowns and the swells in their silk toppers, after dining at El Morocco and quaffing champagne, would wind up the evening with a visit to a dive in Harlem.

And Jimmy was right about the food. It was in a totally different class to what passes for Chinese fare in other restaurants. And to top it all, it was preposterously cheap. Jimmy felt, like my Aunt Gatty, that 'you cannae prize a Scotsman fae 'is last bawbee!'

I had little interest in food before Rudy arrived.

Half an hour after everybody else.

Once I had shaken his hand, my appetite totally disappeared.

What I mean to say is that there was no suspense. From the first second our eyes met, we were in accord. This was perhaps the way it always worked for Rudy.

Fear of rejection is a necessary restraint upon unbridled lust among ordinary mortals, but Rudy had such utter confidence in his magnetism, in his sexual allure, that in his case the usual rules did not apply. Without a word being spoken between us, the naked desire in his eyes poleaxed me completely and swept me right off my feet.

I had a Fan-Club at this time. The films and my pop-records fed its flames. At its height it was, I believe, several hundreds strong. A dear girl called Barbara Holmes organised it, and she has remained a friend to this day. It would be churlish of me not to acknowledge that the loyalty of these fans contributed to my success, but if I am honest, I always found their devotion an embarrassment. I am not comfortable with adulation, either as a donor or as a recipient.

I had seen Rudy dance with Fonteyn in *Romeo and Juliet*. I had seen him in *Swan Lake* and in *La Bayadère*. I had been spellbound and enraptured, like everyone else who ever saw him, so I was without any question a fan.

But when we met, we met as equals. Not in talent, for his talent was stratospheric, but as performers. And our mutual attraction put paid to any notion of 'A Fan' meeting 'A Star'.

I would have fancied him if he had been a plumber.

Since the meal was dirt cheap, Jimmy had spared no expense on the champagne, and as the corks popped, the presents piled up on his plate. We all sang 'Happy Birthday' and made the strip-lights hum. An extended Chinese family looked on in undisguised amazement as the indiscriminate hugs and kisses reached a climax. It seemed to put them right off their Chow Mein.

By the time we got to the lychees, Jimmy was drunk as usual, but it was his birthday and he was paying so nobody minded.

Except me.

I squirmed as he kept squeezing his lips together in a little moue of affection, and blowing kisses across the table at me, while rolling his eyes in Rudy's direction and sucking suggestively on a cheroot.

Dear Alan Bates caught on at once, but he was much too kind and discreet to draw attention to it.

Throughout the meal, Rudy and I had no chance to talk privately. Our eyes had locked together at every opportunity, and the messages we had sent each other had been quite unequivocal. But as the evening drew towards a close, I was desperate to arrange a follow-up to this agonising and almost insupportable suspense.

Fetz, as Svetlana Beriosova was called by her friends, had arrived on Rudy's arm, and he would be accompanying her home. Jimmy was my responsibility.

Rudy and I brazenly held hands much longer than was required for bidding goodnight to anyone. Except a condemned man on his way to the scaffold.

But plenty of wine is always a plausible excuse for a surplus of tactile affection.

'I'll give you a ring!' was all I managed.

I could get his number from my pimp.

When he was sober.

'Tomorrow,' Rudy husked. Even his voice was unbearably sexy. And when he got going with the Russian accent, I would defy man, woman or dog not to fall head over heels in love with him. If you're that way inclined.

Which I was.

'Before nine. I go to class. I wait you ring me, Fraser.'

'Goodnight Rudy.'

'Goodnight Fraser. I like so much to meet you.'

As we climbed into our cars to head westward, he mimed holding a telephone to his ear and mouthed, 'Tomorrow!'

Rudy is dead and I am old and nobody cares any more whether a couple of poofs got together forty years ago, or what exactly they got up to.

I have made passionate love to the most beautiful man in the world, and it was better than anyone can imagine. He was tender, totally uninhibited, and sometimes wild... His body was such perfection that contemplation of it was awe-inspiring.

But there wasn't a lot of time or space for contemplation in our tragically brief time together...

I will be misunderstood, misquoted, and perhaps even reviled if I explain something.

He was scruffy. He smelt sublime, not of deodorant or cologne, but of sweat. And he would often put on a shirt that he had worn the day before, that had a tide-mark round the collar. After class or rehearsal, or after a performance, he didn't always shower straight away. We often made love first. Woody Allen was once asked if he thought sex was dirty. 'Only,' he said, 'if you're doing it properly...'

This icon, this creature of such animal perfection, this love-god to millions, in private had no vanity whatsoever. He was sloppy and neglectful of his appearance – a trait which I found utterly irresistible.

Everyone would know if our affaire had endured; because every move that Rudy made was lapped up by the press and made much of.

I had a terrible six weeks. Hours of anticipation spent in agony; brief moments of realisation in ungovernable ecstasy. Situation normal for lovers. Lies and subterfuge, hurried clandestine meetings... I had to keep our liaison secret from George, because I wanted to have my cake and eat it, and Rudy had to keep it secret from the world.

I should have known something was brewing – but I had no inkling – when our pimp, big Jimmy, summoned me urgently to his office...

He was in a state, as he had every reason to be, since he had been instrumental in opening this Pandora's Box of 'plagues of the body and sorrows for the mind, leaving only hope'.

I wasn't so sure about the hope.

Romantic Love is a delusion and a snare. It is an illness that defies all reason and is the cause, finally, of infinitely more pain than pleasure. I know because I have experienced it too many times. It is my feminine side which is my undoing... My emotions rise up like a whirlwind and engulf me.

Real men can take their pleasures more lightly. They can fuck and forget.

There could have been no possible future for Rudy and me in a long-term relationship. His work – his stardom – was his life. There was no room for any entanglement, no room for anyone at all, ever, in his private life. They would have distracted him fatally from his obsessive pursuit of perfection and fame, in that order.

He was bewitching, vulnerable, generous, flamboyant, and above all, scruffy. He could be demanding, spiteful, sometimes vicious, arrogant and indifferent towards the needs of others.

In 27 BC, Augustus was crowned the first Emperor of Rome. The imperial procession stretched for half a mile. There were musicians, acrobats, Nubian dancers, elephants and tigers, charioteers drawn by plumed horses, and a legion of marching soldiers in gleaming helmets and breastplates, brandishing their swords. The Triumphal Car, ten feet high, was made of gold, and was drawn by sixteen milk-white oxen garlanded with white roses and thick ropes of laurel. The route was lined six-deep with fifty thousand citizens, cheering and shouting: 'We Love You, Great Augustus!'

But Augustus employed a slave to stand behind his throne throughout the whole proceedings, murmuring constantly into his ear – 'You are merely human! You are merely human!'

To exchange almost overnight the privations and the oppression of a totalitarian state for the extravagance and the licence of his life as a megastar in a capitalist metropolis would unbalance anyone.

How many mortals are put to the test of being nightly deluged in applause and pelted with roses by a crowd of thousands roaring its adoration? A mere glimpse of his face, through a car-window, in a restaurant, in the street, was enough to cause hysteria. He had to dash everywhere. As if pursued by the furies…

I believe this constant, indiscriminate idolatry tipped the balance of his mind. In his quiet moments, of which there were many – very many – deathly quiet – I'm not sure whether he knew who he was.

For a very young man, he knew a great deal about music, which is not surprising. But he was also a perceptive connoisseur and a collector of fine art.

Although he was obsessed with the world of The Dance, he still had time to read classics in Russian, and he dipped into English newspapers and glossy magazines. He may not have been wise, but he was highly intelligent. His command of English was improving, although his creative approximations when searching for a word or a phrase sometimes had me on the floor. Within the limits of his vocabulary, he could be cutting and quite inspirationally witty.

It must be clear by now that I was wildly in love with him.

Troubled, but in love.

But it was not reciprocated, for most of the above-mentioned reservations.

And I was in despair. Because the brain-fever induced by my hormones convinced me that I should leave my happy home in Hampstead and set up house in Sloane Square with the greatest dancer in the world.

'Stop it now!' Jimmy shouted at me. 'Stop it! Before you're ruined!'

'You started it!'

'I thought I'd give you a one-night stand! A treat, for the commission on *El Cid*. I didn't expect you to start playing *Tristan and Isolde*! It wasn't part of the plan to break up your marriage!'

'People have no control over these things –'

'No control? NO CONTROL? I'll show you fucking control! If you don't stop this madness instantly, your career will be over, and I will have nothing more to do with you! Finished! You've been SEEN! Thank God it was only Petrina Glenville. [Peter Glenville, a prominent director, who was gay.] This time! It'll be all round London that you're fucking Rudy Nureyev, and you'll be a laughing stock, because you might be the latest, but you'll certainly not be the last! He's a TART! A rabid Russian tart! He'll give you a dose and leave you unemployable with your reputation in tatters!'

Half an hour later, Jimmy was still at it. I was trembling when I got back home to Hampstead. George was visiting his mother so I had the flat to myself.

Plenty of time to brood. To contemplate on the Meaning of Life.

And Death.

It was a low ebb. Not the lowest, but low enough.

I broke it off with Rudy.

It didn't break his heart.

6 THE LONG AND THE SHORT
Roman and Big V

ROMAN POLANSKI is short. Too near the ground to be sanitary. In the sixties he liked to drive around in a sports car with bimbos clustering on the upholstery like bats and to roister the small hours away in night clubs blue with funk and reefers. (The larger hours were the industrious ones behind closed doors.) This is not so surprising when you know that his childhood was spent in a concentration camp. I admired his courage and his talent, but not his style.

I was on holiday with George in Val de Gorbio in the South of France when I was offered the leading role opposite Catherine Deneuve in Polanski's film of *Repulsion*. I had been so impressed with *Knife in the Water*, a film which Roman had made as a very young man, that I accepted the offer without seeing the script.

When I read it on my return to England I was disturbed. Our first meeting was in an office in Wardour Street. It is a great confidence booster to stand a foot taller than one's employer.

Since Roman was credited with being the co-author, I asked him, 'Have you been analysed?'

He laughed. 'Why do you ask me such a question?'

'Because it's sick,' I said.

He laughed louder. 'It's meant to be funny!'

Would you laugh at a girl who for no explained reason goes insane, keeps a dead skinned rabbit in her handbag, imagines babies' hands tearing at her through the soft walls of her bedroom, breaks open her lover's head with a candlestick and leaves him in a bath full of water for a week, before she cuts her landlord's throat? Pure Monty Python.

It was an uncomfortable film to make. In the studio, I had to do take after take, acting dead, fully clothed and with my eyes open under water. The locations were in the thick of the traffic in South Kensington. Total belief in who you are and what you're doing is the bed-rock of good acting; this total belief is hard to maintain when you're rubbing shoulders with real people, who either resent your getting in their way or want your autograph. It was nonetheless fascinating to work with Roman. He is the best director for actors I have worked with.

Like the best of Hitchcock, the film is scary and suspenseful and full of an atmosphere of foreboding. It enjoyed a worldwide success, and won the Golden Bear for Best Film at the Berlin Film Festival.

Catherine Deneuve is the principal French icon, their ideal of French Womanhood. Her portrait was on their postage stamps for a while. At sixty she is more beautiful than ever, and she appears on television interviews to have acquired some warmth. When I worked with her she was sparing with it. 'Glacial' is the trite but precise adjective to describe Deneuve, but this may have been, as it often is, a cover for insecurity.

Tricky leading ladies leads me onto Vanessa Redgrave. She is referred to affectionately by her friends as Big V. She is seriously tall. And she is at the cutting edge of political correctness. She is Joan of Arc at Orléans in defence of the oppressed. I fear she may even call herself an ACTOR.

When Drama began, in Ancient Greece, in Mediaeval England, in China and Japan, the actors were all men. In Kabuki and in Noh, they are so to this day. Historically, for women to display themselves in public was too close to prostitution.

In England this changed with the Restoration. For Nell Gwynne and those who followed in her footsteps, the word ACTRESS was coined. For a hundred years, there was an air of scandal about it. This disreputable connotation, however, had disappeared entirely by the nineteenth century: Duse, Sarah Bernhardt, and latterly in England, Mrs Patrick Campbell, Edith Evans, Sybil Thorndike, Peggy Ashcroft. This dazzling roll-call of women, respected and respectable, brought honour to the title of ACTRESS.

In Italy, everything in creation has a gender. Every human, animal, object or idea is either masculine or feminine. Economy and precision are the hallmarks of civilised, sophisticated language, and I think English would benefit from being *more* gender specific, not less. In my group practice in London, I was allocated a new doctor. For personal reasons, I might have had a preference for a man. To my surprise, this doctor, first name Alex, turned out to be a woman, and I am entirely happy to have her as my doctor; but if I had been offered a DOCTRESS, I would have been freer to choose. LADY DOCTOR is cumbersome. LADY ACTOR is farcical.

And whether we like it or not, in casting, gender counts. John Wayne was baptised Marion. Before he changed his name, one can imagine the confusion in casting departments.

The intrepid Mark Rylance at The Globe recognises that gender need not be constricting. As well as 'normal' productions, with both men and women cast according to the sex of the written character, he does all-male productions, where men play women, and all-female ones, where women play men – in the hope, perhaps, that fresh light will be thrown on familiar texts by this reversal of expectation.

One such production at the Globe, which I did not see, was an all-female version of *The Tempest*. Properly cast and on form, Vanessa is a sublime actress, a jewel in the crown of the British theatre, and a star of world cinema. Mark Rylance was inspired to cast her in the role of Prospero.

She was of course wonderful, in parts. But she was hampered by her delivery. Prospero's daughter, Miranda, was played in this production by a young Scottish actress who is black. Suspension of disbelief is what the theatre is all about, and in telling a story there is no earthly reason why father and daughter should be the same colour. (There was never any question of Vanessa blacking up.)

In rehearsal, however, Miranda had difficulty in adopting received pronunciation to match up with the rest of the cast, so Vanessa, feeling strongly that the family should cohere, insisted on speaking her role of Prospero in his daughter's Glasgow accent.

The result was not happy.

Suspension of disbelief…this sacred mantra. Sadly, there is a treacherous chasm between theory and practice.

I was cast opposite Vanessa in *Isadora*. I first saw her in the set, a Bakst-inspired studio festooned with velvet, overlooking the sea, where she was improvising a dance sequence (as a child, she had training in ballet), isolated against a small mountain range of Turkish cushions. She was oblivious of the crew and the extras whom she held spellbound – oblivious, for the good reason that without her glasses she is all but blind. This may be a clue to her extraordinary radiance in performance. She is a beacon of self-belief blazing at the heart of the amorphous blur which her myopia makes of the whole world around her.

She can still pick out beautiful men: Franco Nero and Timothy Dalton. This was after her youthful marriage to Tony Richardson, the father of Natasha and Joely, who continue the Redgrave dynasty. Perhaps she saw her father in Tony – a bisexual who would treat his wife badly.

Michael Redgrave was a tormented man, whose male lover lived adjacent to the Redgrave home in Chiswick. There was a lot of violence in the men's relationship, of which Michael's wife Rachel and the children, Corin, Vanessa and Lynn, were painfully aware. Lynn was perhaps too young to understand, but I believe both Corin's and Vanessa's politics – Revolutionary Socialism – might stem more from psychological causes than from ideological ones. Their wish to destroy the Establishment, their barely contained anger and their hatred of authority may come from a deep-seated wish to punish their father.

We were on location in Opatia, a faded seaside resort in the former Yugoslavia. Vanessa was playing Isadora Duncan in the lavish film about the dancer's tragic life directed by Karel Reisz; I was playing her biographer.

We were accommodated in The Ambassador Hotel on the brim of the Adriatic, and every evening the cast and the film crew used to file along a little walkway that wound along the very edge of the water, just above the wavelets lapping like cats' tongues on the pebbles, to a restaurant on a point that served food for the Gods, every night the same and plenty of it – Fish and Chips.

The Adriatic is an inland sea within an inland sea, the sea of Odysseus and his voyages, so still and calm when the weather is fine it lies like a mirror under heaven; the horizon dissolves into an infinity of space in which islands float suspended on their perfect reflections. When the sky is overcast it is the 'Wine-Dark Sea' of Homer, and it is awe-inspiring that an epithet from two thousand years ago should describe so perfectly this tranquil sea today. When the wind blows lightly it whips the surface like whisked meringue and the sea turns ghostly white. It is not hard to believe that out there lie the terrible rocks of Scylla and Charybdis and the fearful isle of Circe the Sorceress.

There were about ten of us seated at a long table, tucking into our nightly and decidedly monotonous fare. The group included Franco Nero, who was Vanessa's new lover. He was, and remains, a startlingly beautiful man, and being every inch an Italian – *nota bene* 'every inch' – he has in common with most of his countrymen a degree of vanity.

Vanessa brushed a lock of hair from Franco's forehead, giving him a kiss-puff in the ear while whispering a secret. His nose almost rested on her cheek as he devoured her with his lover's gaze, and I could see with my peripheral vision that under the table he had her thigh clamped in his good hand (one arm was in plaster – from a skiing accident, I think), and he was kneading it like a baker on speed.

Suddenly Big V threw her arms in the air, stretched and opened her mouth wide in an overdone and quite unconvincing yawn, and said to the assembled company: 'Half-past seven already! I must have an early night. I'm on set first thing tomorrow. Will you excuse us?'

Being all but blind, she could hardly reprove her lover, as he stood up, for almost knocking over the table with the tent in his trousers. With one arm in plaster, perhaps Franco can be forgiven for not having adjusted his person, but that sort of solecism is what I call showing off.

Six actors, including myself, were film-tested for the part of Jimmy Porter in the film of *Look Back in Anger*, with Tony Richardson directing, and I was offered the part. I was packed off to the Cannes Film Festival as part of a publicity package, and it was announced to the press that I was to play Jimmy Porter, the original 'Angry Young Man', a hideous character but a coveted role.

This was before Tony Richardson married Vanessa. He was single, and he courted me assiduously. He took me to Paris for the weekend. He promised that he was going to find other vehicles for me and that he would make me a star. I did not find him attractive, but he was persuasive and we were both young. He had yet to make a name for himself as a film director. I already had the part in the bag, I was on the crest of a wave, so I didn't feel compromised in any way, just magnanimous.

Then by chance John Osborne ran into Richard Burton in New York – Richard whom I had worked with in *Henry V*, whom I knew well and liked, who was The Actor of his generation. He told Osborne that he would kill to play Jimmy Porter, so that was it. Who could blame Tony and John Osborne for choosing a star of Richard's magnitude for their film? He was ten years too old, of course. The character's sadistic treatment of his wife is almost understandable, though still unforgivable, if he is very young and 'mixed up'. Richard was in his late thirties, and at that age I believe the character becomes a psychopath. It was not among Richard's best performances.

Tony Richardson went on to great success after his triumph with *Tom Jones*. He married Vanessa and disappeared from my life for many years. When I ran into him by chance in a little French restaurant in Soho, he behaved as if he hardly knew me.

Aunt Gatty's Christmas toast was: 'Here's tae us, wha's like us, damn few an' they're aw deed!'

Mine, which I learnt from a married man I'd just slept with, was:

> Birds do it, and fly,
> Bees do it, and die.
> But I can't. Shall I tell you why?
> I've a sweetheart, and I've promised to be true –
> But I tell you what I'll do –
> I'll lie still, and let you.

7 POLYMORPHOUS PERVERSE
Dennis Price plus Supporting Cast

DENNIS PRICE'S SUICIDE BID did wonders for his career.

Kind Hearts and Coronets had made him a star but his private life was messy. As a young man he had studied theology with the intention of entering the church; instead he turned to acting, got married, had two daughters and became a huge success. He separated from his wife when he discovered late in the day that he preferred a beating-up to intercourse and that men were better at it.

Perhaps indulging in this newly-discovered vice sapped his energy, for the work tailed off after that and he took an overdose. He was rescued and thereafter was steadily employed till his death from cirrhosis of the liver.

He lived on Guinness. He never drank tea or coffee even first thing in the morning. About a crate of Guinness a day was his consumption, starting at breakfast. He was always drunk of course, but he never fell over and could, with occasional lapses and in a general sort of way, stick to the script.

I made two films with Dennis – *Tunes of Glory* and *Tamahine*, in which I played opposite the ravishingly beautiful half-Chinese, half-Scottish actress Nancy Kwan – but we got to know each other well only when we worked together in the theatre for nine months in an American comedy called *Any Wednesday* at the Apollo Theatre. It was a four-hander, starring Dennis, Moira Lister, Amanda Barrie and myself.

In private life Moira was the Vicomtesse d'Orthez, the wife of a French champagne vintner, a nobleman and a millionaire. Moira comes from South Africa where she once went on a date with the sadistic multiple murderer Neville Heath, who used to cut off the nipples of his victims and keep them in the breast-pocket of his hacking-jacket. Moira emerged unscathed. I loved her for her warmth and her wit.

I was living with George up on Hampstead Heath. Amanda was married to an actor, though she didn't seem to like him much (he drank too), and Dennis had a formidable Minder, a shapeless hulk with a curiously high-pitched voice like a dentist's drill. His main job was to heave the crates of Guinness up the stairs to Dennis' dressing-room, but – except when he was on the stage – wherever Dennis went, his Minder was but a step behind, like his shadow.

Dennis was as mischievous as he was charming and we were on extremely friendly terms; he would not accept an invitation to dinner, however, because he never went anywhere without this Minder, and he was sensitive enough to know that 'The Hulk' was not everyone's idea of a sparkling guest.

One Saturday Dennis turned up for the matinee with his right hand in splints.

'What happened?' I asked him, concerned. 'Are you sure you'll be able to get through two shows?'

'It's a bit awkward of course. But I'll put in a line about horses and stables. That should cover it.'

'How did it happen?'

'That's it! Went riding in Richmond Park. Got my hand slammed in the beastly stable door.'

'Dennis!' I am not always noted for my tact. 'You haven't been near a horse for twenty years! You told me yourself –'

'Well, there you go,' he said gruffly and shut the dressing-room door.

Dennis was not a character actor. He always played himself, debonair, elegant and ever so English. When he made his entrance that afternoon, his Minder was clearly visible from the stage, sitting hunched and unmoving in the royal box.

Dennis' 'Charming Cad' personality changed abruptly. He became hard, cruel and vicious. It made my flesh creep. The piece was a comedy, but the laughter died on the audience's lips. They watched in disbelief, while Moira, Amanda and I exchanged thunderstruck glances and struggled through somehow to the end of the first act.

As soon as 'The Rag' hit the floor, Moira turned on Dennis like a wild-cat.

'What are you doing? Have you lost your mind? This is a comedy, not the Nuremberg Trials. I refuse to go on after the interval till you give us all an unqualified apology. And that should include one to the audience. I will make an announcement myself unless you swear to me that you will play the second half as it is intended to be played, and as we rehearsed it.'

Dennis looked sheepish; his anger was spent. The obvious inference was that his Minder had been responsible for the hand in splints, and that in some perverse power-game Dennis had been displaying his ferocity to his tormentor. Now it seemed that he had had his catharsis and was prepared to call it quits.

'Don't be cross, old girl.' He touched Moira with his good hand. 'I'm frightfully sorry. It's this hand, you see – giving me gyp. I promise I'll watch it in the second act – you'll see. Good as gold I'll be. Now. Time for a Guinness.'

He hurried off, leaving the three of us to boggle at his bizarre behaviour.

Amanda said to me, 'Come and have a drink with us after the show.' She tended to act dizzy in a Goldie Hawn sort of way, but her head was screwed on. She was lissom, wildly pretty, and she held her lips in a kissing pout. Her gazelle's eyes were elaborately painted in bruise blue and black, and her lashes were like a thorn bush, spikey with mascara. 'I'd like you to meet my girl-friend.'

I only just avoided falling into the orchestra pit. 'You what?'

'Didn't you know?' She looked naughty. 'I'm finished with men…'

'But Bob – your husband…'

'Biggest mistake I ever made. Kicked him out three weeks ago. Bren's moved in now. She's ever so sweet. And crazy about me. She might not win Mastermind but who wants a genius? We have a lot of laughs. She's just a bus conductress, but she knows a thing or two.' She winked. 'Have a drink with us after. I have a bit of tattle that you won't believe. Tell you later. The Red Lion, okay?'

To say I was flabbergasted cannot describe my astonishment. Amanda was so sexy, so quintessentially feminine… Never in a million years… It was going to be a revealing evening. I had no idea then how revealing. (Amanda, now a household name after many years appearing in *Coronation Street*, has already 'Come Out' all over the *Daily Mail*, to say nothing of her own autobiography, so I am betraying no secrets.)

Being a Saturday night the pub was chock-a-block, with no room to stand let alone to find a space at the bar. I suggested we should all get into my car and drive up to Hampstead. 'We can manage an omelette or baked beans or something.'

Bren wore a smart little suit with a cameo on a choker at her throat. She was moderately attractive and about the same age as Amanda – late twenties – though, on a slight acquaintance, there didn't seem much foundation for Amanda's claim that Bren was 'good for a laugh'. She had a flair for answering leading questions in monosyllables and for chain-smoking, but she seemed happy for Amanda to do all the talking.

Throughout our late-night snack Amanda kept us on tenterhooks and it was only as we gathered round the fire with the claret keeping cosy on the hearth that she delivered the gossip that she had promised earlier.

'Well,' she said, putting down her glass with emphasis. 'Can you wait?'

'Not any longer,' I said, as was expected of me. The story Amanda went on to tell was not true, but it was so gloriously grotesque, outlandish and depraved that I swallowed it, hook, line and sinker, for forty years…

'Then here goes. Bren goes to the clubs and that. It's where we met, actually. Shagarama's. It's fun there. No men allowed. You can dance, and nobody minds if you neck a bit. They're mostly really nice girls. A few diesels of course, there always are, but they're not allowed back if they cause trouble – you know, punch-ups or fighting over the girls. Even if they're wearing suits and smoking cigars – it doesn't mean they're necessarily aggressive. But there's some lovely girls there, aren't there Bren? Real beauties. You'd be amazed. Well. Zarita goes there from time to time.'

'Who's Zarita?'

'You know! Raymond's Revue Bar. Big knockers!' She demonstrated. 'Hair to her waist. "ZARITA!" She does an act with snakes. At Raymond's. A dirty snake act. She's naked, to all intents and purposes. She fondles the snakes and kisses them and strokes them and slides them up through her legs and up the crack between her buttocks. The men go wild. They've no idea of course that she's a dyke. I don't suppose it would put them off. It doesn't seem to. It didn't put Bob off when I told him about me, but by then it was too late, I'd made up my mind. Anyway. Bren – when was it?'

'Last night,' Bren volunteered, quick as a flash.

'Yeah. Last night. She just goes for a dance of course, don't you Angel? No messing about or I'll do you in!' Amanda pointed a finger at her loved one like a gun, then changed the gesture to a ferocious squeeze of her chin. 'Choochy!'

She continued. 'Well anyway. Bren was at Shagarama's and she gets talking to Jane, she's a regular there, lovely girl, models herself on Dusty – *she's* one of us you know – well anyway, Bren gets talking to Jane, didn't you Angel, and Zarita's name comes up. Bren says she finds it depressing how promiscuous Zarita is. Well it's true! At the Club she's always got her tongue down a different chick's throat. And Jane says, "She claims that she was married once." "Never!" says Bren. "Well, sort of," says Jane. "She says they went through the ceremony and everything." "Who was the husband?" says Bren. "You know him," Jane says. "I don't know him!" Bren says. "Yes you do," says Jane.'

Amanda took a deep breath to keep up the suspense.

'"Dennis Price's Minder," she says. Well! When Bren picks herself up off the carpet she says, "I don't believe it! How long did it last?" "Not long," says Jane. "Well no time at all if you're talking official." "What do you mean?" asks Bren. Didn't you Angel? "Well, the marriage wasn't legal," Jane says. "Why not?" asks Bren.

'Jane says, "Because Zarita says – but then she would, wouldn't she, she's a dyke after all – and who can prove it either way? She says he's a woman."'

Amanda was gratified by my reaction. My mouth fell open so violently I almost dislocated my jaw.

It all fell into place. The shapeless figure, the piping soprano voice…

'I've heard everything now. What a fucking festival of polymorphous perversity…'

I still couldn't believe it. 'He's surely – surely he's a man… Just because he's got a high voice! My headmaster at primary school sounded like Gracie Fields, and he had three children…'

'Well,' Amanda gave a wry smile. 'We're all sort of in-between, aren't we? Take a look at us! No such thing as *all* man or *all* woman…'

Amanda plumped herself on the sofa and snuggled up beside her laconic little Bus Conductress.

'Thank God I like girls!' she said.

8 THE DEVIL'S HANDMAID
Bette Davis

JILL BENNETT was not an easy person to rub along with, either socially or professionally, but now that she has killed herself it would be churlish to dwell on her negative qualities. Though she considered herself ugly, she could be very glamorous and was a sparkling conversationalist who was never dull, and I could cope with her treacherous shifts in loyalty since I was never intimately involved with her turbulent life.

Our last 'Spat' was at the Edinburgh Festival in 1985. Jill was playing Elizabeth I in Schiller's *Mary Stuart*, and I was playing Leicester, the Queen's favourite and would-be husband. During rehearsals, I took Jill to task for peevishly slapping the face of our Assistant Stage Manager who was called 'Kerr'. Kerr had a Glasgow accent so impenetrable even I had problems understanding him. Jill always had difficulty learning her lines, and was consequently happy doing an unfamiliar Classic: since the audience were mostly at sea, she got away with talking drivel in iambic pentameters – or Alexandrines, in the case of Schiller. The mystified punters shouldered the blame for not following the gibberish Jill made of the text and attributed the consequent lack of understanding to their own ignorance.

At rehearsals, Kerr was 'On the Book', which means that he was meticulously following the text to supply the line when an actor has dried, which was all the time in Jill's case.

An anxious pause in Jill's delivery, while she clutches vainly at the air... Then –

'Coanseekraytesy reggy sighs,' Kerr suggested eagerly. ('It consecrates the Regicide.') Schiller is not Alan Ayckbourn.

'WHAT?!?' Jill screeched, unable to understand a syllable.

And so it would go on.

Pause... A hand raised – not waving, but drowning... Then 'Stonishmun pissesssess mee ah oan...' ('Astonishment possesses me, I own...')

So she hit him.

If she had slapped a fellow actor, I hope, in return he would have laid her out. But as the ASM is the humblest member of the company, and Jill was the Leading Lady, this was assault, or at best indefensible bullying.

When I remonstrated she accused me of being 'Bourgeois!', presumably because I didn't wallop people, let alone juniors who wouldn't wallop back. As she stormed out I flung a cheap gibe after her, the sort of insult which Prima Donnas like Jill provoke one to, against one's better judgement: 'You're not in one of your tacky B Movies now!'

Which reminds me...

Some years before, Jill had found herself between husbands. Willis Hall had left her, and she was yet to meet and marry John Osborne. She rang me one evening about ten o'clock. She was half-way through making a film called *The Nanny* starring Bette Davis. Jill cooed down the phone –

'We've just been to Ascot, darling, and nobody wants to go to bed. I DON'T MEAN WITH EACH OTHER, of course, I just mean to sleep. I don't have an admirer at the moment, Angel – you know what I mean, bringing me roses, paying me court, shafting me in the doggy position, that sort of sweetness. Could you bear to slip into a dark suit and be my escort so we can all go out to a night club?'

I guessed she was bottled, so I quickly tried to estimate the pros and cons of hitting the town with a gaggle of assorted drunks, even though one of them was Bette Davis. 'Who's all?' I asked quite kindly, 'and what night club?'

'Well there's Seth (Seth Holt, producer and director, whom I had worked with and liked), and Bette and me, and that's it really. And we thought of going to Danny's.'

Danny La Rue made a huge impression in the Sixties as a Female Impersonator when 'Drag' was considered risqué and utterly *à la mode*, and he now had a night club named after him, which was the 'In' place to be seen.

'I'll be there in a quarter of an hour.' I had weighed the possibilities and found them irresistible, Bette Davis being the cardinal incentive.

Jill lived in a mews house off Queen's Gate in Kensington, a five minute drive away from my own house in Ladbroke Grove. The mews had been converted in such a way that when you entered the front door there was no vestibule: the entrance opened immediately into the main room, from which the staircase led to the upper floor. I rang the bell and was admitted to the house by Jill herself.

Before I had crossed the threshold I could see in the middle distance the Legend known as Bette Davis.

She was seated on the stairs, and she was smoking. How could she not be? She wore the sort of pink, beaded dress that only Film Stars can get away with, and anyone would have recognised her from across the English Channel. Seeing her in the familiar surroundings of Jill's mews in Queen's Gate was like bumping into Mister Micawber in the Post Office.

Seth Holt sat opposite the Legend in a lower chair, so that all eyes led upwards to the pink-beaded column of smoke, in the intermittent shadow of which cowered the 'Grey Lady'. I had discovered in Rome with Hedy Lamarr that the first requirement for American Film Actresses with aspirations to being 'A Stawr' is to have a Grey Lady. Bette Davis' Grey Lady would have been more aptly named her 'Side-Kick'. She was sitting several steps below her mistress, diligently cringing within kicking distance and evincing a truly enticing grovel.

The epitome of the Grey Lady is of course Dame Edna Everage's Madge. She rarely speaks, at least in the presence of her mistress, though she usually laughs uproariously at her jokes. She is employed as a companion, a factotum, a secretary, a chaperone, someone to take phone calls, book chauffeur-driven limousines and restaurant tables, dispense alcohol and keep visitors waiting, but her true function is to suffer without a murmur of complaint the spleen of her illustrious Kicker. I can't remember Bette's Side-Kick's name, which is another memorable quality of 'Grey Ladies'.

On the drive over to Jill's I had determined not to gush. A polite introductory remark would be required of me, but I was uncomfortable with the thought of oiling my way through some cliché she had heard a million times before. In the light of what is to follow, I must emphasise that I am an ardent admirer of Bette Davis' performances on the screen. She is among the very greatest of the Old Film Stars, and a true original.

Between snatches at the fag jammed into her upside-down smile Bette Davis offered me her hand. I took it, and delivered my thought-out little gambit.

'If I had been a technician on *Hush, Hush Sweet Charlotte*,' – I offered her like a rare orchid on a salver – 'I would have gone out on strike.'

Now is the time to explain the reason for this cryptic pronouncement which I hoped would intrigue her and open the way to a little badinage, culminating in my delivering a bouquet of compliments without seeming sycophantic. I had seen *Hush, Hush Sweet Charlotte* some weeks before. It is no classic, but I passed an extremely agreeable evening at the pictures, and Bette Davis was, as she always is, hypnotic. The closing credits, naming all the technicians and the workers behind the cameras, were rolled over a close up of Bette Davis. I whispered to my companion exactly the words I had just addressed to the Legend, because I had been so fascinated watching the expressions flickering over the face of this unique performer that I had failed to read who had been responsible for the Photography, the Lighting, for the Sound, for the Design, for the Music... You, dear Reader, will understand where this odd remark was leading since you are now privy to my thinking. She was not.

She erupted like Etna. The fag was ripped from her sneer with disbelief. If you were Bette Davis, would you expect the first comment by a stranger who has been socially introduced in a mutual friend's home to be a savage insult? A normal person, puzzled perhaps, might surely have asked 'Why?', thus opening the way to an amusing dialogue. In my innocence, this is what I had expected. I could then have delivered the praise which I truly wished to bestow and for which, it transpired, she craved with a pathological appetite. I was not, however, given the chance.

'STRIKE! You fucking ignorant RETARD! Nobody on my pictures EVER goes on STRIKE! NEVER EVER!' Her face throbbed danger-red through her makeup. 'I'm a professional! How do you suppose movies get made? You Ass-hole!'

Thunderstruck, unprepared for this insane outburst, I shouted, 'I'm sorry!' I held up my hands to stem the flow of her invective. 'You misunderstand totally –' but I was Canute commanding the waves.

'Go on STRIKE! Jesus Mabel Christ! On one of *my* Pictures!?'

'That Close Up at the end!' I bellowed. 'That Close Up! Of Bette Davis!' I added, as if she were someone else, someone fictional, which in a way she was. With decibels I finally got through to her that what I was shouting about concerned Bette Davis exclusively, with not even a peripheral reference to extraneous irrelevances like technicians or strikes.

'THAT CLOSE UP! THAT FINAL CLOSE UP! It was a wonderful Close Up. How do you expect an audience to read the credits over a Close Up like that! That's all!' I ended lamely.

She behaved like a cat that has mis-timed a spring. She was disconcerted for only a fleeting moment, then she continued as if she had been pulling my leg. She gave me an almost intimate sneer of forgiveness. 'Sure,' she agreed. 'That was a good Close Up.' The Grey Lady's hand had the good grace to tremble when she lit her mistress another cigarette.

From the conversation that followed between Jill, who was anxious but *compos mentis*, and Seth, who was neither, I garnered that Movie Talk was the only option. No other topic was conceivable without causing The Legend grave offence. A reference to the temperature outside, say, would elicit a riposte like, 'Who wants to talk about the fucking weather?'

'You see, Bette Darling,' slurred Seth, his elbow skidding from the arm of his chair and his chin dropping a foot as he leant too far forward to convince The Star of his insight, and of his blazing honesty. 'Garbo rested on her laurels! She was good, but she said "That's it! No more!" She was good. But she stopped. You've gone on! And on! To greater triumphs!'

The Legend thought for an anxious moment about this one, taking too many snatches at her fag before deciding which way to jump. There were several potential insults in there she could pounce on. 'She was good... You've gone on...and on...and on...' She squinted through her smokescreen at Seth, who had been responsible for employing her for the past three months at some astronomical fee, and decided to be gracious.

'Sure. I thought Garbo was a Crock of Shit myself.'

The Grey Lady backed her mistress to the hilt on this one.

'Awe, zip up, you ass-hole. Fill me up for Christ's sake.' Bette thumped her empty champagne glass into the Grey Lady's flabby fist.

I hadn't ventured into the open since I had been peppered by the Davis fusillade, but I was keen not to leave the impression that I was either cowed by her boorishness or in a huff at her lack of manners. The narrow guidelines having been clearly defined, I launched into the harmless Movie Gossip kind of chat with a will.

'Ever since I was little, my hero has been – not a stage star, like Laurence Olivier or John Gielgud, as you might imagine – but the greatest actor in any medium in my opinion is undoubtedly Spencer Tra–'

'TRACY!' She shrieked like a pig being slaughtered. 'That pile of Dog-Mess! Tracy! That ass-hole! He can't act. That drunken bum. That piss-artist. He's knee-high to nowhere. He shoulda played in *Snow White*. He's too short to play a dwarf. He'd have to play a toadstool. That no-good, mother-fucking son-of-a-bitch! Don't talk to me about Spencer Mother-Fucking Tracy!' She snatched a brimming glass from the Grey Lady, spilling half the champagne down the front of her dress; it ran off the beads like rain off a roof and dripped onto the carpet.

The guidelines were narrower than I had supposed. The only acceptable topic of conversation was not The Movies in general after all, but Bette Davis Movies in particular, and they could be spoken of only as a prelude to the most extravagant and ludicrous praise for the actress in front of us and for no one else. If other names in the industry were mentioned, trouble could be avoided only if bowels were emptied over them from a great height; or you could mince them into little pieces, spit them out in disgust and grind them under your heel into a loathsome paste. While Seth was launching into another paeon about one 'Take' Bette had done in *The Nanny*, which held the Dragon spellbound, I managed to propel Jill into the kitchen.

'Dear Jill,' I said to my hostess when we had closed the door, 'I wouldn't have missed tonight for a week in a Bombay Brothel. Which would have been tame by comparison. But that's it I'm afraid.'

'You're not going?' With her cheekbones Jill always looked gaunt, but now she looked haggard. 'You can't leave now…'

'Jill dear!' I stopped her pleading. 'I think the woman is a paranoid schizophrenic, but you ought to get a second opinion on that. She makes Hitler look like Cliff Richard.'

'She doesn't mean it!' Jill begged. 'She's had too much champagne. We've been at The Races all day. She'll calm down. She's just a bit flighty…'

'Too flighty for me.'

'Who's going to take me to Danny's?' She made the prospect of going 'on the town' seem like going to sea on a biscuit.

'Why should I put up with this insane fury? Why does she hate me?'

'You're young,' she wheedled. 'She probably fancies you…'

'Oh, Bollocks.'

'She has to defend her position. She's so insecure…' The Do-It-Yourself Psycho-Analysis kit. Jill flung herself into my arms and hugged me tight. 'Please, Johnny!'

'Just for tonight.' I relented. 'And just for you. But don't ask me to do anything like this, ever again.'

Bette Davis' appearance at Danny La Rue's night club caused counterflow problems. Her whole adult life must have been spent in the eye of this curious cyclone. The people close at hand fall back when they see her, and those further back crane forward to get a closer look. Bette Davis herself is thus left in splendid isolation, while the congestion a couple of feet away from her becomes acute; it also eddies along with her as she moves – exactly like Royalty, I suppose, but they have a phalanx of bodyguards to protect them, and their appearances are scheduled so they don't come as such a shock. For me the experience was new. Difficult as it may be to believe, I have never escorted a member of the Royal Family to a Transvestite Nightclub.

As we were shown to our table, Jill ensured that my evening would be blighted from the start by whispering in my ear: 'You will dance with her! Promise!'

The Legend watched the Cabaret as if she had never seen a Female Impersonator before and never wanted to again. After all those years of taking on the world, however, it was difficult to distinguish her approval from her disgust. After a flurry of moues and a snort, I reckoned it was neither, but rather envy that Danny was the Star of the evening and that she was relegated to darkness.

There was a band at Danny's. The leader sidled up to our table with the familiar grovel that appeared to be the only attitude to appease the Film Star's chronic wrath.

'It's such an honour to have you here Miss Davis,' he babbled. 'Have you a request? Something we could play – specially for you?'

Bette looked around the tables; in the entire night club every eye was upon her. You could not fail to admire her chutzpah. She was a plain woman with a permanent expression of contempt on her face, which did not improve her features. Her hair was mousey, her eyes were poppy, but because of the malice, the bitterness and the rage which drove her, she exuded a threat of danger that made her utterly magnetic. Like a swaying, hooded cobra.

She never said or did anything restrained, modest or considered. In every aspect of her life she had to be the focus of attention. 'Are we ready?' you could almost hear her thinking. 'Okay. Roll it! ACTION!'

She exhaled a plume of smoke and ground her cigarette to bits in the ashtray, then she confronted the quaking band leader.

'Yeah!' she hissed, anticipating his humiliation. '"Mississippi Mud"!'

I was aghast. I had expected 'Smoke Gets In Your Eyes', or 'I Left My Heart In San Francisco', something perennial and easy, something you could count on hard-working musicians in a London club knowing. 'Mississippi MUD'?!?!

But he knew it! The band beader knew it! His musicians also knew it! His eyes lit up, and he skipped away redeemed.

'Ask her to dance!' Jill threatened out the side of her considerable mouth. 'Seth can't stand. You have to dance with her.'

As the band struck up, with as much relish as I might have felt at the prospect of a heart bypass operation, I invited the Gorgon to dance. With a gracious tilt of the head she stood up. I held out my arm and bowed as I had seen Franchot Tone bow in *The Little Foxes*. She responded for the crowd like a Virgin on her First Date.

It was strictly quick-quick-slow. This I understood as she clamped my right hand in the small of her back in the 'Come Dancing' position; this had to be as Fred and Ginger did it. As we quick-quick-slowed round the floor, to my horror it cleared. One after the other every couple left till Bette Davis and I were the only ones left dancing. It was like all the Second Features I had sat through on a Saturday afternoon with my Aunt Gatty, with this difference; in the movies the time is concertina-ed and they cut when the scene becomes boring. In real life the scene goes on. And on. And on. Forever. People started to applaud. My partner glowed, basking in their approval. We would neither of us have got into the beginners' class at any reputable ballroom dancing academy, but Bette Davis' feet, when they weren't standing on mine, were firmly planted in Hollywood's Cotton-Wool Clouds, and she seemed to herself to be playing Scarlett O'Hara at last, dancing the night away at The Ball with Rhett Butler. Applause, even for a decrepit Film Star clod-hopping herself into a spiral, begins to taper off; my face by this time was the colour and texture of the beaded dress after the occupant had chucked champagne at it, and there was still five minutes to go of 'Mississippi Mud' I reckoned, since the band leader was clearly intent on giving his celebrity guest the full Concert Version. In desperation, I searched among the customers for some topic to regale the Gorgon for the remaining, agonising minutes.

'The Beatles are here!' I popped in her ear.

'The Beatles!' She jammed her stilettos on both my feet at once, and her eyes bulged like headlamps. 'Is Ringo here?' She cast a sudden glance over her shoulder, all but knocking us both over, towards the table where I had spotted the celebrated group. I nodded.

'D'you know Ringo?'

'I met him once.' Roman Polanski had thrown a bash after the premiere of *Repulsion* at some millionaire's mansion in Hampstead which the Beatles attended. I had met them all then, but some years had passed and I was sure they wouldn't remember me.

'You gotta introduce me to Ringo. Who needs this shit?' She dropped my enveloping arms and her pose as Scarlett O'Hara for her true role as Clytemnestra, soaked in blood to the elbows. She grabbed my arm and pummelled her way through her admirers like a scrum-half.

'Lead me to him.'

With a lurch in my stomach I thought: 'What if he has no idea who Bette Davis is?' They were from different generations, and if Ringo hadn't been brought up on the cinema he might say 'Betty Who?' in his winning Scouse way, and thereby with one syllable – 'Who?' – unleash Armageddon. I had a fleeting image of tables flying through plate-glass, of crockery being smashed to smithereens, of sneering lips erupting in breakers of foam, of acres of carpets being masticated and torn apart, and of the blood, the undammed rivers of blood…

At any night club in the West End of London, in New York, in Paris or in Rome, the unspoken code of manners is that Celebrities are left unpestered. It was therefore with extreme reluctance that I put my hand on Ringo's shoulder.

'Ringo?' He looked up, instantly on the defensive. 'Bette Davis very much wants to meet you!'

A blank look. Oh God! Here we go. Exactly what I feared was about to happen. 'Fuck off!' I dreaded hearing him say, or something Liverpudlian and infinitely worse. His glance passed over my shoulder to my dancing-partner who lingered shyly behind me, reverting to the role of virgin on her first date.

'BETTE DAVIS!' he shouted, leaping to his feet. Saved! I left them to their mutual massage and did a most ungentlemanly thing. I returned to our table where Seth lay spreadeagled face-down in his garnished Club Sandwich. Jill was nibbling at some nuts like a shop-soiled hamster.

'That's it, pet,' I said. 'I've done my duty by your psychopath. I'm going home. You could call a Black Maria for Seth if a taxi won't take him. You're okay to drive and the Dorchester's on your way. Sorry to leave it all to you – but not sorry enough, I suppose. Ring you tomorrow. Take care.' I'd kissed her and gone before she could swallow.

The Grey Lady phoned me the next morning. Her mistress had evidently experienced post-party remorse. 'Bette wanted me to tell you how much she enjoyed meeting you, John, and she wondered if you would give us the pleasure of your company for supper tomorrow night at the Caprice.'

'Thank you,' I said, thunderstruck, 'but I'm afraid I'm busy tomorrow evening,' which I was not.

I never heard from the Grey Lady or her Dragon Empress again, though fear of a chance encounter disturbed my slumbers for years to come.

9 DEAD DRUNK AND DOWN UNDER
Sleuth *in Sydney*

A horrible woman called Georgie
Was holding a Lesbian orgy.
She said to her chum,
'Let's have less of the bum,
And more of your old Cheddar Gorgie!'

HAROLD LANG COMPOSED the above limerick in the time it takes to eat a sausage roll. It was the summer of 1970, and we were rehearsing for *Sleuth*, a smash-hit thriller that we were taking to Australia. Without spoiling the denouement I can reveal that, though there are four characters in the cast, the play is often done with only two actors. The other actor in our production was Patrick Wymark, who had leapt to fame in *The Power Game*, although he had learned his craft on stage doing the classics with the Stratford Memorial Theatre before it was the RSC.

Patrick was an alcoholic, and by this time, although he was very talented, few directors would work with him. Knowing this to be the case, Patrick demanded Harold as his director, who, as a personal friend, would be more likely to put up with Patrick's problems.

Harold had a shock of white-blonde hair, a cruel slash of a mouth with no lips at all, and a brisk, small-stepping gait which was 'camp' without being effeminate. He was the most fascinating and perhaps the cleverest man I have ever known well, and by a long neck the funniest. I was not alone in prizing his mind and his humour above other mortals', for his devoted admirers included Kenneth Tynan, Robert Shaw, Margaret Drabble, Tyrone Guthrie, John Gielgud, Alec Guinness and many others, including my colleagues Gary Raymond and his wife Delena Kidd, and now myself.

Because I knew of Harold's reputation, because I loved the play and the role of Milo Tindle, and because I wanted more than anything to spend some time in Sydney and to visit Thailand and Bali on the way to the other side of the world – at Harold's insistence we were being allowed ten days for the journey – I reckoned I could put up with Patrick and his problem.

Patrick had been warned by his doctor that if he went on drinking he would be dead within a year. Harold had to start rehearsals earlier and earlier in the morning, so that we could get most of our work done before lunchtime. By the last week we were on our marks by eight o'clock. At half past nine Patrick made his first trip to the lavatory. We would be in the middle of a scene, when he would suddenly remember that he had to make an urgent phone call. By eleven he was mellow, and by noon he was slurring his words and forgetting his lines. I was so determined we were going to get to Thailand, Bali and Australia, and make a success of the play, that after rehearsals I would go home with him to Hampstead and try to help him learn his script. It was a vain exercise. He spent every evening sucking on a tumbler of blue milk. I could see the vodka, almost phosphorescent in the glass, but I wasn't supposed to know. I tried to get him to eat, but nothing could stop him drinking.

Even when he nearly killed me.

Sleuth is a puzzle play, in my view the most brilliant in its genre. It is a spoof of the 'Snobbery with Violence' school of Agatha Christie. There are two crucial revolvers in it, a 'lethal' gun and a 'trick' gun.

The 'lethal' gun is used to establish that the weapon can kill. Flame issues from its barrel when several ornaments on the set appear to get shattered. (Stage Management Special Effects.) This effectively proves its firing power. This 'lethal' gun is then changed by sleight of hand, behind a pillar, to –

The 'trick' gun, which looks the same as the 'lethal' gun, but is safe, since the exploding blank bursts through the side and not out of the mouth of the barrel.

Having swopped the guns, Patrick's character Andrew Wyke places the barrel of the 'trick' revolver against my character Milo's temple and fires.

Patrick was so pissed one night in Sydney that he failed to switch the revolvers. If I hadn't been watching him like a hawk, and hadn't ferociously changed the guns in full view of the audience, these memoirs would have remained unwritten. If I hadn't been killed, I would almost certainly have been blinded.

This episode broke the dam of my tolerance. I waited till the next morning till he was comparatively sober, and laid down my terms.

'My father died of drink,' I told him. 'I know every time you slip off to make a phone call, or pop to the loo, that you're topping up. You're an alcoholic. It's a disease. You can get drunk at lunchtime, if you must. But you must have four hours sleep before the evening performance, and you must do it sober. I cannot and I will not go on stage for two and a half hours, and play to a paying public

WITH HALF THE CAST DRUNK! I'll come out and get drunk with you afterwards, if that'll make you happy. But if you are ever drunk again before we start, either the understudy goes on or we cancel the performance. And that is my ultimatum Patrick. You don't get another chance!'

Without drink, most drunks are frightened and guilty and desperate to please. After our showdown he came to see me every evening in my dressing room before the show, ostensibly to pay a social visit, but in truth, to let me see that he was sober. We became close friends as a result of this debacle, and he never let me down again.

Until the night he died.

Patrick was very short, not much over five feet tall, with a thick neck, a wide mouth and poppy eyes. He looked like a toad, and he had a fog-horn for a voice through drinking and smoking to excess, but for some reason which I could never fathom he was irresistible to women. I knew several of his significantly attractive girlfriends, and he had a beautiful mistress at the end. I can't imagine how he was capable of making love to her, but perhaps drink didn't affect him the way it affects me.

She was called Fifi. I'm sorry, but that's the truth of it. She was Eurasian and extraordinarily sensual and seductive.

After a triumphant season of three months in Sydney, we were about to open in Melbourne, and Patrick and I were due to appear on a television programme on the Sunday prior to our opening night. I had rented an apartment for what I took for granted would be a two- or three-months run, but Patrick preferred to stay in a hotel. I had called his room continuously, receiving no response, and with mounting anger I assumed he was in a drunken stupor and would be unfit to help me with the promotion spot that night.

Finally, I went to the hotel, master keys were used, and we found him. He was half way into a clean shirt, trying to make himself presentable for his appearance on the television, with a gash on his forehead where he had hit the bed-frame on his way to the floor. Felled like a shot Skippy. Or maybe a wallaby. No death struggles. Out like a light.

Australian law requires official recognition of the corpse, and I was requested to identify the body the next day at the mortuary. By this time, Fifi had flown in from Sydney, and we went to the morgue together.

It was raining, and the tram-cars were sloshing their way along the Victorian Boulevards so beloved of the antipodeans who hanker after history. They're welcome to their tram cars and their history and their rain. Give me the crystal skyscrapers of Sydney, the endless sunshine and the silver beaches close-packed with golden sardines.

The trolley bearing Patrick's body was wheeled in beyond the glass panel that divides the living from the dead in such places. Fifi and I clung together.

I signed the requisite forms then drove Fifi through the unremitting downpour to my apartment. I wrote a note to Patrick's widow, Olwen, whom I have never met. She is now a successful playwright.

We had supper from the freezer without candles and almost without conversation, for we had nothing in common except Patrick and he was gone.

There was only one bedroom in my apartment, so I put fresh sheets on the bed for Fifi and made one up for myself on the sofa. At the end of a dismal evening, gently enfolding the weeping Fifi in my arms, I said goodnight to her at the bedroom door. She held my hand for a moment. But then she wouldn't let go.

She firmly led me towards the bed, and I went to comfort her. When she started to undress me, I felt unafraid, for there was nothing required of me except to be there.

I can ascribe my response to Fifi on this occasion to the absence of any necessity to be a good lover. I had initiated nothing, yet I was aroused. Fifi and I made love, and it is the only time in my life that I have achieved intercourse with a woman without experiencing paralysing anxiety. Death, I found to my dismay, is better than Viagra.

I saw Fifi off at the airport the next day, and I have never seen or heard from her again.

On his way home after our opening night in Sydney, Harold had a massive heart attack and died in a Cairo hospital at the age of forty-seven.

Three of us had left England, and I returned alone.

During the run of *Sleuth* in Australia, my Aunt Gatty died. With her tough little legs still peddling her Singer sewing machine, she had ridden into the sunset.

'What's fur ye'll no go past ye.'

'If you don't get whit ye want – WANT WHIT YE GET!'

Apart from good health, what is more important than the incomparable gift of a good education? And that gift to me was paid for out of my Aunt Gatty's sweat-shop wages. What was for me might well have gone past me, without her timely intervention. It's one of the sad aspects of being an atheist that I can't believe she's getting her reward in heaven.

At least she lived to see me in The Pictures.

In autumn 1970 I returned to London full of good intentions, and George left me. We had both been twenty-three years old when we had first set up home together in Hampstead. Later, there had been the halcyon days in Buckinghamshire, where for five years I had played at being a Film Star. Real film stars don't have to do this. It comes naturally with the bank balance. But I had no regrets.

I had plunged straight from analysis into a total commitment, and perhaps there was part of me that felt I had missed out on the wild oats. In 1967 the law had finally been changed, and sexual relations between consenting males over twenty-one in private was no longer a criminal offence. It opened the doors to a future inconceivable in my youth, a life free of fear.

In the theatre, where I thankfully have spent by far the most part of my life, being red-haired, left-handed, tone-deaf, colour-blind, bald, or hairy, causes more consternation than being gay. In the theatre the only condition to be pitied is the resting position.

In the fifteen years that George and I had lived together, there had been some major upheavals in our relationship because I kept falling in love. First, there had been Frank, my Neanderthal Puerto Rican, the Heathcliff to my Cathy, followed by Dany, the Candida to my Marchbanks. Then there was Rudy, my secret rapture, doomed from the start... And finally there was B, a truly volcanic upheaval. We lived together for a year in Manchester, while we were both working for Granada Television in The Stables Theatre. It was cowardice alone that stopped me from leaving George for good. Fifteen years was a long time. I hadn't the stomach to paddle about in the blood and the tears. So I stayed.

Then George went. He was fed up with my peccadilloes.

I took a long time to recover. I went to Rome, rented an apartment near the Piazza Navona, and started work on my first novel.

When I came back to London, I bought two terrace houses side by side in what was then a slum in unfashionable Notting Hill. When they were converted, I lived in one, and George in the other. We remained friends, but went our separate ways.

It was five more years before I met Rod in Africa.

10 WHEN YOU LEAST EXPECT IT
Apartheid, and The Big One

THE AIR IN SOWETO was blue with cooking fires. The rows upon rows of brick bungalows stretched as far as the eye could see, a prison camp the size of a city. A black and white pinto horse was wandering unfettered in a patch of wasteground strewn with rubbish, flubbering vainly with his lips in search of grazing, then pretending to crop the weeds to save face and give him something to do. From the Town Hall came the thrilling sound of thirty violins being bowed in unison by thirty children learning to play the same sweet tune. It pierced through the pervading dust like a gleam of hope, it soared above the corrugated iron rooftops then was lost forever, long before it reached Johannesburg.

This was Sunday, after the carnage. When Saturday comes, deprived of hope and dignity, these segregated slaves get drunk and kill each other on almost any pretext. Powerlessness breeds resentment, and poverty creates thugs and corruption. Xhosa fights Zulu to the death. Ancient tribal hatreds are fostered by a government policy of Divide and Rule. Soweto is not a safe place to be on a Saturday night.

But Sundays, when the thugs are dead and the drunks are sleeping, was when Sam Mangwane held his rehearsals. Sam was an actor and an impresario, with his own company of professional players.

As well as conventional, published dramas and comedies, which they sometimes adapted to a township setting, Sam and his company wrote and improvised their own plays and performed in all the townships of South Africa playing to full and enthusiastic audiences, while making just enough to live on and continue with the struggle. For most of their own plays were shouts of rage against apartheid, even if they were disguised as knockabout farce with interludes of reggae.

I was privileged to work with Sam and his group every Sunday while I was in Johannesburg. This had come about through my friendship with a fearless South African campaigner called Beth Finney, who made it her life's work to circumvent all the rules. As a writer and an actress, she somehow got access to banned plays, and collaborated with Sam on his adaptations; she even snaffled paint and other useful materials for his sets from the scene-dock of the Civic Theatre.

She got me my permit to enter Soweto, which was totally out of bounds to white South Africans.

The acting in Sam's company had a sincerity, an ease, an exuberance, a blazing truth about it that floored me. It was so different from our restrained style that I felt they were teaching me, and not the other way around.

'What the fuck has your white man's theatre got to do with us kaffirs, man?' Joshua asked me. He was right. I was there in Soweto not to bring enlightenment to the poor deprived natives, but to salve my own conscience. But I had to defend myself.

'As much as your kaffir theatre has to do with us white men.' I answered him. 'A lot! If you're interested in people…'

Joshua had a skin like a vegetable plot that has just been weeded, and an outsize attitude problem, for which I could hardly blame him.

'We can learn from each other,' I said. 'The theatre, the cinema, stories in any medium, they try to communicate…'

'Yeah! Don't give me that shit, *wit vark*! "Show us your pass!" Live with that man, day and night! "Get your black arse off that bench! Fuck off, Kaffir! Are you blind as well as black? Get to the back of the bus!"'

'Black, white, deep down we're all the same…'

'Go fuck yourself!' Joshua stormed out.

'What's *wit vark*?' I asked Sam.

He looked embarassed. 'White pig.' He apologised for Joshua's behaviour. I understood his resentment, but it didn't make me like the aggressive bastard.

I did some mime with them, based on the horses in *Equus*, which of course they weren't allowed to see, and this intrigued them. Within minutes they were flesh and blood stallions, as convincing as the ones I was appearing with nightly. I improvised the storm scene from *The Tempest*, with only a long broom handle as the bridge, and beautiful, busty Adela as the Figurehead. I do not think I am fooling myself if I believe this group would have taken London by storm.

Soweto is Africa. The white suburbs of Johannesburg and Capetown in which we had been entertained so lavishly and so often were like Swiss cantons with black servants. I made close and loving friends in Sam's company and would have given anything to have stayed with them in their primitive brick bungalows. Anywhere else in the world I could have done that. Here, all our lives would have been put in danger.

I had opened in The Nico Malan Theatre in Capetown in Peter Shaffer's blockbuster *Equus*, and for the first time in its history we played to integrated audiences.

Capetown has always been less strict about apartheid than the Transvaal. The division between white and non-white there is less clearly defined. The non-white group is composed largely of Coloureds – who are of mixed race and can often be taken for white – and Asians, with a culture older than Europe's.

The Nico Malan, financed by tax-payers, had opened that year for whites only. Since Indians and Coloured people also pay taxes, the whites in Capetown called for a boycott of the building till it was open to all races. The boycott was totally effective: there were no audiences, and the theatre closed down. The government capitulated, and the Nico Malan opened as the first fully integrated theatre in South Africa. This was thirteen years before apartheid was abolished. From small beginnings...

Equus opens in a blackout. As the lights fade up, the psychiatrist – the character I was playing – is discovered alone on the stage. On the opening night, as my eyes became accustomed to the light, on looking out at the audience I was distressed to see that half the auditorium was empty. We had been assured by the press office that the whole run was a sell-out. When the lights were fully up I saw my mistake. The empty seats were not empty at all, but full of eager customers with black and brown faces.

On my first visit to South Africa, two years earlier, I had been in a three-hander called *The Promise* by Arbuzov. With my fellow actor Andrew Ray I had pulled a few strings to meet a politician for whom I have the profoundest admiration, Helen Suzman. She had to go to the Prime Minister to get permission for us to play in the townships of Guguletu, Welcome and Soweto. No white company had ever played there before. Sometimes there were as many white policemen, standing at the back with their guns at the ready, as there were people in the audience. But it was a matter of principle, and another drop of water on the stone.

I am neither an evangelist nor a revolutionary, nor am I arrogant enough to suppose that by visiting South Africa I brought the inevitable demise of the hideous hoax called apartheid a day closer. But the writers who refused to allow their work to be seen there and the actors and others who stayed away were playing into the hands of John Vorster's government. There may be arguments for business sanctions, for boycotts on sport or oil or staple foodstuffs which Nelson Mandela supported, even though they added to the suffering of the blacks whom they were intended to sustain – but I am persuaded by no argument in support of a boycott of ideas.

The Nationalist government was delighted that serious playwrights like John Osborne and Robert Bolt would not allow their liberal views to be given an airing.

This was before television came to South Africa and when the press was heavily censored. The theatre was the only forum for controversial subjects, but plays with anything intelligent to say were banned by their misguided authors, with the result that a diet of *The Secretary Bird*, *No Sex Please, We're British*, *Move Over Mrs Markham* and *Dial M For Murder* was dished up relentlessly for years, and the boat remained unrocked.

After my first visit to South Africa, Vanessa Redgrave berated me. Her films of *Camelot* and *A Man for All Seasons* were playing all over South Africa on the whites-only circuit. So was *Look Back in Anger*, and both Osborne and Bolt had written long, self-righteous articles for *The Sunday Times* condemning writers and actors who had anything to do with the apartheid regime.

Vanessa explained: 'We have no control over the distribution of the films we make.'

'Then until you do, don't make films! Is that too high a price to pay for your integrity?'

It's so easy to wear one's liberal heart on one's sleeve, and blindly to embrace the safe and popular attitudes of Radical Chic.

I travel for two reasons, for my livelihood and because I am hungry to learn. I would have to stay at home if I thought that visiting a country was endorsing its government's policies or condoning an indifference to suffering and injustice. Only fools are certain that they are always right.

I grant that these are matters for the individual conscience, and that there are arguments on both sides.

However.

Nadine Gordimer, the Nobel Prize-winning novelist, believed that to play in South Africa while it was under the apartheid regime was wrong.

Our audiences in the townships hung round our necks begging us to come again and believed that it was right.

Sam Mangwane and his company in Soweto believed fervently that it was right.

That indefatigable campaigner against apartheid, the distinguished playwright Athol Fugard, believed that it was right.

And if any doubt remains, one of the finest human beings it has been my privilege to meet believes that it was right. Apart from visiting her in her home, I marvelled at her courage and her tenacity against fearful odds in both Houses of Parliament, in Capetown and in Pretoria. She was reviled as a Woman, as a Lefty and as a Jew.

Helen Suzman.

She was a beacon of integrity in that dark night of lies and self-interest twenty years ago, and I am confident in having such a paragon as an ally.

These are not men, but lions. More than lions. The essence of lionhood at its most ferocious and noble and frightening. These are men who have learnt to dance not just from their fathers and from their fathers' fathers. They have learnt from lions. They have learnt from observing the Lion King on the plains of Nongoma, the way he holds his head and sniffs the wind. The way he pounces on his prey and savages the beast with his mighty jaws.

From the moment the gut-thumping drums begin you are transported to the primitive heart of Africa. Tribal Zulus wear gigantic head-dresses made of horse hair, which they toss like the manes of charging lions.

Their faces are painted to look like demon gods, and their calves are whirling with monkey-tails as they shake the earth with their thunderous stamping. Brandishing their zig-zag painted shields and feinting with their tufted spears, they are a truly terrifying sight.

And the Zulu dancers at the Vaal Reef de Beers gold mine were just as terrifying, but deeply moving as well, for they were exiles from their homeland three hundred and fifty miles away in the Valley of a Thousand Hills, working long hours deep underground just to keep their loved ones and their families alive, sleeping in dormitories full of strangers, and dancing for the tourists on public holidays.

But dancing is in the Zulu blood. It is their umbilicus to the motherland. It is more than their heritage, it is their identity. The mine-dancers have no monkey tails, so they spend hours sewing strips of rag to the tops of old Wellington boots. They have no horsehair for their head-dresses, so they improvise with plastic straw. They have no animal bones to hang about their necks, so they string Coca Cola cans into chunky, noisy necklaces, and they still shake the earth with their terrible stamping and they are still the most terrifying and the most magnificent sight in the whole of South Africa.

I sat spellbound till the last drumbeat and till the last of the dancers had gone. Three of us from *Equus* had come out from Johannesburg on this crisp bank holiday afternoon, and there was a small group of other actors there from the Market Theatre run by Barney Simons, which was the only company in old South Africa that dared to mount plays with multi-racial casts and even to play to integrated audiences. It was against the law, of course, and they were constantly being closed down, but Barney always opened up again when the fuss had died down, and he got away with murder.

I was introduced by one of our company to a young man who was with the Market Theatre group. I took an instant liking to him. Since the car he had arrived in was uncomfortably full, and since there was plenty of space in ours, we offered him a lift back to the city. On the journey I learned that he was distraught about the political situation, since he was of military age, and he was desperate to leave the country to avoid shooting blacks to sustain white supremacy. He was, I was to learn later, a War Resister, and had this been known to the authorities, he would have been instantly thrown into prison. He was rehearsing with Barney for *Candide*, the Leonard Bernstein musical. This was not due to open for two more weeks, so he had the evenings free.

'Come and see *Equus*, and we can have something to eat afterwards,' I suggested, and he agreed to come the following evening.

That invitation was the start of the rest of my life. There was no thunder and lightning, no yearning and anguish, no heartache, no despair. I liked him from the start, and then I grew to like him more. He came to England, where I had promised him accommodation till he had sorted himself out. There was no expectation on my part of anything further. But he stayed. And he stayed. And I grew to love him. And he grew to love me. And he sought political asylum, for he is an Afrikaaner, with no right to remain in England. And it was pretty dodgy at first. They called him back for three interviews, with agonising gaps in between. And now we were in despair. If he had been a woman it would have been easy. I would have married him and that would have solved it. At last, after four years when he couldn't leave the country for fear of being arrested on his return and deported to South Africa, where he would have been thrown into prison, they allowed him to stay. Now he is a British Citizen.

There was a popular song in my youth which puts it nicely:

> It is when he thinks he's past love,
> It is then he meets his last love,
> And he loves him as he never loved before...

FIVE
A Travelling Player

1 THE GREEN SHEEP
Tuscan Revelry

ITALY. It was the ultimate destination for The Grand Tour.

Byron, Shelley, Keats, Browning, Ibsen, the Sitwells – the list of its famous immigrants goes on forever.

The Alps, the Dolomites, the Great Lakes, the Amalfi Coast, the islands of Capri, Ischia, Stromboli, Sicily and Sardinia, the Necropolis in Genoa, the Etruscan tombs, the Palio in Siena, the primeval forests, the olive groves, the vineyards, the dark majesty of cypresses marching across pale hills.

The Bay of Naples, Pompeii, Ancient Rome, Renaissance Florence, and the most fabulous city ever built on land or sea, the dreamscape that is Venice.

The breathtaking architecture in town after town after town, till the senses reel; the cathedrals, the rich earth colours of the peeling palaces, the frescoes, the statues, the paintings – Giotto, Leonardo da Vinci, Bernini, Michelangelo, Titian, Caravaggio, Piero della Francesca, Veronese…

The beauty, the overwhelming beauty…

And then there is the climate, the wine, the food, Verdi and Puccini, the high fashion, the gilded youth, the music in the squares; the opera festivals, the street markets, the pageants, the *passeggiata* and the tables in the sun, the painted ceilings, the chandeliers, the gushing fountains and the wide marble staircases flanked with cascades of flowers…

Apart from the visual assault on northern senses, what binds me forever to this blessed and magical country is its people, and the society they have created, firmly based on the family.

In Naples and Sicily the notion of 'The Family' has been twisted out of all recognition, into the pernicious and evil secret societies of the Camorra and the Mafia. In Tuscany and Umbria, however, where I live, though the family is at the very core of their existence, they are welcoming to strangers: open, caring, trusting, and quite overwhelmingly generous.

But as several authors have recently been at pains to reveal, there is a dark heart to Italy, which I cannot refute. The purchase of my first house plunged me straight into its infamous cesspit of corruption.

I bought it from The Church.

It was an imposing villa on three floors, badly neglected but fairly sound. And it was vast. It was 3000 feet up an Apennine, and it had been used as a seminary for priests.

My dealings were with Don Sebastiano, a little priest who had lethal halitosis and bow-legs – perhaps as a consequence. The contract of sale was drawn up for a risible price; but I gave him double the amount again in cash. To avoid paying tax. This is the normal procedure in this wickedly corrupt country. Great bundles of 50,000 Lira notes were passed, and I found it hugely satisfying to watch the little cleric hoist up his cassock, and stuff the booty into his underwear.

It had no electricity, no telephone, two lavatories, and a long trough round the back for the novices to wash in. What little water there was came from a spring which dried up completely in the summer. The house was approached by a vertiginous track like a river bed, two miles of rubble with whole stretches of boulders impassable even for my Landrover.

I didn't have the resources to restore the villa to its former splendour, but over the years, we bulldozed the boulders on the approach road. A fairly primitive kitchen and one bathroom were installed, an artesian well was bored, and with the help of friends the inside walls were whitewashed. Simply furnished, the house became a cool and magical retreat during the months of July and August.

To connect the house to mains electricity would have cost a king's ransom, since the nearest pole was at the bottom of the mountain. We had no television, but a battery-operated sound system provided all the music we could wish for. At night we lit the rooms with oil-lamps and candles, which didn't half mess up the floor. It was a small price to pay for a dream.

The house was called 'La Contadina' which means 'The Lady Peasant', or 'The Farmer's Wife'. Since it seemed unlikely that I was ever to have children, I cashed in my Life Assurance policies to buy it. I had reached an age when a wish to consummate my life-long passion for Italy while I was still young enough to appreciate it had become imperative.

I took a month off to look at ruined farmhouses, tobacco towers, overpriced conversions, till my friend Filippo, who was helping me in my search, led me scrambling up through a primaeval forest in the searing heat, higher and ever higher – at every bend in the track I swore that I was turning back – till we rounded the last corner, and there it was.

It stood in deep shadow at the end of an avenue of towering linden trees, a once-proud villa now melancholy with neglect; it had a semi-circular fanlight that had contained stained glass, a vast double-door of panelled chestnut with a balcony above, and serried rows of peeling green shutters rotten at the hinges. Inside were one hundred straw mattresses, ten to each of the ten bedrooms, and each mattress was a home to a colony of mice. It had painted ceilings and *trompe l'oeil* dadoes crumbling with damp because the house had lain abandoned for so long.

No road, no electricity, no telephone, no water.

Perfect.

Filippo accused me of *Illusioni di grandezza*.

The first summer, with a small working-party of friends, we made a bonfire of the mattresses, nearly setting the Apennines alight, and had a tree-felling session to release 'The Farmer's Wife' from the embrace of the forest which was smothering her. During the war 'La Contadina' had been requisitioned and used as the headquarters for the partisans. It was large enough to house an army, high enough to be inaccessible, and completely hidden by trees, so that it was safe from air attack. With all the comings and goings there weren't even any tyre tracks, for the partisans used mules.

I had enough money to repair the roof, to put in two walk-in Tuscan fireplaces, and to make good one bathroom. The hundred budding priestlets had managed with only two, plus the forest for emergencies. And there was a zinc trough all along the back wall outside, with one tap above it for ablutions.

The following year the house was decorated from top to bottom. Out-of-work actors again. We bored a well and bought a generator to pump up the water, but we never used it for electric light, as the noise of it disturbed the peace we had come so far to find. For illumination we used only oil lamps and hundreds of church candles, which we bought in bulk from an ecclesiastical chandler in Sinalunga; we broke them into non-ecclesiastical pieces, and fitted them into hanging chandeliers, wall sconces, little candlesticks with a ring for your finger, and assorted saucers. At night, 'La Contadina' glowed and twinkled in a golden haze. In the morning, getting the grease off the tiles and particulary off the rugs was like the hangover after the party, but it was only for a few months in high summer, and there's no point in having *illusioni* unless you also have *grandezza*.

When the house was full, we put a chemical loo in each stall of the ruined stables, with a fancy drape over the door and a bowl of wildflowers in the empty window, and we rigged up a communal shower outside, which during the torrid heat of August became the focus of everyone's hopes and dreams.

Since we frequently had up to fifteen guests at a time, we all put money in a teapot for the housekeeping, and when it ran out, we replenished it; if there was anything left over when friends were leaving, the teapot might treat us all to dinner in Cortona. People vied to do the shopping and fought to do the cooking, but we operated a strict rota system, as we did with the washing up. The scheme worked brilliantly; no gracious host and no grateful guests; just a self-regulating democracy run on goodwill and a lot of laughs.

I was painting a window frame on the stairs, while George had piled logs waist high in both the fireplaces as a welcome conflagration for our new arrivals. We were expecting ten, a group I referred to as my 'Baa Gooms!', derived from the expression – 'Ee Baa Goom!' Since doing a television series for a year in Manchester, I had fallen under the Northern spell, and ten of this term's best friends were on their way in two hired cars from Pisa airport. (The party included Sue Johnstone, who has in the intervening years become very famous, and her son Joel.)

To my consternation, the weather had suddenly gone mad. Being so high up, the house was sometimes above the clouds, but this time we were *in* them, being fire-hosed from a purple-black cumulus that was trying to wash us away.

A blinding flash, and a bomb exploded at my elbow. All the hairs on my arm stood on end, and as a bough of the great linden outside the window creaked and capsized under the deluge, I realised it had been struck by lightning a foot away from where I was standing. We had no telephone, and mobiles had yet to be invented, or I would have rung my approaching friends to say: 'Turn back before it's too late! Book a flight to Torremolinos! Sunny Italy has stabbed us in the back!'

But they arrived eventually, and the fires were going like Guy Fawkes night, and we had a laugh about it for the first four days; but by the fifth the laughter was ringing hollow. Even Tuscany is subject to weather. It is known as 'The Garden of Italy', and you can't have a garden unless you water it.

Then just as suddenly as the rain had started, it stopped, and the sun on the drenched and verdant landscape hurt your eyes.

And it was Ferragosto.

On the 15th of August every year Italians celebrate this summer holiday, the day on which the Virgin Mary ascended to Heaven, with a feast. For many years Otello and his wife Alfa had looked after 'La Contadina' in my absence. They had recently retired from running their shop and bar at the bottom of the mountain and, bored with nothing to do, had taken this burden upon themselves without my asking them. I paid them only what I could afford, which nevertheless delighted them. In the spring they had cleared the land of brambles, and created a vegetable garden, so we had fresh tomatoes, beans, potatoes, onions, lettuce, melons. Otello was a keen hunter, and during the winter when he was in the mountains with his cronies shooting wild boar, he had my blessing to use the house as a hunting lodge, which gave him status. Status was what Otello craved, and in return for all his labours, I was happy to bestow it on him. Now he wanted to use his status symbol, 'La Contadina', for the midsummer celebration.

The day before the big event a convoy snaked up the mountain with the supplies to throw the party of the decade. From the trucks they unloaded four free-standing gas rings with bottle-gas cylinders attached, gigantic catering pots and several emperor-sized frying pans, an armful of yard-long, slender rolling pins, sacks of flour and a baby's bathful of eggs, five plaits of onions, boxes and boxes of utensils, bottles, condiments, paper plates, plastic glasses, demijohns of wine and wired bottles of Spumante for dessert, and two hundred folding chairs and trestle tables which we laid out all along the avenue of limes. They stretched for fifty yards.

George and I and the 'Baa Gooms!' had spent a day with reams of coloured paper, scissors, gum and bales of twine, making red, green and white bunting to string up in the trees, and a banner to hang on the balcony above the front door:

BENVENUTI A LA CONTADINA! FELICE FERRAGOSTO!

At dawn on the day of the celebration I was wakened by the merry tootling of horns. I rushed to my bedroom window and threw open the shutters. Ten women were jumping out the back of Otello's van, laughing and shouting as Italians do on every occasion, and when they saw my dishevelled head appearing over the sill, they yelled joyful greetings and flung their arms at the sky.

There was Alfa and Marianna and Lucia and Alba and Lorena and Eugenia and Teresa and Rosanna and Richetta and Cleonice. They were in overalls or aprons, ready to knuckle down to business, but without exception their hair was newly styled and set for the party. They must have sat up rigidly all night, or slept with their head in a bucket, because not a hair of those firmly lacquered coiffures was out of place. At six in the morning.

At 'La Contadina' there was a conspicuous lack of bathrooms en suite, so we provided potties, and basins and ewers in all the bedrooms. From the moment the women invaded my kitchen they were in command. They dispatched us all over the house to collect the jugs and the basins – it was clearly common knowledge that we possessed them – and to find half a dozen clean sheets. These we were instructed to drape over chairs in the sitting room in readiness for drying the festoons of fettucini, the dough for which was being prepared in the wash bowls in the kitchen. Amid peals of laughter they crack-plopped the yellow eggs with one hand into the soft white flour, adding a golden wire of olive oil deftly with the other, then with their muscular arms akimbo over the bowl and white up to the elbows, they kneaded the mixture as if their very life depended on it. Then they would slap the dough like a carcass in a butcher's shop onto the big marble table and, dusting the yard-long roller with flour, with little beads of sweat beginning to trickle through their rigid curls, proceed to roll the dead beast out into a thin sheet. This was quickly sliced into six-inch wide strips, which were fed into a cutter operated by cranking a handle, producing long strips of fettucini at the other end. With arms stretched wide as if we were helping to wind a giant ball of wool, in relays we trooped into the sitting room and arranged the long yellow ribbons of pasta over the backs of the chairs and all round the room.

Meanwhile, another noisy group was gutting the chickens and plucking the pigeons and flaying the rabbits and stuffing the pork with fennel and chopping onions and peeling potatoes and arranging it all on blackened baking trays.

'La Contadina' had once been the grand house at the heart of a mountain village, and there were shells of ruined farmhouses to the left and to the right of it. Some were hardly more than piles of stones, but each pile had a bread oven, and with their brick vaulted roofs the ovens had survived and were still functional. Since early morning the men had been lighting roaring fires of broom inside the ovens which they fed with fresh branches till the brickwork glowed white with the heat. When the flames had died down, the trays of meat were shovelled inside with long wooden spatulas to roast on the embers for four hours, the metal doors wedged in position.

The cauldrons were bubbling on top of the gas burners, the sugo was simmering on my stove, I had grated a bing of Parmesan cheese, and the kitchen women were drifting off to slip into their high heels and their party finery which they had brought with them in plastic bags, when Brandino arrived with his green sheep.

Brandino was the shepherd, who owned over a thousand sheep, and he had grown rich making Pecorino. This staple of the Tuscan diet, a delicate and flavoursome sheep's cheese, is consumed in large quantities throughout Italy.

He had a three-ton Mercedes truck for the heavy duty work around the farm, a Range Rover for the look of the thing, but he mostly swanned about in his ruby red Alfa Romeo. And from the boot he produced his contribution to the festivities.

The carcass of a sheep, which smelt like a charnel house and was unequivocally green.

All the meat for the feast was already baking in three ovens, and none of the women seemed keen to start sawing up this disgusting cadaver, so one of the men had the idea for lighting a fire and cooking it on a spit. I was too polite to express my doubts about the edibility of the putrid flesh, especially since Brandino had produced it with such a flourish, and no one had demurred at its state of decomposition. Perhaps they eat it green, I thought, swallowing hard to stop my stomach heaving as two of Otello's hunters shouldered it and took it outside to fix it up on a spit.

The crowds started arriving about noon, eager to be of help in preparing this mighty celebration. Festive meals are a way of life in the countryside. Every Sunday lunch is a festa for the extended family, with three generations round a huge table smacking their lips over each home-made dish, and the women are the stars of the show.

Feminism gets short shrift in Tuscany. These countrywomen would fight to the death to retain what they perceive to be the privileges of their sex. They bear the children and rear them with such unconditional love it ought by rights to produce spoilt and self-centred adults, but it doesn't; because this farming society is almost tribal, and both their work and their leisure time is spent in groups: for their own survival the children are brought up to be considerate of others. Women do all the cooking, they work in the fields at harvest time, they run their households, and keep their homes spotless, they serve their seated menfolk because it is their right to serve, and it is the men's right to be served. Dominant-submissive is not a concept they would understand. The relationship between the sexes is equal and complementary. So long as women rule the roost.

As the guests disembarked from their vehicles, they hung back at first, noting the crumbling stucco, the peeling shutters and the still wild and neglected land with what seemed like disapproval. Then, their curiosity overcoming their reticence, they turned their attention back to the house.

No country person in Tuscany would dream of entering another's house without first seeking his permission. It was comical to see each person, adult or child, hesitate on the doorstep of 'La Contadina' as if about to step off a cliff.

'*Permesso?*' each would ask in turn, and not till I had said, '*Per Piacere,*' would they continue into the unknown. Once they had crossed this politeness barrier at the threshold, they were all over the place like locusts. There was nowhere to hide. My 'Baa Gooms!', who couldn't speak Italian, had to lock themselves in their rooms to avoid being submerged in a scrum of overfriendly strangers and coerced into 'Me Tarzan' kind of conversations. They emerged nervously only when the festivities were under way and the wine was flowing.

Translucent, peach-pink slivers of sweet prosciutto curled round wedges of orange-hearted melons; teams of women ladling pasta onto paper plates with a dollop of the rich sugo on top; basins of salad, great chunks of crusty bread, two-litre bottiglioni of purple peasant wine and pale golden ones of white, jugs of water from the well and labelled bottles containing the bubbly sort. Then, from the distant outposts came the column of hairdos bobbing above the trays sizzling with the baked meats held high before the bearers as if they were offering a sacrifice to their Ancient Gods.

The green sheep which had been spitted above the fire lay still and unturned. The enthusiasm for stoking the flames and revolving the carcass seemed to have evaporated, and it just hung there turning black. No one dared poke a fork in it, or slice off a morsel, let alone sample it, so I realised that my squeamishness was shared by all.

Brandino had roared off in his Alfa Romeo immediately after landing us with the corpse. I suspected he was a snob, and having dumped his rotting largesse, he didn't wish to roister with this bunch of peasants. But Alfa explained later that he had a mistress in Castiglione Fiorentino whom he visited only on public holidays.

Exquisitely decorated cakes – presents from the guests – were produced, one the size of a tractor wheel with an icing sugar motor bike on top, then bowls of fruit, followed by dessert wine and almond biscuits.

Otello had arranged a little band, composed of Nando on the accordion, Angelo on the saxophone, and Beppe on the drums, and once the tables were cleared, everyone got up to dance.

The female 'Baa Gooms!' caused great excitement. There were many elegant Italian women there of course, but women from abroad are thought to be more racy, if not actually depraved: holidays are short, and foreigners don't hang around to cause problems. But Italian Lotharios are all bark and no bite and can be discouraged with a look, so harmony prevailed. When it got dark, we brought out scores of candles in jam-jars and the party continued till midnight.

We all helped clear up and bag the rubbish, and the men took all the perishable stuff down the mountain as they left. They would collect the tables and chairs and the cooking utensils the following morning.

Before dawn I was wakened by the stink of decomposition. I knew at once it was Brandino's sheep, suppurating in the unremitting heat of August.

I rushed out of doors and discovered that the carcass, now black, had fallen off its spit into the embers of the fire and been forgotten. Bluebottles zoomed in from Mars to cluster on the rotting flesh like iron filings on a magnet. I raised the alarm, we chose a shady spot, and retching uncontrollably, five of us took turns with a spade to dig a trench, and we consigned Brandino's contribution to Ferragosto to its shallow grave with a little prayer.

'God Bless our Food, But Make it Good! For Jesus' Sake. Amen.'

But our relief at getting rid of the green sheep was short-lived. We learned by the experience of that dreadful day that 'Six Feet Under' is a reference to the minimum depth essential for disposing of animal remains in a hot climate. By the next day the stench jetted through the topsoil like gas escaping from a main.

We dug another grave, deep, deep this time, and in a maelstrom of disgust, with thick towels wrapped around our faces, we transferred the unspeakable remains from one grave to the other.

Brandino passed by a week later to ask how the party had gone, and to find out how we had enjoyed the *peccore arrosto*. My 'Baa Gooms!' jumped about and kissed their folded fingers then sprung them open, an idea scavenged from movies of how Italians signify 'Delicious!' Even Brandino looked taken aback.

As my friends started up again, patting their tummies and moaning 'Scrumptious!', I had to snap at them to 'Cool it!' Knowing the Tuscan propensity for overwhelming generosity, I was seriously concerned that, with Brandino's flock of thousands, we might be in for a never-ending, unremitting stream of green sheep.

2 A BOY CALLED BONES
Umbrian Grief

A HUNDRED PEOPLE walked behind his coffin. There were four black
horses with nodding plumes pulling a baroque hearse fit for an Emperor. All the
generations were there, from the aged with their harvest-brown faces, to babes
in arms and toddlers with their chubby fists grabbing at their mother's skirts.
Pretty girls sobbed uncontrollably, strong men hunched their broad shoulders,
their craggy cheeks drenched with tears. It was like the funeral of the Boy-King,
Tutankhamun.

In Italy, even death is a celebration of life.

Ossi means Bones. Whether he was given this name before he contracted
multiple sclerosis, or after, when he had to be transported everywhere like a bag
of bones, I have no idea. I didn't like to ask.

I first saw him in the Bar Pantera. I thought I was witnessing a drunken brawl,
the first in all my years out here that I had ever seen. A brawny young man
carried another locked across his shoulders in a wrestling hold, and together
they stormed into the bar and banged into a table. The young man underneath
then heaved his burden into a chair, his arms flailing, and stood up stretching
himself after his efforts. Bones sprawled in the chair like a stuffed guy on bonfire
night. His bearer pulled him roughly upright, and straightened his clothes. He
muttered in his ear, and Bones indicated something. The young man went to the
bar, ordered a cappuccino, and chatted to Marge till it was ready.

Beppe, the handsome young owner of the bar, had recently changed the decor
in his premises from Fifties Streamlined, with orange mirrored ceilings, to Brutal
Chic: all exposed pipes, bare concrete, and swinging zinc lanterns. Internet access,
the right music, and gorgeous young counter staff made the Pantera the most
popular bar for miles around. Marge, a drop-stone-deafer from New Zealand,
had been engaged only the week before.

Adding two spoonsful of sugar, Beppe slid the cup of cappuccino across the
counter, and at the same time handed the young man a straw. Returning to the
table, the young man placed the cup of coffee with the straw stuck in it carefully
within Bones' reach. He gently adjusted Bones' sitting position, patted him on
the shoulder and took his leave.

I glanced over at Beppe, who gave me a collusive smile. Later, he filled me in on the background to this strange and touching behaviour.

There was a gang of five or six of them. They had all been born and brought up in Lugnino. They had gone to the village school. They had played football for the local team. They had completed their compulsory military service, and at the end of it had all returned to their roots – which is the rule rather than the exception in this country – and at the tender age of twenty they were all back in Lugnino where they belonged.

Gianluca was the most handsome, Carlino was the best centre forward, Federico was good natured but not very bright, and Elio was clever, studying law at Perugia University. But Bones had charisma and a wicked wit. He was the star of the group. Four years after returning home, without warning, he was struck down with multiple sclerosis.

He was soon confined to a wheelchair. The disease progressed with terrifying speed, and very shortly his arms lost their strength, and he couldn't propel himself. One of the gang would push him when it was required, but since they were all young and fit, carrying him on their backs was a simpler and more effective solution for short distances and local journeys.

They worked as a team. One would pick up Bones after breakfast, throw him in his car, and dump him in the Pantera with a cappucino and a straw. Throughout the morning, the bar would be thronged with youngsters believing that they were at the cutting edge of fashion in this trendy new environment. Another of the gang would pass by later with a newspaper for Bones, which he would leave on the table for him open at the sports page.

If necessary, he would heave him onto his shoulders, struggle with him to the gents, undo his flies, and when he was done, shake the drips off and zip him up. He would then ferry Bones back to his place at the table, tidy him up again and get him another coffee.

At midday, another member of the gang would pop in to see if he was ready to be taken back home for lunch. Sometimes, if Bones' Mamma was busy (she cleaned and changed the sheets weekly for a holiday let), his friend would buy him a cheese and prosciutto roll and feed him at the table. To avoid either leaving Bones in the lurch, or wasting precious time with a duplication of their services, the gang kept in touch with their mobile phones.

Marge's Dad, Blaine, was over from Auckland, visiting his daughter, and he spent a lot of time in the bar, chatting up anyone who would listen. It hardly deterred this friendly and gregarious Kiwi that almost nobody spoke a word of

English. He was in his early forties, unencumbered, on this trip at least, with a wife; and hell-bent on having a good time.

Which entailed getting rat-arsed whenever possible.

During this period, Blaine made the acquaintance of Bones' gang. Marge had a smattering of Italian, and she acted as an interpreter. Blaine, in spite of his big thirst, was quite clearly a decent chap, funny and affectionate even when sober.

Now, it turned out that one of the gang, Gianluca, was getting married the following week. Prior to the wedding, the lads had arranged a Stag Night, and with the welcoming warmth and generosity which is customary here, Blaine was invited to join their festivities. He had no idea what was entailed, but he liked the boys' company, and he smelt the promise of a booze-up, so he accepted their offer with enthusiasm.

Their rendezvous was fixed for nine-thirty on Saturday evening. By ten-thirty, the guests – about twenty of them – were finally all assembled; including Bones, for Bones was one of the gang, and wherever the gang went, Bones went too.

'Where are we going?' asked Blaine, beginning to panic a little. He'd only managed to down a couple of pints. And in spite of his bluff demeanour, he was of a fundamentally timid disposition.

Marge asked Beppe.

'Rimini,' she told her father.

'Christ Almighty, Margie! That's three hours drive away! It's ten-thirty in the middle of the bloody night!' They do things earlier in Auckland...

The cars were lined up outside the bar, and they were about to pile in, when Blaine grabbed his daughter's arm.

'No one speaks any English!' he yelped. 'And I don't speak a word of Italian. How the hell am I going to manage? What if I get lost?'

'Keep close to Bones!' Marge advised. 'They won't leave Bones. I'll give you my mobile phone just in case. But if you stay close to Bones you'll be all right.'

I got the rest of the story from Marge.

They had set off in a convoy on the three-hour drive to the Adriatic coast in high spirits. An hour into the journey, there was still no sign of the 'festivities' which Blaine had been been promised, so after frantic miming from Blaine, signifying that he wouldn't say no to a stiffener, a can of Coca Cola was found and passed round for the five occupants of the car to share between them. This fell short of Blaine's notion of a booze-up, but more miming proved fruitless, so he hunkered down for the rest of the interminable journey, secretly lamenting his terrible mistake.

At one in the morning they arrived at the holiday resort, geared to late-night revelry, and sat down to a gigantic, pre-ordered meal. Blaine at last succeeded in topping up his liquid quotient with some table wine.

In the middle of the night Marge was wakened by a phone call.

'Margie?' her father's frantic voice enquired.

'Dad! It's half-past three o'clock in the morning!'

They've all disappeared!' Blaine cried. 'I'm stuck here in the middle of bloody nowhere!'

'I told you!' Marge yelled down the phone. 'I told you not to leave Bones!'

'Bones?!' Her father yelled back. 'BONES!?' He sounded apoplectic. 'He's on my BACK!'

'Jesus!' muttered Marge.

'I'm doubled up like a rugby forward! And if I stand up straight, he falls off!'

'Keep calm, Dad!'

'I've been bent double for half an hour! I couldn't get a bloody signal on your phone! I had to stagger two miles up the bloody road with a fucking cripple on my back in the pitch fuckin' dark! Everyone in the town has gone to bloody sleep, the gang's all disappeared and I DON'T KNOW WHERE I AM!'

'Go back to the car, Dad! They'll come back sooner or later.'

Long after sunrise, when the shutters were rattling up on the Alimentari on the corner, Blaine arrived back at Marge's flat, bedraggled and seriously out of sorts.

'You told me to stick close to him,' he snarled. 'That fucking cripple fucked me up!'

The following night Beppe explained the gang's untypical behaviour.

From the very beginning of the outing, Blaine wouldn't be separated from Bones. Everywhere the boys took Bones, Blaine would follow at their heels like a spaniel. He wouldn't let Bones out of his sight for a moment. Blaine had taken the poor boy to his heart. He had bonded in an almost mystical way. He seemed to have practically adopted him as a son.

The gang couldn't believe their luck.

They had chosen Rimini for their Stag Night because it is a swinging resort and a long way from home.

'You don't shit on your own doorstep,' Beppe winked.

It was a Stag Night, after all. The last night of freedom for the groom.

The night clubs in Italy, as opposed to the discos, are almost exclusively for picking up prostitutes. The girls come mostly from Eastern Europe now.

Even with hot totty beckoning, the lads could never, all at once, have left Bones stranded. They would have taken it in shifts to look after him. But Blaine's unutterable devotion to his immobile charge left the way clear. Bones would be safe with Blaine, because Blaine would never abandon the new man in his life.

As soon as the vinsanto was cleared from the table, twenty young bachelors a long way from home shot off to the local night club like a shoal of randy trout up a stream.

And thus it came about that Blaine and Bones were left in the middle of a carpark on the outskirts of a sleeping town with nothing to do but wait till the flower of Lugnino's manhood had all spent their seed, in a shared climax to a memorable Stag Night.

Throughout the remaining week of his holiday, Blaine never betrayed the gang's secret. The language barrier helped, of course. Though the gang was quick to notice that Blaine's special relationship with Bones had cooled.

Since Blaine was about to leave again for the other side of the world, perhaps it was just as well.

In Scotland you are considered a traitor if you abandon your roots. Sean Connery lives in Malaga and Los Angeles, but he espouses and contributes to the funds of the Scottish Nationalist cause, so in Edinburgh he is applauded as a hero. If all the Scots outside Scotland went back to it, it would sink.

The sound of the bagpipes is sweetest from a long way off.

Now that I am an emigré twice over, in Scottish eyes I am doubly-damned. But Rod and I are accepted here without question. We are invited everywhere together, to family meals with peasants as well as to elegant dinner parties with the *intelligenzia*.

Can you imagine the same thing happening with Aldo and young Giuseppe sharing domestic bliss in Kirkintilloch?

3 THE FIREFLIES' WEDDING
All's Well That Ends Well

IN HIS OWN ESTIMATION, Calogero was more than just a communist: he was a visionary. His convictions, however owed more to theory than to practice, for he adhered obstinately to the classic Marxist doctrine, and chose to ignore the collapse of the USSR and the march towards capitalism in China.

He called himself a bricklayer, but he was a highly skilled perfectionist in every department of the building trade. He wasn't a laugh a minute, but driven men seldom are. I called him 'The Rabid Little Red From Palermo'. He laughed at that.

As he converted the cattle-stalls on the ground-floor of my medieval farmhouse into an open plan kitchen and dining room, with Aldo and Mario assisting him as labourers, his craftsmanship, his industry and his gentle but intractable style of leadership earned him my warmest respect.

He had the determination for self-improvement which is the hallmark of the immigrant. He was Sicilian. He had a noble head and stumpy legs. The other day, in the queue at the bank, his noble head was at the level of my collar. It was hard to resist the impulse to scratch his ears, as one would a friendly basset-hound's (an animal he resembled). He was approaching thirty years of age and was as yet unmarried. Being short and a 'foreigner', the local girls had spurned his advances. Their rejection prompted him to find comfort over the hills and far away.

Rod and I were visiting the Fiera Antiquaria in Arezzo, one of the biggest Antique Markets in Europe. This is held on the first weekend of every month, when it fills the cobbled streets and spills into the balconied squares of the Centro Storico of this magnificent renaissance city, fifty minutes by car from home. A spirit of celebration floats like a banner above the heads of the thousands who turn up every month, not only to buy, but to drift with the throng among the stalls stacked high with displays of beautiful, if overpriced, antiques.

And there he was. He was sitting at a table in a shady piazza. And he was not alone.

'Do you think we should say hello?' I hesitated; for in this country, in that place and at that time, it was hard not to form the conclusion that the person with whom he was sharing his table, a young woman of considerable attractions, was a prostitute. This statement is impossible to defend, except in the harsh light of statistics. The girl was very young, pretty, and demurely dressed. But she stood out for one reason, and for one reason only. She was black.

You see a few black faces on the streets of Italian cities, cities like Rome, Milan and Florence, but even there they are rare enough to cause comment. There are traders from Ethiopia – the Abyssinian connection – and some American tourists. But there is no indigenous Afro-immigrant population in Italy as there is in England.

The exception to this state of affairs is evident in sparsely-populated rural districts outside cities, on trunk roads often bordered with woodland and punctuated at intervals with lay-bys for picnics and for viewing the scenery. As the traffic cuts through the softly rolling Apennines, drivers are assaulted by the spectacle of clutches of prostitutes in miniskirts, standing in all weathers, or collapsed astride kitchen chairs, importuning for business at ungodly hours of the morning even in the dead of winter. Almost without exception these girls are black.

That prostitution is rampant in Italy is a legacy of the Roman Catholic Church. Divorce was illegal until 1970. But why Italian motorists, when succumbing to their ungovernable urge for sexual release, should prefer black skin to white is a mystery that only sociologists or psychologists will ever be able to answer. (The night clubs, on the other hand, are full of white women for hire. These indoor girls are mostly from Albania.)

The reason why streetwalkers ply their trade along the country roads and not in red light districts in the city is because of a legal discrepancy. The laws against persistent importuning do not apply in rural constituencies. It would appear that the authorities do not anticipate the peasant class offering up their cherries for financial gain.

In Italy, Women of the Night are euphemistically called *Lucioli*, or Fireflies. No one has yet coined a more suitable epithet for Women of the Broad Daylight.

'I feel murderous, when I see those poor girls dumped along the roadside like traffic cones!' I said to Rod. 'They're not doing it because they like it. Or to get rich. It's the pimps who take most of the money. It's the slave trade all over again. The Mafia is probably behind it all.'

'They lure them to Europe with the prospect of an easier life,' Rod agreed. 'They break them in, and threaten them, get them addicted to drugs and beat them up regularly to keep them in line.'

Calogero glanced up and spied us muttering in the shadows at the edge of the square. Failing to recognise us in an unfamiliar environment, and taken aback, perhaps, at being discovered in a compromising situation, it took him a long moment before he raised his hand in greeting.

During three months of building work, we had established a firm and trusting friendship. Throughout our many discussions, I had confessed to him that as a youth I had been attracted to the ideals of communism. Although I made it clear that I no longer shared his views, I believe he felt that I was nonetheless a kindred spirit.

He also must have known – as most of my friends and neighbours out here know – that Rod and I are lovers. It is never discussed, of course. The nature of our relationship is our business and no one else's. As actors on our travels, our vagabond status had worked in our favour, gaining us acceptance across the whole spectrum of society. This hint of the disreputable proved yet again an advantage in my friendship with Calogero, for I believe he saw me as a fellow outcast: since my private life was beyond the pale of bourgeois respectability, he guessed that I would not be judgemental about his.

'Giovanni!' He motioned me towards the table with a downward flapping of his hand, which to non Italians would signify 'Go away!' We embraced warmly, and there was a hiatus while we worked out which course would cause least offence. Should we sit down? Or would this embarrass them? Would it be discreet to leave them alone? Or would this appear unfriendly?

Calogero pulled up two chairs from a nearby table, and indicated that we should join them. He still had not introduced us to the young woman, but those drawing-room niceties are not always observed, even in the highest echelons of Italian society.

Over cappuccino, it was no surprise to discover that the girl was Nigerian. Many years ago, a wave of female immigrants arrived from Nigeria to pick tomatoes. Coming from a culture which devalues women, some of them discovered after a while that there was an easier way to make money. This was the start of what has become a flood, and Nigeria has a monopoly on this new slave trade.

The girl's name was Kofo and she came from Enugu. She spoke little Italian, but her English was good. There are so many tribes in Nigeria, each with its own language, that English is the lingua franca, and the only means of communicating across the tribal barriers.

On learning that I had spent a month travelling round her country, that I knew the Igbo city of Enugu well and had stayed for a whole week with Mrs Okongwu in her mud compound in Nnewe, Kofo's glum expression vanished, and she gave me a radiant smile. She claimed that she had relatives living in Milan whom she had come to visit. There were inconsistencies, however, in the brief account she gave us of her reasons for being in Italy, so I quietly let the matter drop.

We left them shortly afterwards with an invitation to come to Scopeto anytime for a swim, and a cup of tea should they feel like it.

On a balmy Sunday afternoon in May, Rod was in his studio, and I had just settled down with a book under the pergola by the pool, when I heard Calogero calling me from the terrace. I climbed the steps to meet him.

When in the past we had been discussing building work, after shaking hands Calogero was wont to retreat to a respectful distance and hail me as if he were electioneering at a rally. This might have been something to do with his lack of stature, or with his wish to keep business on a formal footing, or perhaps even to get some practice in for the day when he would be marshalling the comrades to man the barricades against the capitalist exploiters.

He had heard that I knew where to find old railway sleepers. These were now being replaced with concrete, and they were prized for their robustness in making rustic steps, and for a multitude of building purposes. They could be bought for a fraction of the price of new timber. I supplied him with the information he required, but he seemed reluctant to leave. I made some coffee, and dropping his hectoring stance, he sat down opposite me at the big table on the terrace with a frown knitting his patrician brow.

In the light of what was to follow, it must be remembered that he was a long way from his tribal roots and from his family. He was a foreigner in Tuscany and he was quite alone. Even in this generous, tolerant and xenophile community, Sicilians are looked down on. They are sometimes referred to under the breath, as 'Arabs'. At times like these, Calogero must have felt isolated.

'Giovanni,' he said. Country people address you here by your name in every sentence and at every opportunity. It establishes familiarity and cements your friendship. Conversations are therefore like 'Pete' and 'Dud' exchanges; and the repetition is soothing like a mantra.

'Calogero,' I replied.

'Giovanni. Can I speak to you about a very personal matter?'

'Of course, Calogero. Your secrets are safe with me. You have my word of honour.'

He lit a cigarette and examined the grounds in his empty coffee cup like a gypsy reading tea-leaves.

'I've asked Kofo to marry me.'

In the thirty-odd years I have been coming to Tuscany, I have not heard or seen evidence anywhere of an inter-racial marriage. During a very long pause, I hoped he would continue, for I was lost for words. Then – to leave the silence any longer would have seemed like a reproach – I asked him:

'Has Kofo accepted?'

'Like me, Giovanni...she's worried about people's reactions.'

He gave me what, in another man, I might have described as a wistful smile. But there was nothing wistful about Calogero. He had left his village family when he was fourteen years old to seek his destiny in the slums of Palermo, where he got up to God knows what in order to survive, joined the communist party, then, having learnt as much as he could of the building trade, he set off for the lusher pastures of Tuscany, where he has established himself over the last ten years with an ever-growing reputation for excellence and reliability.

'It may not be easy, Calogero.'

I explained my misgivings. The local people are generous and kind, honest, good people, but many of them have rarely seen a city. They might have visited Arezzo or Perugia once or twice, but they have never been to Rome or to Florence. Many have never set eyes on the sea. Their knowledge of the outside world is limited to what is shown on television. They accept foreigners with open arms when they contribute to their economy, like the English, Germans and Americans, who spend great quantities of money and provide employment. But they are not so keen on the Moroccans and the Albanians who come to work in the fields or on the building sites. These manual workers are essential for agriculture and for maintaining the infrastructure, but the people in this area don't always see it like that, because these immigrants are poor. They might be giving their labour, but the locals just see them as foreigners taking their money.

'When I marry Kofo she will be Italian, Giovanni,' said Calogero. 'Like me. She will be contributing to the economy by looking after me.'

'Simple country folk are prejudiced, Calogero. It's not their fault that they are ignorant of the world elsewhere. Tuscans think of Umbrians as foreigners. As a Sicilian, living and working here, you must have had problems. And in Sicily, you are prejudiced against Arabs.'

Calogero ground out his cigarette on the heel of his shoe and left the stub in the saucer of his coffee-cup. I fetched him an ashtray, adding –

'But there is a much bigger problem and we can't shrug it off.'

He thanked me for the ashtray, with a wary, sideways glance, as if I were about to strike him. He lit another cigarette.

'Rightly or wrongly, Calogero, Nigerian girls in Italy are perceived as being fireflies.'

He rose and left the table, greatly agitated. I had no idea how he had met Kofo, and I did not intend to ask. By now it was irrelevant. But I had to be honest with him now. There was too much at stake for both of them.

'In a farming community like this one it will be hard for you to share your life with a girl, who simply because of the colour of her skin, is assumed to be a firefly.'

He was only too clearly in emotional turmoil, struggling with himself, in an agony of indecision, as to whether to confide in me.

'Kofo's a good girl, Giovanni. It's not what you think. It's not at all what it appears to be to those who don't know the truth. There are evil people in this world, Giovanni. Wicked men. Wicked women. Evil beyond anything you can imagine. They take advantage of innocent girls… Kofo's life is in danger… But I am not a lily-livered, mild-mannered Tuscan farmer. I am Sicilian! I will stop at nothing. They will soon find out who they are up against. I have nothing to lose. I will take Kofo to Africa if I have to… '

Gradually, throughout the afternoon, bit by bit, a morsel at a time, he revealed a dreadful story. In the field beyond the pool, Rod was in his studio where he spends hours happily painting and listening to music. It was dark before I called him on the intercom to say that Calogero had gone at last and that a light supper lay waiting for him on the table.

And these are the bare bones of Kofo's ordeal.

Enugu is the biggest purely African city in Nigeria. In the 1970s, when I was touring the country with *Macbeth* and *The Merchant of Venice*, there was a saying among the small European population – there, briefly, only to make money: 'Lagos is the arsehole of Africa. And Enugu is a hundred miles up it.'

Given an opportunity, young hopefuls will make their escape without a backward glance. Such an opportunity was offered to Kofo by a friend of her mother's, a Mrs Adewale, who ran an 'Employment Agency', with promises of lucrative jobs in first world countries.

Pretty girls like Kofo were assured that there was no limit to their prospects in the 'service industry'. Model, hairdresser, air-hostess, receptionist, shop assistant, waitress in a high class hotel… Kofo's mother's friend, Mrs Adewale, out of the kindness of her heart, would lend Kofo the money for her passage, with the promise of employment in London at the end of it. Once she had found a job to her liking, Kofo would repay her benefactress in instalments.

For good ju-ju, Mrs Adewale demanded that Kofo should give a phial of her blood, a curl of her crinkly hair, and some nail-clippings. This was to weave a powerful spell, that would bring her good luck and protect her on her journey.

'Kofo is a simple, uneducated girl, Giovanni, deeply superstitious, as all her countrymen are even today, and she believes implicitly in the terrifying power of witchcraft.'

She was then sent with three other girls on a circuitous smuggler's route, by rail and lorry, through Ghana and the Ivory Coast, and then by cargo boat to Germany. Six weeks after leaving Africa they were dumped on the Swiss border, where a man took away their passports. Kofo was bundled into a van. Two days later she arrived in Gubbio where she was met by two Italian men who raped her. Then they told her what she would be required to do. Her first instinct was to run away. To keep running. To keep running till night came, so she could hide in a ditch like a dog. She was in a strange country, in a teeming city, unable to speak a word of Italian, without documents, with no one to turn to for help, with no means of support, nowhere to sleep, no means of buying food. What chance did she have of survival, if she refused to do as she was told?

She was introduced to other girls, who lent her suitable clothes till she could buy her own. They showed her how to protect herself, what she should allow and what she should refuse, and how best to present herself for sale. She worked on the golf-course road for some months. She lost count of time, and of the number of men she went with. She tried to save, but most of her money went to the thugs who had brutalised her.

Then messages came through from Mrs Adewale. '2,000 Naira now. Or your little brother will be scarred for life.' So she sent her meagre savings to Nigeria.

A month later: '3,000 Naira immediately, or your mother will lose her eyes.' So she borrowed from the other girls, and sent everything she had, and more...

'There are estimated to be 30,000 Nigerian fireflies in Italy today,' Calogero said. 'Nearly two hundred were murdered last year alone. They never find the killers. Many girls are as young as fifteen or sixteen. Kofo is twenty, but she's wise beyond her years. She always refused to have unprotected sex with punters. By a miracle she has escaped HIV and AIDS. It's enough to make you believe in Saint Mary Magdalene de Pazzi and all the Angels...'

I rested my hand on Calogero's shoulder. No words could express my horror or my sadness. I was stunned that he had taken me into his confidence. But who else was there in this village community to whom he could open his heart? I could see no resolution to this terrible story, no outcome that would not be calamitous.

From the first day, Kofo had dreams of escape. But – her blood, her hair and her nail-clippings – the ju-ju... And above all the terrifying threat of hurting her mother... The work is horrible, but the worst part is living every day with the fear – the never-ending fear of disease, of abuse, of violence by the clients, of beatings by the pimps, of not making enough money to satisfy their demands; of the threats of mutilation against your family.

But gradually, reason began to overcome her paralysing fear of Mrs Adewale and her ju-ju spells. If the woman hurt her little brother, or put out her mother's eyes, she would never get Kofo's money. There is a big difference between threats, no matter how horrible, and carrying them out. Particularly if it's going to cut off your source of income. And what was the worst that could happen to Kofo if she defied the magic of the ju-ju? Nothing could be worse than the life that she was living now. Death would be preferable.

Her mind now made up, she started begging clients to help her. Finally, one of them took pity on her, and drove her north. Fifty miles north. He dropped her outside San Sepolcro, where one of the fireflies had told her that there was a convent that would help her. Il Convento Santa Maria della Misericordia.

Madre Maria Teresa took her in. The nuns saved her life. They fed her, and she slept in a cell for a week till they found her a room in the town. She still does housework there for a doctor and his family, who know her story. They are happy to take care of her till her legal status is sorted out.

There is help at last for the Nigerian women from an organisation called La Gruppa Abele, based in Turin. If the girls give the names of their abductors, and how they were smuggled into the country, they are automatically given six-month residence permits. They then receive visas that entitle them to study, or to seek regular employment. Most of the girls are too frightened to denounce the pimps and the Mrs Adewales and her ilk in Nigeria.

But '*Grazie a Dio*,' said Calogero, 'they helped Kofo. And next week we go to Rome. To the Nigerian Embassy, to collect her new passport.'

He stood, preparing to leave. Then he added: 'You can't get married without a passport.'

'Are you marrying Kofo to rescue her, Calogero? Is that the only reason? And if she agrees to marry you, is it only for legal reasons?'

I knew him so well now. I knew that behind his fervent communism, bred of the abject poverty in his childhood, lurked a thwarted passion to save the world. Would it satisfy his missionary zeal to save one poor child from a life of degradation and fear? And would marriage offer either of them the remotest chance of happiness?

'Next week she will have a passport, Giovanni. She doesn't need marriage to make her legal. She will be a human being again. They will give her a work permit. She can pick tobacco. She can work in a shop. The nightmare is over. I don't have to rescue her. But if they come after her, I will kill them. I have a hunting gun. I am a Sicilian, and there will be a nasty accident. I will look after her. She needs looking after. She wants to look after me. Perhaps I need looking after too. We want to look after each other. And to do that, we must be married.'

The sky was blood-red and the bats had started to swoop and squeak round the cypresses. In the dying light I could see that Calogero's eyes were glistening.

'Will you give her away, Giovanni?'

'I will never give her away, Calogero. You must know her secret will go to the grave with me.'

'I meant – will you give her away at our wedding?' He smiled, and reached up to put a hand on my shoulder. 'She doesn't have a father. Will you take her on your arm, Giovanni, and give her away? Will you lead her down the aisle and give her away to me – to "The Rabid Little Red from Palermo" – at our wedding?'

I took him into my arms. He wasn't a demonstrative man, but there are times in one's life which call for extreme measures.

'I will be proud to, Calogero,' I promised him.

For eight years Calogero had rented accommodation in a half-derelict hamlet just above the village. His two rooms, bathroom and kitchen were squeezed between the cottage of a blacksmith's widow and the shell of a larger house which was falling down. For a single man, it had sufficed. But the imminent change in his status required urgent action.

An affordable alternative, worthy of his new bride, would not be found in a hurry, so as a stopgap, he bought a mobile home. This vast, glittering confection would not have disgraced a fairground. He parked it in the shell of the tumbledown building, alongside his bachelor pad, since like most of us, he is territorial; he was also on affectionate terms – purely filial – with the blacksmith's widow.

Nothing would persuade Kofo to live in sin with Calogero. She categorically refused to cohabit till they were married. As we have discovered, she was superstitious. She quoted an adage from her extensive collection of Igbo sayings: 'Nobody buys the cow when they can milk it for free.' While still lodging in the doctor's house in San Sepolcro, however, she lovingly decked out the dormobile as a honeymoon suite.

Viewing the preparations of his wife-to-be, Calogero was plunged into a rich stew of bewildering emotions. Excitement, disbelief, trepidation, protectiveness, desire, utter devotion and dismay. And for 'The Rabid Little Red from Palermo', it was profoundly dismaying to see the caravan transformed into the Roman Catholic version of a ju-ju shrine.

'It's her way of thanking the nuns,' Calogero confided to me. Then he added, a little ruefully: 'I thought I'd left all that shit behind me in Palermo.'

'That shit' was a two-foot-high plaster Madonna with a halo of coloured fairy-lights and a vase of plastic roses at her feet, several crucifixes, some rosaries, a Technicolor print of Santa Maria Magdalene, and another of The Sacred Heart of Jesus festooned with garlands of more plastic roses, red and white and yellow: there were electric candles on every level surface, all fitted with Vera Fiamma flickering light bulbs, and a thurible stuffed with incense which filled the mobile home with fog and made your eyes water.

'It's a fire hazard!' Calogero's smile of bemused indulgence indicated that the threat of a major conflagration was a small price to pay for his young fiancee's joy in her new-found religion.

Communism and catholicism in Italy have long been compatible, and the priest had agreed to marry the couple, since Calogero, though an outsider and a Red, was popular in the village. The fact that the bride was Nigerian, and consequently a woman with perhaps a questionable past, was – to Don Ottorino, a simple man of good faith – irrelevant.

In the absence of the bride's family, Calogero was footing the bill for the reception, a traditional meal of crostini, fettucini al ragú, followed by roast chicken and salad, laid out on trestle tables in the car park. Angelo had volunteered to provide the music afterwards, with his combo of electric guitar, keyboard and drums. The blacksmith's widow had baked a three-tiered cake, iced in the colours of the Italian flag. A sawhorse would be set up bearing a log and a double-handed rip saw, so that after the ceremony, the bride and groom could saw the log, one at each end, and thus symbolise a lifetime of working together in harmony.

And of course there was The Frock. The Frock was the subject closest to Kofo's heart.

'If you do not have The Special Frock for bridal purposes,' she assured me, 'there is no need going into it. I have not pretended! It is too important.'

'I think she's only marrying me so she can wear The Frock,' Calogero said one evening as we discussed the practical arrangements.

'It must be costing you a fortune,' I commiserated.

'More than the caravan!' He laughed. 'She's happy!' Then his smile clouded over. 'Babo and Mammina are coming up from Sicily,' he added. 'They've never left the island.'

He was visibly apprehensive. I truly believe that Calogero, in the racial sense, was colour-blind. There was no guarantee, however, that his parents would be similarly impartial. I only hoped that he had made it clear to them that the bride was of a dusky hue, otherwise their shock might mar the celebrations.

The month of May is for the veneration of the Virgin, and August is considered inauspicious for a wedding, so we fixed the day for a Saturday in June, and the hour for the ceremony late in the afternoon. This would allow ample time for the preparations and for the guests to arrive, and there would be no awkward pause between the church and the party.

The weather is at its kindest in June, before the torrid heat of summer. Breakers of yellow broom pour down the hillside filling the air with a heavenly scent, while poppies and wild orchids spread a jewelled carpet over the wakening land-scape.

Nine of Kofo's girl friends were coming from Gubbio for the big day. Nine bridesmaids. That's what I call a contingent.

'I'll pay their fares on the train,' Calogero explained. 'Kofo needs their support.'

I briefly wondered if Don Ottorino would look so pious and serene if he knew what a churchful he was in for.

Signore and Signora Farinelli, Calogero's parents, arrived on the eve of the wedding, looking a little ragged after their eighteen-hour journey – sitting up overnight on the ferry from Palermo and then the slow train to Terontola. After a pizza in the village, Calogero tucked them up in bed in his bachelor pad – he was sleeping on the floor, since country folk work too hard to need sofas – where they all passed the night packed like sardines.

Which was apt since Sicily is famous for its sardines.

Since Calogero's glittering new home was a mere kilometre from the village and downhill all the way, we had agreed that it would be fitting and fun for the bride and her entourage to arrive on foot, and that I should be in charge of the procession.

But first, the entourage had to be assembled. I volunteered to collect the girls who were due to arrive at the station from Gubbio at midday. I borrowed Calogero's van, which he used for carrying his building materials. It was inches-deep in rubble and cement dust: after I swept it out, I covered the floor with plastic and threw in some cushions. I even borrowed some kitchen chairs. I winced at the fireflies' all-too-familiar roadside seating arrangements.

Kofo insisted on coming with me, in case, as the girls descended from the train in the noonday sun, I should fail to recognise nine black prostitutes dressed for a wedding. (As it turned out, they were each carrying an overnight bag and were saving the best for later.)

There was Bolanle and Lolita and Ademola and Flora and Ekubo and Jasmine and Ojunkan and Adumi and Betty. After the introductions, with whoops of joy, they crammed into the scruffy van and started to sing in ravishing harmony all the way home. They were practising the wedding songs.

I unloaded them at the bottom of the rickety steps that led up to the honeymoon suite of the Carnival Caravan, now a shrine to Mary Magdalene, the Holy Virgin, and Our Lord Jesus Christ the Son of God. We can only imagine the scene that followed as they transformed themselves from their chrysalises of ragged jeans and holey sweaters, to emerge as gorgeous butterflies to adorn this unforgettable wedding day.

Bolanle and Ademola wore traditional robes, dazzling wraps in colours that hurt the eyes. Their head-bandannas were piled two feet high, and they wore rings in their ears the size of saucepan lids. The other girls had raided the tart's dressing-up box. They emerged in gold lamé, purple satin, scarlet velvet, sea-green sequins. Jasmine was all fringes, like a tassel-dancer. When she breathed, she shimmered.

They were, to be honest, a mixed bag. Inevitably, there were quite a few scrubbers, hard-faced little whores, battered by life before and after, and two or three nice girls, really sweet and heart-breakingly young – so young – and one Dame of the British Empire. This was Ekubo, whose regal grace would have shamed an Empress.

But there are no words in my vocabulary to describe the spirit of these girls, these tragic slaves in the world's oldest profession, universally despised and feared, even by the men who use them and discard them like toe-rags. Just for this day – a day the like of which each one in her heart prayed would be repeated for every single one of them – they were putting aside the degradation of their pitiable existence, risking disgust and derision from these upright country folk, who have no reason to be tolerant or understanding of the stark choices that face the poor in Africa. All this courage, this good humour, this generosity of soul, for the sake of the one girl in all their number who had made it across the troubled waters of their sordid life to the far shore of marriage and respectability: Kofo Adeola from Enugu, their sister.

As the bridal party assembled, it was too late to have misgivings about the kilometre walk to the church. If the stilettos wouldn't stand up to the rough gravel on the unpaved road, they would all have to arrive barefoot. They could scarcely look more pagan. Fore and aft, the African shape puts its European counterpart to shame. The rumps alone would be worth the entrance money.

Ekubo and Flora, appointed as bridesmaids, remained inside helping Kofo to dress. At last a blurry vision arrived in the doorway of the caravan. You could pick out a little black hole at the centre of an avalanche; this was Kofo's face submerged in a frothy cumulus that would fill the sky.

This was The Frock.

With Ekubo and Flora struggling to support the bulk and the weight of the train, the bride emerged, and it was clear that The Frock was the size of a football pitch. At full stretch it would reach the horizon.

I thought, 'They'll never get it into the church!' But I was soaring on the wings of their infectious elation and I didn't care. Don Ottorino could conduct the ceremony in the car park.

The women started singing a lovely song. Putting Kofo's arm through mine, I squeezed her hand. She was trembling like a fern. The procession hobbled and tripped and squealed and whooped its way down towards the village, collecting dogs and children and frantic chickens along the way.

Accompanied by Mario as his best man, Calogero, in a shiny new suit, was inside the church, standing nervously at the altar.

His parents Signore and Signora Farinelli were waiting outside till the bride arrived before taking their seats. Standing side by side, they looked like a condiment set. They were both tiny, nut-brown, stocky and packed solidly into their clothes. Signore Farinelli was being throttled by his tie. He looked as if he wouldn't last out the afternoon. He wore a black formal suit, which had clearly seen some action. It could have been a waiter's, or a family heirloom. His bald head gleamed like a newel post, his eyebrows looked like two dead mice and he had a Hitler moustache.

Signora Farinelli wore a floral print dress, with a man's white dinner-jacket – the sleeves turned back – worn over the top as a coat. Her crinkly hair was pulled tight off her face. She had an eager expression (due to deafness, Calogero explained), and the sweetest smile you ever saw, marred by large gaps in her teeth. Every time I checked them out, they were holding onto each other for dear life.

Their Sicilian dialect was so strong, I couldn't understand a word that either of them said.

At every stage the wedding was a carnival. The women sang their wondrous songs in glorious harmony, swaying their big black shiny breasts and rolling their mountainous backsides in front of the popping eyes of the village elders, while Don Ottorino fought to be heard above the hullabaloo.

Somehow the ceremony was accomplished and the register signed. The cheers and the ululating threatened to dislodge the roof beams. Then everyone trooped out blinking into the sunlight. Mario's wife Gina threw a handful of rice. Rosetta threw another. Finally, in a hail of the stuff, the village wives demonstrated their goodwill for Calogero's sake. Aldo had borrowed a camera, and all the girls fought to get into the picture with the bride and the blushing groom.

If the bride was blushing, you couldn't tell.

Such a riotous kaleidoscope of clashing colours, of unbridled exuberance, of sumptuous shiny blackness, and of dazzling, toothsome whiteness. As a memento of a great day, these undistinguished, amateur snaps captured the distilled quintessence of a truly singular joy.

Too stunned to register disapproval, the villagers watched with dislocated jaws.

The young Farinellis, one black, one white, led the way to the carpark, followed by the old Farinellis, still hand in hand. There, the young couple sawed the log in half to raucous shouts of encouragement from everyone, and more singing from the girls whose musical stamina was inexhaustible. They were both hot and sweaty by the time the log surrendered, but they embraced and kissed so tenderly, the audience united in a sympathetic 'Ahhh!!'

Then the feasting began. All the villagers came, of course, the women to keep their men in check, the men to see how much they could get away with.

When the band struck up, Calogero and Kofo led the dancing. No man was brave enough to ask a firefly to dance. It was their wives and their sweethearts and their mothers that they were afraid of. Particularly their mothers. (There was more than a glint of murder behind the women's smiles.)

But gradually curiosity and good manners overcame shyness, and the girls were being invited to dance by males of all ages, from cheeky little boys up to dirty old men – posing as venerable grandfathers – and even by the intrepid from the dangerous ages in between.

The honeymoon was booked – five days at The Jolly Hotel in Rimini – but since Calogero was driving Kofo there, they were staying till the end of the festivities.

I had promised to take the girls to the railway station, so they could catch their train to Gubbio (only forty miles away), but they were in no hurry, it seemed, to get back on the beat. They were having too good a time.

They were singing a lullaby now that dusk was falling. A pinprick of light appeared in the dense shadow cast by the moonlight under the poplar trees. Then another. Then another. Then another and another. Soon the dark was dancing with them, a myriad day-bright sparks that floated lazily against the velvet backdrop of the dark hills, bleeping gently, indicating turning right and turning left towards Fairyland.

'It's like *A Midsummer Night's Dream*,' I said to Rod, as we watched this heart-stopping display. 'Peaseblossom and Mustardseed.'

'*Lucioli*,' Rod said. 'Fireflies… Do you think it's a good omen?'

'I hope so,' I said. 'They last for such a short time. Three weeks and then they're gone.'

'But they're so beautiful while they're here.'

'Nothing lasts forever.'

I heard the next day that Domenico and young Francesco had come home later than expected. As far as I could make out, the girls slept overnight in the ju-ju shrine to Jesus. God knows what happened after that.

Or perhaps He doesn't.

Calogero and Kofo have been married now for four years. Kofo works in the tobacco fields, alongside the other villagers. They are both well-liked, and after some difficulty in conceiving, Kofo is pregnant with their first child.

4 MY PASSPORT TO THE WORLD
The London Shakespeare Group

IF I HAD LIVED a thousand years ago I wish I could see myself as a hard-working chap, up at dawn, coaxing my hairy team through the furrows or hammering white-hot iron and singeing the great beast's bunions; daubing wattle or dowelling and trowelling and scything the ripening corn. But I lack the skills and the enthusiasm for taming the wilderness. I am a dreamer, and I would have been ensconced at a busy street corner with a cap for coins at my feet telling stories of princes and dragons and damsels in distress.

When I was compulsorily serving my nation for two years in The Royal Signals, a story circulated about a recruit who appeared to be severely mentally disturbed. He spoke little. He picked up every scrap of paper his eyes alighted on – a grocer's receipt, an old bus ticket, a discarded chip-bag. Whether he was on the parade ground, in the barracks, or off-duty in the NAAFI canteen, he would stop whatever he was doing and approach the piece of paper that he had spied as if he were a cat and the scrap of paper a venomous snake. Once the fragment was in his hand he would lift it cautiously to his nose and sniff it; he would turn it over and do the same again, letting the puzzling aroma linger in his nostrils for an endless moment; then he would hold it at arm's length with a reproachful look in his eye as if the little piece of paper had been maliciously pretending to be something that it was not. Then he would shake his head and mutter almost inaudibly, with a searing sense of loss, 'That's not it.'

This disturbing behaviour did not go unnoticed. The soldier was summoned by the Commanding Officer, whose quarters had been temporarily relinquished to a civilian psychiatrist. On entering, all the squaddie could see was the banquet of litter on the desk, each item of which, piece by piece, under the psychiatrist's earnest gaze, had to be subjected to his patient's olfactory test, all with the inevitable – and for the soldier – tragic outcome. 'That's not it.'

After a short while the psychiatrist had confirmed his diagnosis: 'Compulsive Neurotic. Unfit for Service.'

'You need professional help, which is not available in Her Majesty's Service. I will arrange for you to see a colleague of mine in your home town of Doncaster. This is your formal discharge.' He signed and handed over a document to the young conscript. The soldier saluted politely and made his exit. As he shut the door behind him, he raised the document to his nose and sniffed it. His eyes lit up and he whooped, 'This is it!'

I said, 'This is it!' when I saw Peshawar.

Kathmandu is full of Hippies. Kabul, even before the Afghan war, was a scarred wreck of a once great city. But Peshawar on the border of Afghanistan, veiled in smoke from a thousand cooking-fires, has hardly changed since the middle ages; only camel-carts clog the streets, and black-tented women hover round the market stalls like daleks; henna-ed pilgrims returned from Mecca flaunt their crimson beards and jostle with lesser fry in the mud lanes between the galleried ancient tenements that lean towards each other as though sharing a secret. The town is a fable from the *Arabian Nights*. Pathans, with inbred hawk faces and blue eyes, descendants of Alexander's armies, prowl the alleys swathed in bullet-belts with rifles casually slung across their shoulders.

In Peshawar there is a street of the knives. There is a street for vegetables, one for sweetmeats, another for silk and for gold-embroidered shawls; there is a street for bangles, one for utensils and hardware, another for pulses and for spices in lurid hills between the samovars dispensing pale tea flavoured with cardamom; there is a street for chadors and for sandals and for gilded slippers with curly prows.

And there is The Street of The Storytellers. To this day crowds gather spellbound round these men spinning their tales.

Pathans pay no allegiance to anyone, maintaining a fierce independence which makes the bureaucrats of India and Afghanistan despair. Descended from warriors, for two thousand years they have been fighting-men, as they are to this day. In their castles up the Khyber Pass, behind fortified walls two metres thick to protect extended families numbering a hundred or more from their warlike neighbours, they have every modern comfort. Including television. They can watch soaps to their heart's content. But still they come to the bazaar and sit at the feet of these storytellers, because the stories they tell are about them, about their ancestors, about great battles fought and won, of natural catastrophes overcome. They celebrate their heroes and extol their virtues, they define who they are as people, what their fears are, and what are their aspirations and their greatest triumphs. The listeners identify with these stories which have been shaped over centuries because they speak to them in their own language of a history and of a life they are still living and that is as relevant to them today as it was a thousand years ago.

Tales extend our horizons. They may enthrall us or perplex us; Jesus and other prophets used stories to teach us; they burgeon in the mind and survive us all. The Bible, The Koran, the *Iliad*, the *Aeneid*, the Icelandic Sagas, the Upanishads, *A Thousand And One Nights*, *Beowulf*, *The Canterbury Tales*, all orally binding spells when none could read.

Actors are the direct descendants of these tellers of fables, and I am privileged to have spent my life as a weaver of dreams.

My twin passions are acting and travel; since time immemorial they have gone together, but now instead of a donkey and a cart, we take off in an aeroplane.

I feel an almost erotic frisson when I am invited to sleep in a mud hut in Enugu, or to share a blanket with an Indian in Ecuador. If I am offered a cup of mint tea in Marrakesh, Wilfred Thesiger must look to his laurels; a puff on the communal hubble-bubble in Aleppo, and T E Lawrence can go home.

This passion, however, does not embrace Belgium. I yearn for the exotic, a way of life as different as possible from that of my childhood on a council estate in Glasgow; preferably hot, though I am not dogmatic about the temperature, since in my northerly peregrinations Stockholm, Helsinki and Reykjavik come high on my list – despite the smorgasbord.

In the old days actors were vagabonds beyond the pale. Rootless, itinerant vagrants, who instead of working for a living, played to survive; they consorted with pickpockets and prostitutes, and were considered no better. Playing was mostly a family business, and youngsters followed in their father's footsteps, much like fairground folk today. In China and Japan this tradition continues with the Beijing Opera, the Kabuki and the Noh. No matter how bourgeois our pretensions – honours lists, titles, tax-havens in Switzerland – no matter how many fortunes are amassed from the big screen and the small, actors are still perceived as being beyond the pale of normal society, which is why I found my home among this band of gypsies. And it is the reason, on our travels, why we are welcomed by princes and paupers alike.

We are seen as frivolous outsiders with a talent to amuse, who are only passing through; we will be gone forever by tomorrow…

Gone forever… It took me till my thirty-seventh birthday – why my thirty-seventh, and not my thirty-fifth or my fortieth, shows how random was this insight which assailed me with Damascene suddenness – to wake up from my torpor and do something about the rest of my life.

I had had a taste of film stardom as a young man, but it had stopped well short of international acclaim, and I was now a middle-aged, well-considered actor who earned a living, but who would never make it to the pantheon of theatrical gods I had set my sights on when 'Poor Tired Dick Had Hot Toast For His Tea' and Percival Dodds was in intercostal-diaphragmatic heaven paddling his thumb between Doris Wylie's tits.

I was not going to sit at home waiting patiently for an episode of *Doctor Finlay's Casebook* or a provincial tour of *Middle Age Spread*. While I still had my health I would throw caution to the winds and see the world, or my unresolved passion for travel would start to gnaw like an ulcer at my duodenum.

I had no ties (George had left me), I had no dependants. 'Think of all the advantages of being on the scrapheap of life!' I told myself. I was going to sell up and take the golden road to Samarkand.

Then I had a better idea.

The Dance and Drama Department of the British Council promotes tours all over the world. The National Theatre, The Royal Shakespeare Company, The Royal Ballet, The London Philharmonic, Cheek-By-Jowl, one-man shows. No company is too small or too large to be considered to represent British Culture wherever and whenever the occasion and the venue are fitting.

I rang them up and made an appointment to discuss my project.

I had yet to write it, but I had had an idea for a two-hander for myself and a black singer/actress, dealing with a history of the slave trade, punctuated with negro spirituals since I can play five chords on my guitar.

'The slave trade?' The British Councillor's eyebrows disappeared behind her fringe, before withering me with an indulgent smile.

'With two-handers and one-man-shows – we're talking of small venues. Out of the way places. And that means the Third World.' She paused, then nodded along with me as the penny dropped and we said in unison: 'Africa'. She continued, 'I feel the subject might not promote Anglo-African relations.'

'It would be taking a risk. It could be wonderfully exciting.'

She remained unconvinced. She nevertheless contacted me some months later suggesting a two-handed tour of Sierra Leone, Nigeria and Cameroon, doing scenes from Shakespeare, and I was ecstatic. (I wrote *The Bard in the Bush* about this trip, when Suzan Farmer and I performed excerpts from *Macbeth* and *The Merchant of Venice*, sometimes in clearings in the jungle; and at my request, we stayed throughout with African families, often in mud huts.)

My colleagues and my agent thought I was committing professional suicide by making myself unavailable for 'proper' work, *ie* high-profile exposure on film, television, the West End, or either of the subsidised Behemoths, The National and the RSC. I had had my chances there, but life is not a dress rehearsal, and I prefer a pie in the hand to pie in the sky.

Out there, I felt, over that hill, across that sea, was where my future lay.

I could do nothing about war and famine and catastrophe, about mighty empires disintegrating, or rainforests disappearing. I have shared the planet with Hitler, Stalin, Papa Doc, Idi Amin, Pol Pot, Ceaucescu, Saddam Hussein. And I should worry that Michael Billington called my Malvolio 'cheap'?

In some situations, acting is up there with teaching or with poetry. It can't compete with healing, or the fight for justice, as embodied in Nelson Mandela.

But the greatest genius who ever lived did it. Acting. He wasn't much cop at it, I suspect, or he wouldn't have stooped to writing. And if he hadn't, we wouldn't have *Hamlet, Macbeth, A Midsummer Night's Dream…*

Osborne and Pinter the same. They couldn't persuade the adulators in the stalls that their pretending passed muster. So they took up the pen.

Joining forces with my oldest friend Gary Raymond – we had spent six months playing wicked brothers in *El Cid* – and his brilliant wife Delena Kidd, we formed our own company: 'The London Shakespeare Group'.

We recruited other actors as we needed them, and for two months at a time – the rest of the year we scrabbled for better-paid work to keep our heads above water financially – and for sixteen glorious years we toured the world.

Our sponsors were an unlikely combination – the British Council and the *Tokyo Shimbun* newspaper. Our Japanese impresario, Kenichi Watanabe-San provided the production costs: we opened each play in Japan, touring there each time for a month or six weeks; then the Council would take over our travelling costs for the rest of the world.

In sixteen years we played in over sixty countries, including: China, Japan, Korea, the Philippines, Sarawak, Singapore, Hong Kong, Malaysia, Indonesia, Canada, Iceland, Norway, Sweden, Finland, Kenya, Cyprus, Lebanon, Jordan, Syria, Iraq, Bahrain, Abu Dhabi, Kuwait, Dubai, Qatar, Pakistan, Nepal, India, Sri Lanka, the Maldives, the Seychelles, Mauritius, Tanzania, Uganda, Ethiopia, Sudan, Sierra Leone, Botswana, Swaziland, Lesotho, Malawi, Zambia, Switzerland, Cameroon, Nigeria, Zimbabwe, Tunisia.

All this because of the greatest writer the world has ever known.

Irving Wardle, the esteemed critic of *The Times*, called The London Shakespeare Group 'our most world-famous theatre company'.

When we opened with *Twelfth Night* in Beijing, ten thousand people were turned away because they couldn't get tickets.

Shakespeare has been my passport to the world.

On the unlikely anvil of an idea for a two-handed musical about the slave trade, I had forged my destiny.

And for the rest of my acting life I became what actors have been since the beginning of time... A TRAVELLING PLAYER.

5 EATEN ALIVE
Soldier Ants in Nigeria

WILLIE WAS CROAKING GRACE when we got back home to our jungle-compound near Ondo.

After six weeks 'On the Road', in Sierra Leone and Cameroon (we had been staying throughout in mud huts), we were lodging briefly with Adam and Angela Farley of the British Council, and we were looking forward with breathless excitement to a few days of British Colonial plumbing. Suzan Farmer and I had travelled 3,000 miles by landrover on dusty laterite roads, performing excerpts from *Macbeth* and *The Merchant of Venice*, just the two of us, for over 60,000 children.

We had just given performances at two schools thirty miles apart, driven by our trusty Yoruba driver called Filament, who looked like Clement Attlee rolled out thin and covered in bitter chocolate. We had lost a wheel in a crater on the way to the second venue, so we had had to hitch a lift in a 'Mammy Wagon' with 'God's Grace' painted on the side. These are open trucks, bulging with 'Mammies' taking livestock and assorted produce to the market, that can be hailed like a taxi; for a small fee you can then climb aboard if there is room. All have mottoes on them – 'Queen Mummy Ju-Ju', and 'Ever Onwards – Yes and Backwards' or similar 'thoughts for the day'. Filament had triumphed in getting the landrover repaired while we were giving our second performance, and he had navigated through the maze of confusing tracks in the jungle about an hour away from the great African city of Enugu, to deliver us to Adam and Angela's brick-built homestead.

In Nigeria, English is the only means of communication between the many tribes, each with its own language, so that when children first go to school, in addition to their Yoruba, Ibo or Hausa names, English ones are usually adopted.

Originality is esteemed above tradition when rechristening a child. In my view Filament is a marvellous name. There is beauty and dignity in the sound of the syllables. That alone would make me a proud possessor of such a sobriquet. But consider the meaning: an individual strand of light, a modest illumination on its own, so there is no place for hubris. But combined with other Filaments, from many such tiny strands of light a beacon might blaze, to banish forever the dark night of ignorance from the face of the world.

Not all the choices of names were so felicitous. In two months we came across Hitler and Samson, Lovemore and Hyacinth (for a man), Flobert and Menthol, identical twins called Plastic and Plaster, and an elfin little albino with ribbons in her ginger hair called Astonishment.

But my favourite of all was a diminutive steward who looked after a household of Irish nuns in a fever hospital in Owerri, and who rejoiced in the name of Paraffin Sandwich.

The Farleys had a small menagerie of animals, including a baby genet; the cat who had adopted him, along with her five kittens; a wiry-haired hound of mixed ancestry; and a parrot called Willie, who said grace before meals and at any other time he felt religious.

Their house stood on its own in the middle of the forest in a garden bright with hibiscus and Pride of Barbados and white star-like jasmine. When the waxy insect-eating plants by the front door twitched, the dog barked. The Farleys had two stewards called Christian and Cosmos, which seemed propitious.

Adam said grace again before dinner, and Willie took umbrage in such a stream of Yoruba that Angela put the cover over his cage which shut him up like magic.

My mouth was full of avocado when I felt a sharp stab on my big toe. I cursed under my breath that I had changed from my desert boots into flip-flops for comfort. Everything that flies and creeps bites in this part of Africa, and I wanted to stamp the wretched parasite under foot, but I could see nothing except my pink swelling toe when I searched under the table.

Cosmos was serving the lemon mousse when Christian burst in from the kitchen.

'I think we have some trouble, sir,' he said to Adam in a voice too calm to be comforting.

'What's wrong?' Adam asked.

'Ants,' was all he said, and I went on eating till I saw that the colour had drained from Angela's face.

Without a word Adam rose from the table, and we followed him into the kitchen.

From the windowsill, down the wall and across the floor was a faint, shimmering smear about a foot wide which disappeared under the larder door. Each ant was almost an inch long, but the numbers of which the trail was composed relegated the individual to an insignificant part of a relentless whole which moved in a curving sweep across the vinyl tiles. The sill was wet with insecticide, but, as if mocking the efforts to deter it, the procession swarmed over the empty canisters which had been discarded in its path.

Angela ran to the larder and opened the door. The shelves looked as if lumpy treacle had been poured all over them. There was no longer any shape to the neat piles of tins and sealed containers in which a careful housewife in Africa stores food, but the crumbs and specks which may be invisible to the human eye were enough to attract the insects' attention. For the moment.

Adam ran to the garage and returned with a can of petrol. Regardless of the herbaceous border and the flowering shrubs, he drenched the ants outside in a torrent of it. They seemed to disperse a little, floundering in the pungent fuel, but then they converged again out of the darkness in even greater numbers and continued on exactly the same path up the outside wall to the window, though the smear now seemed darker and wider. Throwing caution to the winds, Adam shouted at us all to keep clear. With reckless courage, he threw a lighted match onto the patch of dark earth where he had emptied the can, but it blew out before it landed. He tried again. And again. But the parched earth had soaked up the petrol immediately, and all he could raise was a small burst of flame which died even as it ignited. Cosmos appeared with some paraffin, with which we had more success. We lit a barrier of fire across the advancing column, and though hundreds of the creatures plunged into it and sizzled, a squirming hill of them piled up on the far side as the vanguard turned back on the advancing army.

While Adam attended to the fire, we returned to the kitchen. Angela and Christian were knocking the tins off the shelves in the larder into plastic bags, and throwing them, still swarming with the tenacious insects, out into the garden. Another sharp stab on my toe was the reminder I needed to charge upstairs and change into my boots.

Suzan was wielding a broom when I returned, sweeping wriggling mounds out the back door, while individual ants swarmed over the head of the broom and scuttled up the handle. With a dishcloth she flicked them off between strokes. There was still a mass of insects everywhere, but they were no longer in an organised column. With a feeling of the utmost relief, we realised we had routed them.

Then we heard the dog squeal. It was a continuous, terrified yelp of pain. Adam reached him first. He was chained up for the night by the front door and already his paws were crawling with ants. Adam loosed him from his chain, and he cavorted on the spot, whimpering pathetically and snapping savagely at his own feet. There was no time to go to his aid, for while we had diverted the column from the rear part of the house it had reformed, and was now pouring through the front door in a river four feet across and inches deep in layer upon layer of slithering insects. Like molten metal or black lava it slid sluggishly, inexorably forward, invading the house with no possibility now of stopping it. We were struck quite powerless with horror.

'The kittens!' Angela gasped. We ran back through the kitchen to the box under the stairs where the kittens were nesting. The mother cat was standing, her striped fur on end, snarling and spitting at the millions upon millions of ants as they passed within feet of her lair.

'There are only two here!' Angela cried. The baby genet and three others had gone. The tabby jumped into the box, seized one of the two remaining kittens by the neck in a ferocious bite, and leapt onto the fourth step of the open staircase, banging the kitten's bottom on every tread all the way to the top.

'She's moved them!' Angela groaned with relief. 'I hope to goodness they'll be safe.'

For we could not ascend the stair to ascertain their whereabouts without crunching through the loathsome flood that still poured like a vengeance through the house. We put the last kitten on the stair when the cat returned, and joined Adam outside, who was standing disconsolate in a group with Christian's wife and their two children, whom the steward had collected from his house at the end of the garden. No one knew in which direction this monstrous phenomenon would flow, so Christian was taking no chances.

'There's nothing we can do,' Adam said, 'except wait.' But the advancing column stretched back as far as one could see into the darkness, and he told us they frequently go on for miles.

We collected the dog, whose paws were raw and bleeding. We piled into two cars, and drove to a neighbour's house. Their children were at school in the UK, so they had rooms for us all, though none of us slept a wink.

In the morning we returned to a desolate scene. The kitchen was more or less as we had left it and upstairs was untouched. The food in the dining room had all gone, however, and the plates were grimy with the insects' excreta. A few half-eaten dead ants lay crinkled in the sticky wake of the army's passage. The curtains were tattered round the edges and three limp pieces of string were all that remained of the candles.

With an intake of breath, Angela whipped the cover off the parrot. Willie had said his last grace, for all that remained of him was a pile of green feathers and a skeleton picked clean on the bottom of his cage.

6 HAMLET IN BABYLON
And an Infidel in The Golden Mosque

NORTH EAST OF JERICHO lies the country now known as Iraq, a delta between two great rivers, the Tigris and the Euphrates, once called Mesopotamia. There is a well at Jericho which never dries up. Since the beginning of time, and even now in the torrid heat of an Arabian summer, it has produced an abundance of sweet water. This well was the nipple which fed the infant civilisation in the cradle.

No civilisation on earth is older. Not even China's. The empire of Ur of the Chaldees, Sumer and Nimrud and Nineveh. With its mighty Ziggurats. These stupendous mud-brick pyramids were the origin of the legend of the Tower of Babel. With the global migrations of early man, the first settlers arrived in Mesopotamia, so they say, from Turkey, spreading over the vast mud flats of this fertile land. But they yearned for the mountainous land of their birth, so to ease their transition they built those earthen monoliths to remind them of home, and they have survived for six thousand years.

Hammurabi, Ashurbanipal. Winged bulls the size of elephants. Civilisation was born from mud. Man no longer had to roam and kill to eat. Seeds scattered in the mud flourished. And by mixing the mud with straw, and drying bricks of it in the sun...

Babylon.

The great Kings Hammurabi and Nebuchadnezzar created Babylon, with roof-beams dragged a thousand miles overland from Lebanon and bound with copper mined in Anatolia. The strength and length of the trunks of these fabled cedars made it possible, for the first time in man's history, to build not only high but wide. Hammurabi's kingly palace, with its great wide halls and its majestic vestibules, crowned with its magnificent Hanging Gardens – blooming high above the surrounding desert, planted on the great roof terraces and tended by an army of slaves – made Babylon the first wonder of the ancient world.

But six thousand years before Babylon, when man was still a hunter-gatherer, the bounteous spring at Jericho gave him another option; it gave him the chance to cease his wandering, to domesticate wild animals, to grow crops and to produce not only enough food for his family to survive on, but a surplus, a blessed surplus. And this gave him the most precious gift known to man, after food and water. It gave him Time.

Time to think, time to question, time to marvel. Time to reason, to imagine, to entertain concepts beyond brutish existence, to envisage beauty, to paint indelible images, to carve icons, to build temples dedicated to a pantheon of implacable Gods – Anu, Enlil, Enki, Marduk – and time to build the fabulous City of Babylon. Time to make music, and to respond to this, the most sublime of all the arts, to create the science of numbers, mathematics, to chart the movements of the stars and to invent astronomy.

Time to devise symbols to represent sounds.

And to record language.

And with the beginning of recorded speech came the means to write down the oldest story ever told.

The Epic of Gilgamesh.

And if the breath of a butterfly's wing in the rain forest is the birth of a tornado in the desert, so Gilgamesh leads inexorably to Shakespeare.

And here we were in Babylon bringing the greatest play ever written to the land of Ur. *Hamlet.* Or bits of it, at any rate, since everyone was agreed that a morsel of the masterpiece was better than nothing at all. There were bits from *Macbeth* as well, and *Twelfth Night* – with music, since I can play five chords on my guitar, remember?

This time there were only four of us, the founder members of the London Shakespeare Group: Gary, Delena, Suzan, and myself.

At this time, long before the Gulf War – let alone the invasion of Iraq – Saddam Hussein was keen to start a Babylon Festival. It may come as a surprise to hear that this worthy project never got off the ground.

Saddam rebuilt Babylon as it was four thousand years ago. It looks like a Magic Carpet Ride in Disneyland. Every tenth new handmade brick is stamped with his name, just as the original mud bricks were carved with Nebuchadnezzar's, so that the most fabulous civilisation of the ancient world has disappeared forever under a twentieth-century monument to a monster.

The tomb of Sheik Abdul Qhadir al-Ghailani, a descendant of Imam Ali Bin Abi Talib, who was both cousin and son-in-law to the Prophet Mohammed, lies in a mosque under the biggest brick-built dome in Iraq. It is commonly referred to as The Golden Mosque. It is a mythic place of pilgrimage and great sanctity, and as such, of course, quite forbidden to Infidels.

In the British Council office there was an Anglo-Iraqi woman called Hilda who had been most helpful in arranging visits to the grand Ziggurat and the temple of Nimrud.

'I suppose there's no chance of going inside the Golden Mosque?' I asked her. This seemed to put her on her mettle.

'You're the only problem,' she said to me.

'What do you mean?'

'The girls can put on the veil,' she said. She meant the black tent that covers a woman from head to foot, with only a slit or a grill to see out of. Both Delena and Suzan are blonde. 'And Gary looks just fine.'

Gary is a Romany gypsy, with colouring dark enough to make him convincing as an Arab. His father worked in the Music Hall as the straight man to various comedians, and since he always wore a top hat, white tie and tails he was billed as 'The Immaculate Feed'. Gary's twin brother is a butcher in Stepney, yet Gary has the air of an ex-public schoolboy.

'But you're so fair!' Hilda complained to me. 'Rosy-cheeked and English-looking.'

'I'm Scottish.'

'Or whatever.'

'You're not taking them without me! We go as a group or not at all!' I said peevishly.

There was a glint in Hilda's eye. She was improvising. 'If anyone approaches you, you must say "*Turki! Muslim!*" Have you got that? "*Turki! Muslim!*"?'

'*Turki. Muslim,*' I repeated. 'Does that mean you'll take us?'

'It's a terrible risk. Provided you stick to your guns and remember you're Turkish. If anyone blows your cover, I can't vouch for your safety.'

'*Turki, Muslim. Turki, Muslim. Turki, Muslim...*' I babbled. '*Turki, Muslim...*'

'Just pray there isn't a bus load of tourists from Istanbul,' she admonished me.

In the morning she arrived with the chadors, and Gary and I watched in high excitement as our Anglo-Saxon womenfolk disappeared inside the forbidding garments till only their eyes peeped out at the world through a narrow slit. Their pallid, sandalled feet contradicted the disguise, but Hilda was reassuring.

'You look just fine,' she said, as the five of us squeezed into a taxi in Old Baghdad.

The Golden Mosque lived up to its name. The glitter of its dome was a beacon above the higgelty-piggelty metropolis while the sun was up. At sunset a miracle occurred: under the violet night sky, sparkling with stars, the dome turned silver; but the gold returned with the dawn just as the wailing cry of the Muezzin from the minaret summoned the faithful to the first prayers of the day.

Inside the gates of the mosque there was a forecourt where the pilgrims fore-gather. It teemed with secular, almost pagan, life. Families were gathered round little cooking fires boiling tapioca or roasting goat on a spit; though veiled from head to foot in black, mothers succeeded in suckling their babies. Older children played noisily in the dust, while conversation among the groups of men and other groups of women and children was conducted at a most irreverent volume, producing a hubbub one would expect in a street market and not in a place of worship. These pilgrims had travelled far, endured much, sacrificed even, and spent a lifetime saving, to visit this holy place.

Hilda and the girls were ahead, and Gary was off, as he frequently is, on his own. I was rapt in the richness of the drama all around me, till I suddenly saw two uniformed soldiers bearing down on me. I was alarmed for a moment, till I saw that they were very young and smiling, and it touched me to note that they were walking hand in hand. In Arab countries this sight is common, and it signifies only friendship and affection.

'Where are you from?' one soldier asked in clear, well-pronounced English. His face was open and warm, without guile.

I was about to answer as I usually do, 'I live in London, but I come from Scotland.' In the very nick of time I remembered Hilda's injunction. Lamely I answered, '*Turki. Muslim.*'

The soldiers' expressions changed instantly, and I could see that their friendli-ness had been feigned. Their young, almost beardless faces registered first shock, then narrow-eyed disbelief, then knowing cynicism, as if to say, like the school bully, 'We'll be waiting for you, and we'll get you outside the school gates!' They left me abruptly, with a hostile sneer.

On our three tours of Iraq over several years we made many friends. We found great kindness and courtesy, as indeed we found in almost every country we visited. The Golden Mosque is by its very nature frequented by religious zealots, and my experience there has to be understood in this light.

Chastened by my encounter with the boy-soldiers, and considerably more cautious, I ventured into the Inner Sanctum. In doing so I entered a hell which I could never have imagined.

The scene I am about to describe is not peculiar to Islam. I have never been to Lourdes, where I am told the fevered atmosphere is demented. I have witnessed religious hysteria in the Philippines, where the communicants fall to the ground in rigid, thrashing fits; Christ is adored in Alabama by votaries festooned in rattlesnakes; and I have seen Hindu firewalkers in Malaysia with skewers through their tongues, dragging carts with chains attached to hooks embedded in their flesh.

My experience in the Golden Mosque in Baghdad was a gut-wrenching experience of such horror I can only try to describe the degradation which poses as religious fervour.

On our television screens in 1989 we saw the Ayatollah Khomeini's corpse torn from its bier and all but savaged by the mob, not in hatred, which is what it looked like, but in religious ecstasy, which looks the same. During the Iran–Iraq war, we saw the fountain of blood in the main square of Teheran, cascades of water dyed red to symbolise the blood of the faithful, blood gushing in the streets to inspire fourteen year-old martyrs to throw themselves in front of the enemy's guns and into the arms of Allah before they had begun to live. They were slaughtered in their thousands. All this tragedy and evil carnage at the command of twisted old men drunk on religious mania and the power it bestows over the weak and the credulous.

Moses, Buddha, Jesus, Mohammed. With the world in the state it is, why did they bother?

The Holy of Holies was a Maelstrom. The area was surprisingly small – about the size of the courtyard of a modest town hall – and in the middle was the Shrine. The Shrine that housed the tomb of Sheik Abdul Qhadir al-Ghailani. It was tabernacled in silver. Under the Golden Dome a Silver Tabernacle. The intricate and exquisite silverwork was now worn smooth by the kisses of the faithful. The pilgrims swirled in a clockwise direction, kissing the silver edifice as they went, mouthing it, eating it, while beating their breasts and weeping and pounding the marble floor in their passage. They tore their hair and wailed; they knelt, kissing the silver catafalque like a lover, moaning and shrieking; in this emotional holocaust it was impossible to distinguish love from hate, joy from sorrow, pain from pleasure, or goodness from evil. They knelt there gobbling the tabernacle till they were kicked aside and almost mashed underfoot by the juggernaut that pounded relentlessly on.

I felt ill. I felt iller when a man who wore the djellabah of authority pinned me against the wall with his right arm.

'*Ach wullah vi sudduch mu cha wucka succhein!*' He spat at me. Or words to that effect.

I said weakly, '*Turki. Muslim.*'

He paused, eyeing me up and particularly down. I was afraid he was going to demand to see if I were circumcised. Then he let me go.

I was now frightened. I continued to shuffle round with the juggernaut since there was no alternative. I cast around for Hilda, but among the scores of women in black tents she was indistinguishable from the rest. If I could just make it to the far side, beyond this frenzy, there had to be an escape into the open, where I could breathe again the pure air of sanity.

Another Mullah pounced on me. This time there was no mistaking his violent intentions. He grabbed my shirt and wrenched me from the demented mill-race. His eyes blazed, and he spoke English.

'You are not a Muslim!' he snarled at me. 'You desecrate our Mosque!'

'*Turki! Muslim!*' I shouted at him, surprising even myself with the conviction in my voice. '*Turki! Muslim!*' I cried again, playing the part to the hilt.

The Mullah wavered.

A black tent suddenly appeared at my side spouting a torrent of Iraqi Arabic, and Hilda proceeded to try to extricate me from my dire predicament. She described to the Mullah in detail the village I came from in Turkey, where the people are all fair-skinned and often red-haired; she emphasised from what a distinguished line of Arabs my parents were descended, what diet I favoured, and the mosque I frequented in Istanbul. She rhapsodised about how devout I was and how I had saved to make this historic pilgrimage since I was fourteen years old, a poor shepherd tending my sheep in the mountains of Anatolia. She spoke of my needy family, my crippled mother who was so proud of her son in Baghdad –

The Mullah held up his hand. With a smile truly beatific in its plentitude he took my hand. He laid it tenderly to his heart. Bedlam was all around us, but his forgiveness and his grace made a bubble, a tiny vacuum in the hubbub, and he accepted my false credentials with shaming humility.

'Forgive me for doubting you my friend, and my fellow Muslim,' he said. 'Welcome to Baghdad. *Allah Akhbar!*' He kissed me slowly, ritually on my left cheek, then on my right; then, cupping my head in his hands and lowering it, he kissed me on the forehead. Finally, still holding my head, he kissed me gently and chastely but full on the mouth.

The black tent by my side shot out an arm and dragged me at last out of the wailing mob into the courtyard.

The Ambassador at the Embassy two nights later went white.

'That was a very misguided exploit, Hilda,' he said. 'I forbid you to do it again. I have been in Baghdad five years. I have never contemplated for a moment trying to enter the Golden Mosque. In Muslim eyes, it is sacrilege of the highest order for a non-Muslim to enter these Holy Places.'

He lowered his voice, which was a common phenomenon in Iraq, for all official residences were bugged in Saddam's time. Since everyone knew that telephones had a device concealed in them, any conversations which might be construed as subversive were conducted in the open air.

His Excellency continued in the *sotto*-est of *voce*-s: 'A year ago an American bluffed his way into the Golden Mosque. He got as far as the Holy of Holies and took a flash photograph. He was torn limb from limb.'

7 THE NAUGHTY SAILOR
Romeo and Juliet *in a Japanese Convent*

'DEFENESTRATION is the most popular bethod of suicide.'

We were on tour for the very first time with our expanded, much improved, sponsored company, The *Tokyo Shimbun* newspaper's very own London Shakespeare Group, consisting of a stage manager and eight actors – five men and three women. We had opened with *Romeo and Juliet* at the Shinjuku Bunka Center in Tokyo the week before, and we were now playing in a Catholic college for young women in Nagoya.

Kenichi Watanabe-San, the spokesman for his newspaper, had laid down two rigid rules from the beginning. The productions would be traditional, and we would present only the popular plays. There would be no *Troilus and Cressida* or *All's Well That Ends Well*, let alone any of the histories. I preferred the description 'classical' to 'traditional', but try explaining the difference to a Japanese.

Our public performances would be presented in modern Art Comprexes (Art Comprex is Japanese for Art Complex), which seat up to two thousand people. These vast auditoria were invariably full, as were the special performances we gave for students, a statistic which I found humbling. I could not imagine a Japanese-speaking company playing in England to such numbers. Ken emphasised that it was Shakespeare that the customers wanted to see, that they had no doubt read the play but that they would see it performed only once in their lifetime.

'It is hard enough for Japanese to understand ancient Engrish, Johhhhh... You must not confuse us further with revorutionary re-thinks and anachlonisms. Swords and terrifones together, rock music in the Follest of Arden. This is all very well for Stratford-upon-Avon. But not for Nagoya... Ah, so.'

'Ah, so!' means the same in Japanese as it does in English. It is a 'filler' like 'Really?' which you often hear Japanese using among themselves.

Outside the windows of our dressing-room, the giant maples flung their autumn splendour at the sky, tumultuous storm clouds of gold and scarlet and pale yellow. There is nowhere in the world so beautiful as Japan in autumn, except Japan in cherry blossom time. And, perhaps because you spend so much time stuck in traffic jams in the great cities, the sight of trees of any sort uplifts the spirit.

There was a fusillade of sneezing, and a bubbling of mucus being evacuated noisily into paper hankies.

To a man – and to a woman – we were all afflicted with what was truly the common cold.

'Defedestration? Is it contagious?' Capulet asked.

'If they fail their exabs,' Mercutio explained, 'rather than disappoint their parents, students throw thebselves out of high buildings. Whed the results are published, in a bad year… It's like an eclipse of the sudd.'

Standing on one leg to remove a sock, Mercutio's underpants had ridden up the cleavage of his buttocks just as a little Japanese student appeared on her knees at the sliding door to the dressing room with a tray of tea cups balanced in one hand. She was faced with such a close up of a *Gaijin's – ie* a Foreigner's – intimate regions that the tray slid from her grasp like a bar of wet soap.

'Oh, sorry!' She dipped her head, blushed, and dipped again, picking up the cups which had been empty and none of which was broken. 'Oh, sorry!' Hanging her head she scuttled to the table, the cups dancing a jig on their saucers, and ditched the treacherous crockery like a hot potato. With her eyes downcast, bowing to all and to no one in particular, she scurried from the room.

'That gave her a nasty turd!' Tybalt blubbered, helping himself to a tissue from Romeo's dressing table.

'Feel free,' Romeo said, folding his jeans and laying them on the piano.

We were preparing to play in a well-equipped theatre in a Women's Christian College run by Japanese nuns. The students were from the best families, and they had all stepped out of a sailor's bandbox. They wore uniforms in navy blue and white with a square sailor's collar complete with lanyard.

'If I'd known we were going to have visitors in the dressig-roob,' Mercutio swiped a tissue from Romeo's dressing table –

'Feel free,' Romeo said.

'I'd have worn my party pantdies.' He blew his nose crossly.

'Which wudds are those?' Romeo asked, unwrapping new tights, since his old ones had expired from third degree darns.

'The Y-fronts. With the motto on the bottob.'

'The botto od the bottom?' Tybalt snaffled another tissue as Romeo had turned his back to climb into his jockstrap.

'Feel free,' said Romeo.

Mercutio drew a finger across his backside. "Kiss Be Quick!'

'Very pithy,' Tybalt conceded.

'Very pithy!' we all agreed.

The door slid back, and once more on her knees our little damsel reappeared, who had quite recovered her composure – till she was confronted with Romeo's pudenda waving about as he struggled to stuff it all into his jockstrap.

'Hello sailor!' said Mercutio. 'You aggedd!'

'Oh sorry!' the child gasped, and sidling crab-like with her back to Romeo's thrashing limbs as he got tangled in his new tights, she dumped a jug-flask of hot water by the tea-tray and fled.

'Quite an eventful day for a sailor in a Japadese codvendt,' I suggested, passing round the Meggezones.

The door slid open once more and the poor child was saying 'Sorry!' in anticipation of some unimagineable gaffe before she had crossed the threshold. Her tray was loaded with instant coffee, green tea bags, sugar and CREAP, their non-dairy creamer, and she kept her eyes fixed in dread upon the floor.

'You daughty little sailor!' Mercutio whispered. 'Come over here at wudce and sit od my face!'

The Stage Manager popped his head round the door. 'Begidders please!' he said. Then: 'Eddy wudd got a tissue?'

'They're all godd, I'm afraid,' I said, taking Romeo's last one.

Snatching up the box in disbelief, Romeo cried: 'Subwudd else can bloody well steal the dext lot!'

'It's dot stealing!' Tybalt protested, returning from the loo. 'They're supplied by the hotel. Ad eddyway!' He threw a a soft toilet roll onto the table. 'There's plenty bore where this cabe from.'

After five curtain calls we retired modestly to the dressing room where the naughty sailor, having learnt a thing or two from her traumas, had laid out a sumptuous tea in our absence: palisades of prawns around a lagoon of tartare sauce; chunks of sweet and sour fried chicken, with salad; ham and rice and croissants and bowls of fruit sliced and peeled and decorated to look like exotic birds; apple and papaya and segments of persimmon, and both red and white Japanese wine.

There was a commotion in the corridor and we made a concerted grab at articles of clothing to cover our nakedness – in the nick of time, thank heaven, for the door burst open and a Japanese nun, her wimple like a swan in flight, landed in the middle of the dressing room emitting sounds which seemed unequivocally to denote enthusiasm.

'This place is a fuckid assault course!' Romeo squeezed his naked arse against the wall with Benvolio's hat clutched between his thighs. Throughout the world,

I have noticed that elderly nuns, with the notable exception of Mother Teresa, remain childlike. This nun, who it transpired was not only the Mother Superior but the Head of the College, was like a larger, more rumbustious version of the naughty sailor.

'Ohhhhhh! It was wonderfoohhh! You were marverohhhh!' she cried, clasping her hands as if in prayer. Then she cocked her ear towards the stage. 'Just risten!' she commanded.

We ristened.

'The ghirrrrrrrrrrrs!'

'Yes. The girls. What about the girls?'

She swept her arm towards the auditorium. 'My ghirrrrrrrrrs!'

'Your girls! Yes! What about your girls?'

She yelped, 'They are still crapping!'

The Singing Crocodile

(A sonnet composed after playing in a Women's College,
where the students arrive and depart in orderly lines.)

The crocodile emits high atmospherics,
The uniforms are black to match their hair.
Its members are in uniform hysterics,
A blend of joy and uniform despair.
An hour before the show they're in their places,
In serried rows struck dumb they sit and quake.
Inscrutable they're not, it's in their faces,
Such slanty-eyed amazement you can't fake.
There's bouquets at the end, and breathless muttering,
A handshake like a mouse inside a trap.
They gathered not a word that we've been uttering,
They sit there till the last before they 'crap'.
Hai, Arigato,* little voices ringing…
As we depart the crocodile starts singing…

*Yes, thank you.

8 BACKSTAGE WITH AN AGED JUVENILE
At Kabuki-Ka

'SNOW FLAKES ARE SQUARE,' our American guide hissed, as we huddled on the floor in the National Treasure's dressing room.

There was Macbeth, Lady Macbeth, Banquo, the American woman and me. We were on a return visit to Japan with the Scottish Play, and as fellow professionals had been granted the supreme privilege of access to the Inner Sanctum, backstage at Kabuki-Ka.

The guide held up a piece of tissue paper to illustrate her thesis, while with the other hand she sifted through the litter that had drifted to the tatami matting from the actors' voluminous costumes and produced another scrap. 'Cherry blossom is blossom shaped!' she pronounced in the reverent tones of an acolyte affording us a glimpse into the mysteries of a cherished religion. This daftness is common among some occidentals who have clasped to their earnest bosoms the incomprehensible society that is Japan.

They may be unfathomable, but the Japanese are volatile to the point of hysteria. It took me three visits to Japan before I discovered the key to their schizophrenic behaviour.

They are touch-deprived.

When we played in universities and colleges, it had puzzled me to find lines of girl students waiting to meet us afterwards, not begging for autographs, which is quite usual in the West, but anxious to shake our hands. When we complied with this request, physical skin-to-skin contact provoked storms of giggles, a kind of prelude to orgasm. It was only after a conversation with Toshie – our interpreter, and in time our friend – that this phenomenon was fully explained.

Among themselves the Japanese never shake hands. Both in greeting and in parting, everybody bows as if their heads are bound together with strong elastic. The last one to bow is the most polite, and politeness in this congested society is the paramount virtue. Farewells can therefore be interminable and can spread out over a great distance as each party tries to sneak in a last little bob. I guessed that our fans enjoyed the Western practice of shaking hands, but I failed to grasp the deeper significance till Toshie revealed to me that, after an engulfing but proscribed infancy, the Japanese never touch at all. The exception to this, sexual love in private, is snatched and furtive since whole families sleep, if not in the same room, then in rooms divided by literally paper-thin walls.

'When I was studying overseas,' Toshie told me, 'I returned home after two years and I bowed to my family and they bowed to me. As a child, when I was ill my mother touched me, but only to wipe my brow and to attend to my needs. To embrace or to show physical affection is not in our code. We find it embarrassing even to watch it in the cinema. It looks weak and uncontrolled. A young child is forgiven for such primitive responses, but adults should maintain their dignity.'

The repression which results from this inhibition may explain their complex nature. Their rigid code of manners, the structure of their language, which demands differentiation between 'Superior' and 'Inferior', male and female, family and stranger, the importance attached to clothes which amounts to a fetish, their formality, the ascetic restraint of their art, the whole inflexible system which lays down guidelines from the death of an Emperor to the folding of a napkin, they are all like the icy ribs converging at the apex of the perfectly symmetrical cone of Mount Fuji.

They contain and adorn a volcano.

In business, some firms provide 'Rumpus Rooms' with an effigy of the boss, where workers who have a grudge can go and vent their fury on this stuffed puppet, and thus avoid confrontation with its prototype.

But we were squatting backstage at the Kabuki-Ka, the vast purpose-built theatre in the Ginza district of Tokyo where nothing but Kabuki plays are performed, from ten in the morning till nine at night throughout the year.

Theatre is composed of two elements: storytelling and ritual. The earliest form of theatre as we know it, Ancient Greek Drama, was performed at religious festivals, so the ritual element is strong. It is said that when the Persians invaded Japan in the eleventh century they brought Greek drama with them, which influenced Japanese storytelling profoundly.

Noh employs a chorus and all the actors wear masks, which seems to verify this theory. The texts of Noh plays are incomprehensible even to the Japanese, since the language is so ancient. In the audience, you see many devotees referring to translations in their laps, like concert-goers following the score. These texts are 'sung' in such a bewildering cacophony that the performers sound like cats being flayed alive. Noh is almost pure ritual, quintessentially Japanese, bleakly austere, astoundingly beautiful and so slow that watching it is like witnessing giant sloths coming round from an anaesthetic. It summarises, to me, how alien are our cultures.

As in Kabuki, the company is exclusively male. Since it is so esoteric and such hard work to understand, Noh has tremendous snob appeal. There is a school attached to all Noh theatres where the elite send their daughters at vast expense, to learn how to be perfect young Japanese ladies. They are taught flower arrangement, the tea-ceremony, how to walk and move and how most gracefully to kneel. They are taught, in a word, how to be feminine. And they are taught this by men. By Noh female impersonators.

Kabuki is to Noh what Operetta is to Chamber Music. It is totally accessible, sweeping in its epic scope, and it is wonderful entertainment. The atmosphere backstage is nonetheless religious, and this is not too strong a word. When visiting Japan, you need a suitcase of clean socks. Shoes are never worn indoors. But it wasn't simply the business of leaving one's shoes at the door that reminds one of a mosque. We were on holy ground backstage at the Kabuki, and we were fiercely enjoined to keep silent. We were instructed to cling to the corridor wall when performers passed us on their way to the stage, and to conduct ourselves as reverently and as invisibly as possible.

We huddled in a corner of the dressing room not daring to converse even in whispers while 'The National Treasure' prepared for his role.

Utaimon was seventy years old, with a hip severely damaged by arthritis. He was playing 'Juliet'. Or the equivalent in the drama we had come to see. He had always played young ladies, and in this gerontophile society, he would go on playing *jeunes premières* to delighted fans till he joined his ancestors. As we hadn't yet seen the performance, I wasn't able to judge whether the illusion of Young Love would be helped or hindered by the fact that 'Romeo' was seventy-five.

Utaimon sat cross-legged on the floor in front of a triple-mirrored dressing-table with no legs: one of several such disposed about the room, all donated to their favourites by adoring fans. His wispy white hair, which we had seen in photographs in the foyer – a reticent elder statesman – was trussed up in a complex system of bandages and bows, which his dresser fixed at the nape of his neck with sticky-tape. Though there were ten strangers squatting in the poor man's private space, Utaimon addressed himself to his *toilette* as if he were in outer space and the world was a memory.

The dresser laid swathes of gleaming white pigment across the old man's shoulders and across his hairless chest up to the ears at the back, and at the front, right up to where the jaw line might have been in a younger man. In the Kabuki tradition, this pristine whiteness signifies unblemished youth, and the colour alone conveys this to the audience without further artifice.

In the old days the paint the actors used was lead-based, so that madness was as endemic in Kabuki companies as it had been among the Roman Emperors – and for the same reason, though Nero and Caligula got their lead from their drinking vessels and the plumbing. Perhaps this taint of insanity added glamour to an art that was already called 'Strange' (Kabuki means Strange). It would doubtless appeal to a people whose reaction to their strait-jacket society is to crave release in the chaotic, the violent and the grotesque.

Three youths with powder-blue pates appeared on their knees at the doorway, briefly kissing the tatami with their bald wigs before they scuttled noiselessly into a corner and knelt in submission. Their attitude was in stark contrast to their appearance, for they were costumed as Samurai, historically the most savage of warriors; but they were only actors after all, humble members of this feudal company, in which the stars are paid a king's ransom (for it is they whom the public clamours to see), while the supporting players receive a pittance, and in serving their apprenticeship they are required to assist in the elaborate ceremony of dressing the leading players.

No outsider can ever be employed in the Kabuki. You have to be born into it. The father's position determines forever the position of his sons: the son of a bit-player will remain a bit-player all his life, with no chance of advancement to playing more important roles. As in the Caste system in India, your role in life, as on the stage, is pre-ordained and irreversible. There are, however, a few examples of talented youngsters, the sons of actors low down in the pecking order, being adopted by distinguished fathers to overcome this obstacle.

'They miss all the fun of the dole queue!' Banquo whispered. Our American guide gave him a ferocious look.

Over the tannoy came a medley of growls and clicks and shrieks and a twanging of stringed instruments, which kept Utaimon and his colleagues backstage in touch with how the marathon performance – at ten fifteen in the morning already in full swing – was progressing. During the twenty-five-day season in each of the major cities, the company arrives at the theatre at nine in the morning and does not leave it till ten o'clock at night every day of the week including Sundays, so it is little wonder that the actors sometimes allow a few privileged visitors backstage to relieve the relentlessness of their schedule, which would have the same effect on me as lead-based paint.

Utaimon acknowledged no one's presence and, with the dedicated concentration of a priest performing a mass, he communed only with the faceless skull in the mirror and seemed to pray for inspiration to transform it into the image of the beautiful young heroine he was about to play. With a long brush he shadowed his nose and his cheekbones with rouge; then little round dabs at the centre of the mouth, so that it looked as if was fastened with three scarlet buttons, two above, one below. The teeth he left alone. If he had been playing a married woman he would have painted them black, which was all the rage for wives at the time of the Great Shogun.

Utaimon tapped a cigarette from a packet of 'Peace' on his dressing table, and before he could unpop his painted pout one Samurai leapt from the corner, maintaining his kneeling position in mid-air, and landed at the Star's side with a match, while another Samurai alighted on his other side with an ashtray. The Star took a deep puff and surveyed his handiwork in the glass. Evidently satisfied, he dropped his cigarette in the proffered ashtray and uncurled his legs from under him. A third Samurai sprang at him from behind, brandishing the Japanese version of a shooting-stick – one leg with a little padded seat on top – and succeeded in wedging the padded end under Utaimon's sagging buttocks just as the Star seemed about to try sitting on fresh air.

A platoon of cringing Samurai removed Utaimon's cotton kimono and wrapped him in a silk one that reached the ground. They belted and girded their master with a series of straps tied in elaborate bows, though they were completely hidden by the next garment, another kimono made of richer stuff. The wrapping of sashes and tying of sheep shanks and the criss-cross of ribbons and the hitching of grannies continued, till the bald doll was trussed like a Christmas Turkey; then came a truly sumptuous kimono with train, which would have stood up by itself. It taxed the strength of four Samurai when they staggered with it from the rack, and when they draped it across Utaimon's shoulders it nearly knocked the old man over. A spare Samurai just managed to jack him up with the shooting stick in the nick of time.

The Perruquier arrived with the wig on a block. It was built on a cage-frame of copper, made of thick coils of raven black tresses pierced with ivory pins, and was less like a wig than a fireman's helmet. Under the wig-man's gentle persuasion, Utaimon's old bandaged head disappeared slowly inside the deep bowl of hair, and the transformation from Elderly Pillar of the Establishment into Legendary Maiden was complete. Or as complete as it would ever be. If you suspend disbelief. And if you're Japanese. And if you know the form.

With as much dignity as he could muster under the crushing weight of his multiple kimonos, Utaimon stood awaiting the final touch. Five Samurai attached a bow the size of a hiker's rucksack across his back, then they all threw themselves on their knees at his feet with their foreheads on the mat. The Ceremonial Robing was complete.

'He's on in five minutes,' our American guide reminded us, 'but if you'd like to ask him any questions, go ahead.'

'How long have you been playing this part?' Lady Macbeth asked.

The guide translated. 'Only thirty years,' she said.

'He's played in, then,' Banquo muttered.

'Is your son going to take over your role?' asked a student who had clearly done his homework.

The old man twitched his little rosebud.

'His son plays only male roles. You have to be specially gifted to play the female roles.'

As Utaimon inched imperceptibly towards the door, ANOTHER garment was put on top of everything that had gone on before, obliterating the inspiration of the designers and the dressmakers and the painstaking efforts of the Samurai which had taken half an hour to achieve. The rucksack-sized bow strapped to his back now appeared as an unsightly hump.

'Maybe he's going to do a striptease!' Banquo suggested.

'He's a grandfather!' our American guide protested.

As Utaimon left to make his entrance Banquo waved and cried, 'Blake a regg!'

But the National Treasure had disappeared through waves of bobbing heads that divided like the Red Sea before him as 'Juliet' made her triumphal progress towards the Land of Make Believe.

9 THE GEISHA AT THE DANCING HIPPO
My Farewell Present

NO SELF-RESPECTING Japanese Lothario would be seen dead without a lovelock. This badge of fashion consists of a strand or two of straight and heavy hair which appears to have escaped from his otherwise immaculate coiffure to swing like a pendulum before his eyes every time he turns his head. Even the unyielding wigs of the young lovers in Kabuki plays have these flying buttresses built in. The smallest gesture in Japan is imbued with deep significance, so there is meaning to this carefully contrived artlessness. Like the flaws that Persian carpet-makers weave into their rugs in case perfection should offend Allah, who alone is infallible, this errant hair, while at a far remove from anything that might be described as being unkempt let alone dishevelled, is nonetheless clear evidence that the wearer is on the safe side of vanity.

When a man reaches middle age, however, he is expected to restrain this symbol of impetuous youth or lose respect.

When Kenichi Watanabe-San's lovelock came to rest, it plumbed straight to the level of the Windsor knot in his tie. This raffish excess was to compensate, I suppose, for his lost opportunities. He had kissed goodbye to his heyday, if he had ever had one, twenty years before, and he had never married. Ken – as he encouraged us to call him, since he understood westerners' aversion to formality in the theatre – was our impresario in Japan, a senior saralyman with the *Tokyo Shimbun* newspaper, which over a period of fifteen years had subsidised new productions of *Romeo and Juliet*, *The Merchant of Venice*, *Twelfth Night*, *Macbeth* and *Hamlet*.

Ken had variegated brown teeth set at random angles in his gums, the better for crunching on his sea-weed biscuits and masticating a variety of substantial snacks. These, prettily packaged in boxes like chocolates, came with one single, plastic-wrapped wooden chopstick which you snapped down the middle to make two. Thus equipped, he munched pretty well continuously throughout his waking hours. He was a good advertisement for eating little and often, for he was only moderately plump, which was just as well as he was only five feet tall.

The majority of his compatriots wear glasses, but not Ken. This was another example of his vanity, because his eyesight was not good enough to tell a sake-dispenser from a petrol pump. Like brothels in Victorian London, in Japanese cities there is an optician on every corner. The islands of which Japan is composed are densely populated and short of space, with mountains in the middle and high-rise urban sprawl all round the coast, so there are few far horizons. Only foreground-focus is required for city life and office-work, and without exercise eye muscles grow weak. Farmers and fishermen don't wear glasses.

Although Ken was fluent in English, he was hard to understand, not only because of his intonation, but because he was in such a constant state of excitement that in conversation with him pleasantries and platitudes assumed an urgency which they did not merit. For this reason his company was unrelaxing.

'Ah, Johhhhhh!' We had been sitting side-by-side in the bus, stuck in the usual traffic jam for two hours, but he suddenly hailed me with a catch in his voice as if he had glimpsed me across a crowded room after a long absence.

'Fifteen years is a wrong time! Fifteen growlious years of Rondon Shakespeare Gloup! Speaking on behalf of *Tokyo Shimbun* newspaper,' – he carefully packed the wooden chopsticks and the litter he had accumulated from his grazing into his hand ruggage to bin later – 'I invite you for a spesher occasion to commemolate your invaruabre contribution to Japanese Curturo...Ahhhh!'

We were in the last week of touring *Hamlet* throughout Kyushu and Honshu with Rob Edwards playing the prince, and I had been anticipating our diminutive impresario's invitation to supper, which was by now a ritual, when we would discuss the details of our next presentation.

Then he would get down to the serious business of loading me with presents.

'I offer you a prayer!' Ken was able to joke about the 'L' and 'R' difficulties. There is no 'L' in Japanese, and those who speak English understandably get confused. They sometimes see 'R' and, anxious to avoid a solecism, they pronounce it 'L'. A common sign in hotels points to the 'Lestaurant'.

'A cassette prayer! I hope you rike it!'

Without wishing to seem ungracious, the Japanese custom of presenting gifts to everyone all the time quickly becomes onerous. Even when the presents are small, like a paper wallet or a pencil blazoned with a motto 'Happy Animals, Tutti-Frutti', the onslaught is so relentless that the gesture of giving becomes meaningless, and one's protestations of gratitude ring hollow.

At dinner on that last night, no mention had been made of what our next production was to be, though after *Hamlet*, I felt that a comedy would be fitting, and was keen to suggest *Much Ado About Nothing*.

In spite of Ken's continuing affability throughout the meal, he seemed to be striking a final note... 'Fifteen years! Five wonderfuhhhh productions! Such a fruitfuhhh corraboration!' I could not rid myself of the feeling that the *Tokyo Shimbun* newspaper and the London Shakespeare Group were about to part company.

What I did not know was that Ken was dying.

He told me he had been ill during the winter, but he made it sound like flu. He had lost weight and looked better for it, but his Japanese reticence forbade him to confide in me that he had inoperable cancer and had only months to live.

In the light of his death some weeks later, his courage that evening and his unflagging good humour were heroic. It left me feeling sad that I had not made my fondness for him clearer.

The waitress had removed the thimble cups and the empty sake flasks, the bill had been unobtrusively settled, and I was looking forward to an early night before our last two performances at the Bunka Arts Comprex in Shinjuku.

'Now the fun begins!' he said. As I looked puzzled, he explained.

'It is my honour to invite you with my boss Toshiro Natsame-San and my distinguished correague Hideo Miyama-San, the sub-editor of our newspaper, to the famous Night Crub, "The Dancing Hippo". All Tokyo is talking about it. We are meeting up with my business associates in half-an-hour. The Crub is in Roppongi district, so we take a cab, and you are in for a big surprise! This is important night for internationarr...re-raytions! Tonight, tonight!' – With an impetuous toss of his head, he flung the lovelock from his puckered brow and burst into the refrain from *West Side Story* – 'Tonight! Tonight! Won't be just any night!' Ken was the Star of any Karaoke Bar, and liked to sing romantic ballads, mostly in English. 'I reft my heart in San Flancisco', and his favourite of all, Tom Jones' signature tune, 'The Gleen Gleen Glass of Home!'

I had met Ken's colleagues after our opening night, and although I had found them charming I was less than enthusiastic about sitting up late at a Night Club in their sober-suited, top-executive company without a single word of any language in common between us. But my imagined discomfort was as nothing compared to the reality of what turned out to be the most excruciating night of my entire adult life.

As I have said, The London Shakespeare Group was always a small company, never exceeding ten in number and run on democratic principles. The star of the show, and the only box office draw, was Shakespeare. From the beginning we had decided that for people travelling and living together for two months or more at a time, it was essential that everyone should be paid exactly the same whether one was playing Hamlet, carrying a spear or managing the stage. Rather like a circus troupe, we all assisted with the set-up at the beginning of the performance, and with the pack-up at the end. Each production had to fit into three trunks, but within the strictures of space and mobility every one was as colourful as we could make it. We had magnificent costumes and ingenious settings designed for us. For *Twelfth Night*, which was done in an Arabian Nights style, we had a revolve. It consisted of articulated bamboo poles and acres of silk but it was a revolve just the same; it served as a shipwreck, two sumptuous tents, a prison, an orchard, a street, a distant view of minarets.

And for all our productions we used lots of music, just as Shakespeare did. In his day, when the only music to be heard was live music, people often went to the theatre regardless of the play and the actors, just to hear the music.

For our audiences worldwide, English is a second language, often read and spoken only at a rudimentary level. 'A plank and a passion' is the very basis of theatre. But 'Minimalism' – a ladder and a bucket and all the actors in track-suits – is not appreciated by people who hardly understand a word.

There was a misprint in our Japanese programme which caused no little consternation.

'It is hard to believe,' it said in bold letters on the front page, 'that the London Shakespeare Group travels the world with only three drunks.'

The orientals could not accept that our company had no leader. Gary, Delena and I were a triumvirate. I directed the plays by consent, not autocratically, and since Delena was our able administrator, she was most qualified to be considered 'at the helm'. Neither the Japanese, nor later the Chinese, could accept that I was not The Boss, since I was credited with being the Director. I was always the one required to make the speeches.

And to endure the hospitality…

In Roppongi, Ken and I squeezed into the lift which was the size of a London telephone box and to my surprise I saw him punch the button for the tenth floor. My rare visits to Night Clubs had been passed in more grounded establishments – frequently in the basement – and low-level seemed somehow more appropriate for nocturnal shenanigans than high in the sky. But the tenth floor was where the Hippo was Dancing – there was a little logo of a hippo wearing a tutu pirouetting on point by the lift button to prove it.

On consideration, ten floors up was pretty near the ground for Tokyo, where the tallest buildings have express lifts to the fiftieth floor; thereafter, for higher floors, you change to a local.

As we arrived at the landing outside the club, Ken put his hand on my shoulder and assumed a confidential tone.

'Johhhhh. I want you to understand one thing before we join the others. This is our speciar pleasant to you for all your wonderfuhhh productions. And since we are more than correagues now – we have become fast friends – I will confide in you. We are so rucky *Tokyo Shimbun* newspaper is picking up the tab! Oh Wahhhhh! You would never berieve! It cost an alm and a regg! Ahhhh!'

These incomprehensible people, the Japanese! They have raised politeness and form to an almost religious plane, and yet here was Ken warning me that the Night Crub, to which I had come reluctantly and at his insistence, was prohibitively expensive. This came as no surprise to me, since Tokyo is the most expensive city in the world. But I was dismayed that he should feel it necessary to inform me of how much the evening, which I was not looking forward to, was going to cost his blessed newspaper.

'I'll be happy with a glass of water,' I assured him.

His face screwed up in frustration, and he held his hair aside to gimlet me with his earnest little eyes.

'The Geisha! I am talking about the Geisha. We have not one, but two Geisha. Tonight we are entertaining you Japanese style! Come! Ret me introduce you!'

At last I understood. Like nuns, Geisha are a dying breed, and I had heard that the few who still pursue the ancient profession command astronomical fees for their services. What those services are, or more precisely, where their services stop, is not a question with a clear answer. The most accurate reply would be – 'It depends'.

He indicated the lockers provided, and we removed our shoes. My big toe popped out through a hole in my sock like a thumb through a doughnut. Curling it up made it worse, as I hobbled when I walked and it drew attention to my feet. I prayed that the lighting would be low, especially at floor level.

'The Dancing Hippo' was not a Disco, so we did not walk into a wall of sound. There was some tinkling music being played on the long-stringed shamisen lute, the girl musician nodding like a toy dog in the rear window of a car as she read her up-and-down music.

The room was divided round the walls into open-ended booths crowded with squatting customers. Waitresses in traditional kimonos pattered like toddlers on the polished floor between the tables (a gait which seems to be considered fetching), before glissading to their knees to serve the clients.

Ken led the way to a low table round which our party was gathered. The men, in their business suits, were sitting cross-legged on buckwheat-filled cushions on the tatami-matting, while the two women knelt by their sides ready to top up their glasses and murmur in their ears.

They all rose to their feet at our approach, and I greeted the newspaper magnates with a civil, Western handshake. The two women, tightly trussed into magnificent silk kimonos, bowed and bowed and twittered and giggled, and I found myself staring, for the one whom Ken had introduced to me as Mimou and whom he seemed with a very un-Japanese lack of subtlety to be foisting upon me – all but, in fact, pushing her into my arms – was not at all to my taste. Sexually that was no doubt to be expected. But I'm talking about aesthetically. Hygienically. Medically. Contagiously.

The dense white pigment that all Geisha paint on their faces is startling at close quarters, and perhaps may even have been the cause of Mimou's problem, for the woman was suffering from galloping acne, truly carbunculous, volcanic acne erupting in bubbles like the surface of the moon all over her exposed areas from her decolletage to her hairline. With the blinding white cosmetic plied an inch thick on top of this epidermal epidemic, her skin looked like a newly-distempered rough pebble-dash wall.

The touch-taboo does not extend to Geisha, which may go some way to explaining their popularity.

The theory is that while wives are left at home in their tiny houses or apartments with paper walls to look after the children and do the housework, the menfolk stay away as long as possible in bars and tea-houses, and even Night Crubs when the occasion merits big spending. Male-only gatherings with business associates soon pall, and when held on a regular basis they become stodgy, so hostesses are employed to leaven the dough and add spice.

Further comfort is negotiable.

Mimou had evidently been primed to treat me as a VIP. I had barely struggled into a squatting position with my legs tucked under me to hide my naked toe, than I found my Geisha's disconcerting complexion within an inch of my nose. She wore an exaggerated expression of pop-eyed amazement at her own effrontery while her fingers scrabbled at my lips to insert a piece of gristle between my teeth.

This unidentifiable morsel was no doubt some hideously expensive delicacy, probably the pickled appendix or the lower intestine of the puffer-fish, a virulently poisonous fish which to this day claims the lives of over a thousand Japanese a year. It is still eaten, provided it is prepared by a licensed chef. These chefs have to have five years' experience of preparing the puffer-fish without a casualty before they are given their certificate. There are still mistakes. A thousand a year or so to be precise. And still the Japanese eat the poisonous puffer-fish in quantity. Dicing with death appears to add to the flavour.

The other Geisha looked human. She was an apprentice, Ken told me. Her face was not painted white, her hairdo and her kimono were modest in comparison with Mimou's, and she was taking care of the entire executive staff of the *Tokyo Shimbun* newspaper to their evident satisfaction, while Mimou devoted her exclusive attention to me.

Ken, who might have acted as an interpreter, had left me to my own devices, and altogether understandably seemed entranced by the younger, prettier and blemish-free apprentice who was flirting herself into a spiral among the business suits.

I was clearly not the first foreigner that Mimou had dealt with. Even without the inestimable advantage of verbal communication, she had a repertoire of tricks to make the evening go with a swing.

There was the game with sesame seeds and sake cups, much like the dice under the egg-cup game played at fairgrounds, except that in between each foxy pass, Mimou would stir her fingers in a large plate of crisp-fried offal, and having chosen an irresistible fragment, would pop it merrily into my mouth, then pinch my lips together between her thumb and forefinger, giving me a little kissing moue of encouragement and ending all with a treble pit-a-pat on the tip of my nose.

During this ritual she kept up a low murmur of what I could tell, even with the language barrier that stood like a fortress-wall between us, was baby-talk.

'*Oooo! Doosie-Poosie! Woochi-poochi-Ha-Ka-Wa!*'

In goes another ghastly chewy thing.

'*Urrigat-Urrigat-Urrigat! Ticka-Ticka ticka!*'

Squeeze the lips together.

'*Poo!poo!poo!*'

Playful patsies on the nosey-wosey.

It was while she was engrossed in her prestidigitation for my delectation that I noticed to my further dismay that the shawl collar of her exquisite kimono was grey with dandruff. It costs so much to construct their elaborate hairstyles, pinned together with chopsticks of carved ivory, that a thrifty Geisha will visit her hairdresser only once a month.

To the sound of irrepressible laughter and stifled giggles, at the far end of the table the Managing Director of the *Shimbun* newspaper folded an aeroplane out of a paper napkin and the sub-editor improvised a pair of binoculars out of two empty glasses and trained them on the apprentice's cleavage, while at our end Mimou disdained such childish games and instead we played clap-handies.

Till my enthusiasm ran away with me and I spilled my Coca Cola.

And that was when Mimou found the hole in my sock.

It was while she was engaged in the unbridled hilarity of introducing my naked toe to the entire nightclub, and interfering with me all the way up my trouser leg, and twirling my leg-hairs to the 'Ooh!s' and 'Wahh!s' of the spectators – Japanese men are almost hairless – and patting me on the nosey-wosey when she wasn't tickling my toesy-woesy, that I decided to get drunk.

With tiny baby steps a waitress scurried across the floor and delivered a large scotch for me and a microphone for Ken, who had clearly requested to sing. Oriental popular music, whether Japanese or Chinese, is curiously tuneless to Western ears, but Ken always chose American songs, and once the backing track for 'The Gleen Gleen Glass of Home' was on, I was unutterably grateful for the diversion. It was a respite from the limelight and from Mimou's increasingly lewd attentions. But not for long.

Since I was the guest of honour, my whole party would brook no denial: I had to sing. The list of backing tracks was entirely in Japanese. Ken was by now scarlet in the face and too pissed to be of any help. When I think of how he must have been suffering – mentally, even if he was not yet suffering physically – I am awed by his courage, and his selfless determination to give me a night to remember. He succeeded, but not in the way he intended.

I was handed the tome that was the list of backing tracks, and I scanned it eagerly hoping to find a song I knew – 'Around the World...' or 'Smoke Gets In Your Eyes...' or 'Roll Me Over...' or anything; but page after page of pictograms swam before my vision without the relief of one recognisable title written in Roman script. The ghastliness of my situation combined with the whisky gave me, if not a sort of Dutch courage, then a sort of Dutch resignation.

I have found in my travels that England is always considered to be closely associated with America, and it has thus a double chance of being unpopular. But Scotland has a ring to it. It is a small country, nobody knows exactly where it is or what it stands for, and in Japan they like tartan plaid and they adore whisky, so I always emphasise my Scottish roots.

I threw the incomprehensible list over my shoulder, took the microphone and stood up, raising one hand for silence.

'Rabbie Burns!' I said, and the only response to this exciting announcement was the microphone whistling.

Natsame-San swivelled me a little, and I tried again.

'Robert Burns wrote this song, Ladies and Gentlemen, which I am going to sing unaccompanied.'

There was a hush. The sort of hush that you encounter in dying rooms.

And I launched into 'My Love is like a Red Red Rose', which I happen to think is the loveliest of Burns' songs, though 'Maggie Cock-a-bendy!' would undoubtedly have been jollier. The only thing that kept me going was the thought that the hideous ordeal would soon be over, that I was flying back to London the following week, and that I was not doing anyone any harm, at least intentionally.

I think those at my table applauded my dismal rendition enthusiastically, but then they would, wouldn't they? I slumped on the tatami matting next to Ken, and citing two performances on the morrow, asked him if it would be indefensibly rude of me to ask to be excused.

'Take Mimou with you Johhhh!' he cried. It's what he had been planning all along. My farewell pleasant. 'She rikes you! She rearry rikes you! And when Minou rikes you, there's no ploblem! I already tell her it's on the *Shimbun*! You don't have to worry about a thing! It's all taken care of!'

I know now that Geisha are hard to come by, but surely – is anyone that desperate? Is it just 'any place to put it'?

Ken tried unsuccessfully to rise to his feet while I said my thank yous and goodbyes to Toshiro Natsame-San and Hideo Miyama-San and the apprentice, but it was as I feared. Mimou would not be left behind.

All the while I struggled into my shoes, she hovered, murmuring endearments. They may have been imprecations, but they sounded like endearments. She donned her wooden platform sandals, and clicked and clacked around me like a little girl masquerading in her mother's outsize high heels.

In the lift the size of a telephone box, she pressed the rigid armour of her traditional garb hard against my linen suit and in the short distance to the ground floor she managed to slip in a few more affectionate taps on my nosey-wosey.

I fled the building with my arm already raised to hail a cab, for they were fortunately plentiful at that hour. As one swept up to the kerb, I bowed to Mimou and delivered a stream of polite Japanese – or the nearest I could ever approach to a stream in the circumstances.

'*Arigato goẓaimasta! Domo! Doẓo! Koni-chiwa!*' And for good measure as I gave the driver the card for my hotel and leapt into the safety of the back seat, I leant out of the window as we took off and shouted, '*Sayonara!*'

The poor woman clicked in a daze right out into the middle of the fast-moving four-lane traffic, and was almost hit by several speeding motorists as she stood there disbelieving, jilted, scorned, with a hand suspended motionless in the air as if she was caught in the flash of a photograph.

This inscrutable Japanese gesture could have meant 'Come back', 'Goodbye', or 'Go fuck yourself'.

But at least she was being paid exorbitantly by the *Tokyo Shimbun* newspaper for her confusion.

10 THE FINAL BOW
Our Revels now are ended...

WE WERE flying home, nursing our grief. The lights had dimmed and darkness had fallen on the last night of The London Shakespeare Group. The applause had faded to a distant ripple like water trickling over the stones of all our dear performances now passed away, wrapped with love and buried in our memories; all that remained of the cheers was a ghostly echo... 'Bra – vohhhh...' The tears were dry on our cheeks. The three battered trunks had been packed and loaded onto the carousel and had disappeared through the hatch like coffins in a crematorium.

> Our revels now are ended. These our actors,
> As I foretold you, were all spirits, and
> Are all melted into air, into thin air;
> And, like the baseless fabric of this vision,
> The cloud-capp'd towers, the gorgeous palaces,
> The solemn temples, the great globe itself,
> Yea, all which it inherit, shall dissolve,
> And, like this insubstantial pageant faded,
> Leave not a wrack behind. We are such stuff
> As dreams are made on; and our little life
> Is rounded with a sleep.

Buried in our memories...

How many actors get to feast on newly slaughtered goat in a fort at the top of the Khyber Pass?

We had sat cross-legged on charpoys, while beardless boys washed our fingers over silver basins with a thin stream of water from tall silver-spouted jugs, while the girls were allowed into the women's quarters. The black burkhas worn in the bazaar are discarded within the sanctum of the family, to reveal scarlet skirts slit to the waist, gold high heels, jewels, lipstick, and bangled arms as ready to cuff a husband as caress him.

Westerners who had been stationed for years near this outpost of the Hindu Kush on the border of Afghanistan had never been offered hospitality such as this by these tribesmen, nor had anyone ever been invited to penetrate the fastness of their mighty castles.

But we were travelling players, vagabonds from the market place. We were storytellers, not civil servants in pin-stripe suits or military personnel in uniform.

And we were only passing through…

This has been the *Open Sesame!* in all our travels. We are harmless entertainers like performing dogs, who can amuse you for a brief moment before we move on, and 'leave not a wrack behind'.

Do you remember, my fellow thespians, do you remember the hippos spouting round our dugout on the wide Zambesi above the Victoria Falls – *Muse O Tunya*, The Smoke that Thunders, while the Great Litunga – whose son goes to Eton, skimmed past us in his war canoes to the thunder of apocalyptic drums, bearing him to his summer palace guarded with towers of elephant tusks? And after we had left our boat stranded in the mud where the waters had receded, will we ever forget the three-hour hike across the flood plains, our arms and faces the colour of pewter under a blanket of flies impossible to beat off, fording trickling streams below circular palisades high up on their banks where long-horned cattle were penned, passing villages of thatched rondavels straight out of *King Solomon's Mines*? The villagers came out to meet us, offering us home-brewed beer as thick as porridge, which in moderation makes you drunk and in excess will surely kill you. We found the Chief seated on his throne, a Maples wing-chair mounted on a box wrapped in swirly patterned carpet, his courtiers in shiny lounge-suits squatting on the ground at his feet, deferentially clapping their hands.

'*Enisha!*' they murmured respectfully as we approached, and as we bowed and held up our hands in embarrassment, they continued to applaud.

This custom explained why our *Merchant of Venice* had been met with a deathly hush in Livingstone.

'They hated us!' we had said. We had never before been greeted with total silence at the end of a performance – never once in all our travels. But clapping your hands is the normal greeting in Zambia. When we took our curtain, we could hardly expect the audience to break into a chorus of 'Hello! Hello! Hello!'

In Sarawak in the west of Borneo, the British Council landrover took us out from Kuching to the very edge of the rain forest for the start of our arduous trek to the headhunters' longhouse.

Gary, Delena and I skidded in single file for five hours through the drip-ping jungle along a plank-walk above a leech-infested swamp, while macaque monkeys swung down on us from the gloom above our heads, getting closer at every swoop, chattering angrily and threatening us with bared teeth. At last, frightened and exhausted, we came to a wide, fast-flowing river: across a rope bridge stood the longhouse. Our relief was short-lived, as we were spotted by the village dogs, who were forming into a pack to tear us apart. The chief's son, alerted by their barking, leapt to our rescue in the nick of time. After delivering our token presents of sweets and cans of soft drinks, we sat down cross-legged on the worn wooden floor to wait patiently while the cooking-fire was lit.

The headman's son had a smattering of English, so, using him as his interpreter, his father – a middle-aged little man in a loin-cloth with a pudding-basin haircut – invited us to stay for supper and to spend the night. We had been advised that among the Dayak, good manners dictate that strangers who turn up unannounced cannot be turned away. Having made the long journey, we too were obliged to accept their hospitality or cause grave offence. We had also been told that payment for these services so freely given was welcome, though we had to tread carefully or risk offending their *amour propre*. We decided to leave the money to be discovered after we had gone; thus the proprieties were observed, and any appearance of a transaction was avoided.

While supper was being prepared, we bathed in the river with the chief, his sons, and a bevy of jungle beauties. They washed themselves from top to toe inside their sarongs, which they kept decorously wound over their nakedness like Victorian Belles in their bathing machines.

After a dinner of bushmeat, rice and palm wine, the headhunter's wife and daughters rolled out rush mats in two neat rows facing each other at one end of the hut, and indicated that we should do likewise at the other end. Before the lamp was dowsed, as I lay on my back utterly exhausted, in the shadows above my head I could just pick out what looked like an abandoned harvest of brown, shrivelled gourds, unequivocally head-sized, hanging in bunches high up in the rafters.

The fighting cocks, tethered by the door of each family's quarters at regular intervals all along the verandah just outside, crowed incessantly through the night, as if the high-pitched whine of the mosquitoes and the tickling all over our bodies of unidentified insects were not enough to ensure that we stayed wide awake till morning...

Did we really take Fortnum and Mason's Earl Grey tea with the Baroness d'Erlanger in her Islamic palace in Carthage, with its fretted screens and gold-leaf ceilings, tinkling with perfumed fountains? This hostess to Princess Margaret and others of the international beau monde was an aged Southern Belle, her arthritic fingers carbuncled with rings, who beguiled us with tales of Lady Hester Stanhope in an accent like Scarlett O'Hara's. Her first questions to me were: 'Are you married? Do you have a lover? Or do you just fantasise like the rest of us?'

We have shot the *Apocalypse Now* rapids in the Philippines, looking in vain for the shade of Marlon Brando.

In the endless night of the Icelandic winter, we have boiled in the Hot Pots of Reykjavik, then rolled in the snow in the Stygian darkness of noon.

At a wedding in Lahore, we were stormed by a troupe of grotesquely painted eunuchs, who assaulted the guests with lewd gestures, till, in order to ward off the bad luck they threatened, we had to stick rupees to the rivulets of sweat that trickled between their padded breasts.

In Ethiopia we have been stoned by horsemen firing with slings from their perky little Arab mounts sumptuously caparisoned like the steeds of mediaeval knights, on our way to the rock churches of Lalabella. An ancient patriarch who might have been a priest lurched towards us waving his ceremonial staff, his white hair standing up in woolly spikes. Since none of us spoke a word of Amharic, the impasse was total and it would surely have ended in our being turned away.

Then, seeing how old he was, I had a stroke of inspiration.

'*Parla Italiano?*' I asked him.

His face was a study. '*Si,*' he said.

After Mussolini's invasion of what was then Abyssinia, his troops had occupied the country for six years, from 1935 to 1941, and this clever old remnant of a shameful chapter in Italy's history could still speak the language.

He showed us round his church, buried deep underground and carved out of the living rock; above the altar was the painting of a beautiful black Madonna.

'*Grazie. Auguri,*' we said as we parted good friends.

At the Ambassadorial Residence that night I met the vet, a tiny little man with a beard so bushy and black you felt you could dig your fingers into it, pick him up and swing him round your head. As soon as Emmanuel told me his profession, I knew we weren't talking hamsters and budgies here, but cattle, horses, camels. I asked him if he would consider taking me out on his rounds.

'Can you get up at five in the morning?' he asked me, with a sceptical smile.

'Of course,' I assured him.

At dawn Emmanuel collected me in his landrover from the Haile Selassie Hotel in Addis Ababa and transported me back a thousand years into the past. We followed the mighty caravan of the animals, a moving menagerie shrouded in a golden mist raised by their passage as camels, horses, hump-backed cows, donkeys, sheep, goats, plodded along the bottom of a deep gulley worn by their hooves since the beginning of time in their trek to the wells.

We had answered the call of a half-naked boy clinging to the branches of a dead tree, wailing his message over the roadless desert to guide us to his village. Arriving there, Emmanuel was greeted like their saviour. The little vet dug his hand into the rectum of a sick cow, right up to the elbow. It looked for a moment as if he was going to climb inside himself. Then he brought forth a fistful of steaming dung. It would be analysed back at his lab. A blood sample removed from a goat was injected straight away into a guinea pig, taken from a cage in the back of our vehicle. This must have seemed like powerful magic to these primitive people.

We were persuaded to enter a dark, evil-smelling hut where, in gratitude for Emmanuel's ministering, we were presented with a feast. It was composed of their bread made from the grain of a tough desert grass called Tiv. The resulting bread is grey in colour, and looks rubbery, like a rotting bath mat. Then the tray of meat was offered to us – torn up morsels of dead animal, completely raw and still bleeding, with yellow lumps of fat and waving blue veins. Knowing how I would feel about this repast, Emmanuel excused my lack of appetite on the grounds of my religion…I think I even crossed myself…

In Malaysia during the Festival of the Seven Gods at Seremban, the noise of fireworks was so deafening, we stopped our performance of *Macbeth* and helped the revellers to hurl their flaming effigies into the river while holy madmen scourged themselves with barbed, serrated flails.

We have taken part in camel-racing in Al Ain, where the keepers literally beat the shit out of the long-legged camels to make them lighter for the race. The jockeys are little boys no more than five or six years old, and they are secured to their saddles atop the humps of the camels with Velcro sewn onto the seat of their trousers.

Sultan Qaboos of Oman is a fine looking man of sixty, a reformer, a liberal ruler, who has used his oil revenues for the good of his own people. His only marriage, when he was a young man, lasted no time at all, and he reverted once again to being a bachelor. He is escorted everywhere by a bodyguard of twenty or so spectacularly handsome young men who always dress in tribal regalia, with a silver jewelled dagger at the waist. They travel in a fleet of Mercedes limousines, and because of their flamboyant headgear, they are known as The Rainbow Boys.

Sultan Qaboos is a great patron of the arts, and, alongside the most beautiful and luxurious hotel in the world – The Al Bustan Palace, where every bathroom has gold fittings – he has also built a spectacular theatre. He will not allow vulgar commercial entertainments to be shown there. Derek Nimmo's companies had to make do with the InterContinental Hotel. But since we were presenting *Hamlet*, we not only played in this glorious venue, we were accommodated in the Al Bustan Palace as well.

There was a tumbledown fishing village standing on the most spectacular site on the coast of Oman just outside Masquat. Sultan Qaboos razed it to the ground to build the Al Bustan Palace Hotel. At the same time, however, on another bay just along the coast – an equally beautiful site – he built a model village for the displaced fishermen and their families, and he built it in the old Omani style. It is one of the loveliest seaside developments I have ever seen.

The Sultan did not encourage tourism, and for many years no foreigner could enter Oman without a sponsor.

This fabulous country of fairy-tale castles and rugged mountains, where the Sultan's retainers ride bareback with daggers in their belts and hooded falcons on their wrists. This Biblical land of gold and frankincense and myrrh. The most sumptuous and beautiful hotel in all the world, alongside the theatre of our dreams.

We have our Will to thank for that.

You have never smelt a Panda till you've smelt one in a Chinese circus.

I suppose it got a lather up riding the bicycle, but from the ringside, as it ped-alled round the sawdust as if warming up for the Tour de France, the pong just about knocked you over and made Delena gag.

We had spent the day at the Beijing Opera School for young performers, marvelling at the panache and the precision of these jumping beans. These little acrobats defy gravity; they handle swords bigger than themselves with dazzling aplomb. But in the end, no matter how breathtaking their skills, it's always personality that marks out a Star. Even at eight or nine years old, we knew who the Stars would be. And what's more, they knew themselves. Which is probably why they will be Stars...

We have sat in the Mother House in Calcutta, while Mother Teresa delivered her benediction. When hearing that we were a troupe of travelling actors, she said, 'Very good. Very good. You do the playing, I do the praying.'

We spent the morning in her home for unwanted babies and paid a visit to her hospice, where the terminally sick are allowed to die with dignity. Afterwards, an earnest member of the company – a lad who takes life, and particularly death, as seriously as he should – asked the little nun a question.

'What advice would you give us?'

She looked at him for a moment, and paused before replying. Then she said gently, 'Try smiling more.'

All these countries, all these people, all these life-enhancing experiences, and more.

All because of the greatest writer the world has ever known. All because of Will Shakespeare.

And if I needed a further reason to love him, it would be this. No fewer than thirteen of his plays are set in Italy...

INDEX OF NAMES

Note: References to the photograph section are given after the main text pages, in uppercase Roman numerals.